The Ceramics of Ráquira, Colombia

The Ceramics of Ráquira, Colombia

Gender, Work, and Economic Change

Ronald J. Duncan

University Press of Florida

Gainesville Tallahassee Tampa Boca Raton Pensacola Orlando Miami Jacksonville

03 02 01 00 99 98 6 5 4 3 2 1

Library of Congress Cataloging-in-Publication Data
Duncan, Ronald J., 1941-
The ceramics of Ráquira, Colombia: gender, work, and
economic change / Ronald J. Duncan.
p. cm.
Includes bibliographical references and index.
ISBN 0-8130-1615-0 (cloth: alk. paper)
1. Pottery industry—Colombia—Ráquira. 2. Pottery—Colombia—Ráquira.
3. Potters—Colombia—Ráquira. 4. Women potters—Colombia—Ráquira.
5. Sex role—Colombia—Ráquira. I. Title.
HD9615.C73R363 1998
331.4'8663986137—dc21 98-11727

The University Press of Florida is the scholarly publishing agency for the
State University System of Florida, comprising Florida A & M University,
Florida Atlantic University, Florida International University, Florida State Uni-
versity, University of Central Florida, University of Florida, University of North
Florida, University of South Florida, and University of West Florida.

University Press of Florida
15 Northwest 15th Street
Gainesville, FL 32611
http://nersp.nerdc.ufl.edu/~upf

Dedicated to

Ana Inés Avella and Nola Ellen Duncan

Mothers and craftswomen who lived the crafts of the Americas

Contents

Illustrations

Preface

The purpose of this book is to describe the contrasting systems of women's and men's ceramics production in Ráquira, Colombia, and to analyze the tension between tradition and economic change in these gender-based cultural patterns. The intersection of gender ideology, ethnicity, and social status has altered the relationships of both women and men in Ráquira to the national and global economies. This study provides information for practitioners and scholars interested in indigenous traditions in the Americas, gender and work, crafts, domestic economics, Latin America, the social effects of capitalism and economic expansion in rural areas, and indigenous and mestizo ceramics traditions in the northern Andes.

My interest in this subject springs from various sources, one of which is being part of a Colombian-American family; another is a professional background in both anthropology and studio ceramics. My wife Gloria De Duncan and I have long been interested in the anthropology of crafts, and in the 1970s we began doing fieldwork in Colombia and Peru on traditional weavers and potters. Between 1972 and 1975, we did extensive visual anthropology, including photography and films, which was supported by the International Development Research Centre of Canada and the Ford Foundation. In 1983 I received a USIA-Fulbright grant for Colombia, and we renewed our anthropological research in the country. From 1984 to 1990 this work was supported by UNICEF, the International Development Research Centre of Canada, and the Andean Pact countries. Local support was provided by the Museo de Artes y Tradiciones Populares (Museum of Popular Arts and Traditions) and the Universidad de los Andes (University of the Andes), both in Bogotá. During that period we also did research on the ceramics community of La Chamba and visited traditional potters in other parts of the country.

Gloria and I carried out most of the fieldwork for this research jointly, and in this project we mixed marriage and professional life. In addition to sharing the photography for this project, Gloria had an important role in the field research, particularly interacting with women potters. She helped gather interview data and brought special social and visual insight to the art and craft behavior that we observed.

I would like to thank Professors David Bidney and Paul Doughty, who introduced me to many of the ideas that are developed here, and also Cynthia Cone, Greta Friedemann, and Andrew H. Whiteford for reading earlier drafts of this text and making important recommendations for corrections. I thank Professor Val Cushing of Alfred University for emphasizing to me the importance of studying village ceramics. I appreciate the anonymous readers for the University Press of Florida who read this manuscript and made helpful recommendations to improve it, and I thank Gillian Hillis for her skill and insight in editing.

The staff of Artesanías de Colombia (Crafts of Colombia) was helpful to me in various stages of this research, and I want to thank Director Cecilia Duque, Subdirector Lucie Cajiao de Ruan, María Gabriela Coradán of CENDAR, the Centro de Investigación y Documentación (Center for Research and Documentation), and Angel Custodio Hernández in Ráquira. I thank Ligia Wiesner, former director of the Museo de Artes y Tradiciones Populares, for field support of this research, and I thank the current director, María del Carmen Benavides, for permission to use photographs of material from the collection. Robert and Nina de Friedemann also gave critical support for a trip to Ráquira in 1995. I especially thank the people of Ráquira who admitted us to their homes and took time to share their lives and knowledge with us. I also owe special appreciation to my parents and grandparents, who gave me the life lessons of indigenous America and who showed me that cultural heritage lives in what we are today.

Introduction and Fieldwork

In the millennial old pottery town of Ráquira, Colombia, men and women have contrasting systems of pottery making: a women's domestic craft tradition and a men's semi-industrial, capitalism-based system. The women potters work primarily in the countryside and use indigenous styles and hand-working techniques that have been consistent with local pottery making since before Columbus. They work part-time, making traditional cooking pots and water jugs in the hours not devoted to domestic tasks. In contrast, the men's workshops, which have emerged in town in the last fifty years, employ a mass-production approach to making planters, tableware, and decorative ware using molds and potters' wheels.

In the town workshops, capitalism has combined with the male-dominated family organization to transform women from independent potters into assistants to their husbands. The fact that men can be full-time workers, control capital, and have greater mobility in marketing has made them the primary beneficiaries of "economic development." Although men and women have the same craft in common, their designs are different, the technology is different, the work patterns are different, and the economic organization of their work is different.

This study shows how women and men work with two contrasting cultures within the same society. The women preserve the indigenous tradition and are more family oriented in economic decisions. Men pursue a Spanish-derived behavioral pattern and do commodity-oriented production with the purpose of maximizing profits. The marginalization of women as independent potters by the economic expansion of the twentieth century leads to the question of whether the ultimate impact of capitalism will be the disappearance of traditional women's ceramics and women's style of economic decision making, which is oriented toward sustaining the family as a collaborative work unit. In this period of economic expansion, men have combined their gender power in the patrifocal family organization with capitalism to gain control of ceramic production in the town, subordinating the work of women to an insignificant position. The women's ceramic system is being rapidly replaced by a new capital-based system of workshops run by men.

Gender, Work, and Capitalism in Ráquira

The chapter plan of this book traces the differences between women's and men's ceramics in Ráquira through five major areas of behavior: history, social organization, ceramic design, work organization and technology, and economics and marketing. They are discussed in the order in which they occur in the life of the potter, starting with history.

The history and theory of Ráquira ceramics are explored in chapters 1 and 2, which explain the role of gender in the economic expansion of recent decades and look at the historic development of the craft in the town. While women have retained traditional design styles and working organization, they are also beneficiaries of the expanded markets that have been created by the men. On the other hand, men have transformed the assumptions of the domestic women's craft in Ráquira into incipient industrialism. The indigenous-Spanish tension in Ráquira's history is embedded in the gender differences today.

Second, the social organization of the family and community establishes the social context of work (chapters 3 and 4). In Ráquira, understanding the role of gender in the family is essential to understanding the organization of the ceramics workshop. In the indigenous-influenced rural areas, women have a stronger, more independent role in ceramics and in the family, but in town the woman's role is more subservient in both work and family. Town women are excluded from important work roles by the men whose concepts of hierarchical work patterns dominate, but in the rural areas women's cooperative work patterns are the norm.

Third, the ceramic designs produced by women and men are different (chapters 5 and 6). The stable repertoire of women's domestic pottery contrasts with the shifting repertoire of men's commodity ceramics, which are made in response to the urban markets. Both men and women do figurative ceramics, but each expresses a different view of life in their figures.

Fourth, work organization and technology reflect the contrasting patterns of gender and division of labor in the rural women's workshops, traditional family workshops in town, and industrial workshops (chapters 7 and 8). Organization within the ceramics workshop correlates with gender ideology and economic orientation. Technology is largely a result of ethnic heritage, with indigenous influences manifest in the rural workshops and Spanish/Andalusian influences in the town workshops.

Fifth, the differences between women and men in economics and marketing (chapter 9) are notable, with the historical orientation of women's ceramics being local and domestic and men's ceramics being urban and mass produced. In recent decades, the purpose of making ceramics has gradually shifted from subsistence to commerce, and to understand Ráquira crafts today one must understand its commercial potential, especially for younger generations who see crafts primarily as an income-producing activity.

The cultural theory of craft making discussed in chapter 10 explains how potters make a series of complex decisions about life and work according to their economic orientation. The potter makes design decisions (whether to make cooking pots or planters), technological decisions (whether to use traditional hand-building techniques or mold-based mass production), and economic decisions (about investments in infrastructure and sales channels). In making each of those decisions, the potter learns the cultural traditions of pottery in the community or chooses to adopt new ways of working from the outside.

This study traces the emergence of men as the dominant force in Ráquira ceramics and the loss of status among women potters. It asks questions such as why gender symmetry is lost when capitalism expands and what the differences are between men and women in working styles, technologies, and economics. How do the cumulative decisions of hundreds of men and women potters in Ráquira lead to predictable patterns of production and design? The cultural construction of gender, the differences between the generations, and the contrasts between rural and town behavioral patterns interweave to form the fabric of Ráquira gender and work. It was our interest in understanding and explaining these behaviors that led us to this project.

Fieldwork in Ráquira

I first heard about Ráquira in the early 1970s, during the early stages of the change that introduced mass-production techniques to the town. At that point, I knew only that it was a traditional ceramics center, and I was interested in documenting the dynamic between tradition and change. Although our attempts to obtain complete funding for a research project in Ráquira were unsuccessful at that point, my wife and I were able to do initial observations in 1974–75, including photography and film documentation of the ceramic process. This initial research focused on describing ceramics making in town workshops.

After an interlude of ten years, we returned to Ráquira in 1984 as part of a survey of village ceramics in Colombia (Duncan 1984). Finally, in 1989, we were able to initiate the project that led to this book, and the information we gathered was then supplemented by follow-up trips in 1992 and 1995. During this period we did participant observation, interviewed individual potters, attended meetings, and observed the intermediary system. In Ráquira and Bogotá, we interviewed the directors of Artesanías de Colombia (Crafts of Colombia) and the Museo de Artes y Tradiciones Populares (Museum of Popular Arts and Traditions) and other professionals working with Ráquira ceramics, and we researched the extensive collections and archives of both institutions. We also carried out research in the Archivo Histórico Nacional de Bogotá (National Historical Archive of Bogotá) on the history of Ráquira and the department (province) of Boyacá.

By the start of our 1989–90 work, it had become apparent that women and men were engaged in two different cultural systems. So we focused our research on gender and social change, comparing the processes of ceramic production, the forms produced, and the influence of the social aspects of ethnicity and gender on work patterns. In addition to studying town workshops, we observed and interviewed women potters in the *veredas* (rural districts) of Pueblo Viejo (Old Town), Resguardo (Reservation), and Candelaria Occidental (West Candlemas). Gloria played a major role in interviewing the women potters because it was not appropriate for me, as a man, to spend extended periods alone with a woman. We also had a car that we could offer for the purpose of transporting rural people home or carrying pottery to town, which permitted us to give as well as receive during the research process.

In 1989, the Museo de Artes y Tradiciones Populares in Bogotá invited the two of us to exhibit our one-of-a-kind ceramics in a branch of the museum in Ráquira. In conjunction with the exhibition, we were invited to demonstrate our working techniques to local potters, a reversal that placed us in the role of subjects. Part of the philosophy of the education program of the museum was to introduce different approaches to ceramics to the Ráquira potters, and as part of that program I was asked to demonstrate the use of the wheel in making one-of-a-kind pieces.

In 1994 we consulted the General Archives of the Indies in Seville, Spain, for historical information on Spanish ceramics that were shipped to Colombia, evidence of Spanish ceramists who traveled to Colombia in the colonial period, and ceramics technology that might have been transferred there. In the follow-up trips of 1992 and 1995 in Colombia, we were able to collect recent data and additional visual materials. We did interviews on the changes in rural pottery production, figurative art work, and the small industry movement. Out of those interviews, we recorded information from younger potters to document the changes that are occurring among them. These case studies give empirical examples of the choices individual potters are making in design and working patterns.

Our early contacts in Ráquira were limited to town workshops because they are the most easily accessible to visitors from the outside. Town potters who have showrooms are accustomed to visitors wandering into the workshop to observe the work and even to take an occasional photograph. It was Doña Otilia Ruiz and other women potters in Resguardo Occidental who first introduced us to the rural pottery traditions. Our first visit to Doña Otilia's house is instructive because what we observed about her and what she told us about her life make a good introduction to the ceramics of Ráquira.

Doña Otilia Ruiz de Jerez

One afternoon in 1989, Gloria and I encountered Doña Otilia in Ráquira in the Museo de Artes y Tradiciones Populares, and she talked with us about the Christ figures she was making. She was dressed like most other country women of Boyacá, in a rumpled fedora hat, a straight dress, a sweater, and the ever-present *ruana*, a Colombian-style woolen poncho that is open in front. When she was ready to leave, we offered to drive her home, knowing the long, steep climb that lay before her. After we drove as close to her house as the road would take us, she invited us to walk the rest of the way to see the pieces she was making. As we continued along a winding path, her adobe house seemed to emerge from the hillside, its walls made of the same earth on which they stood. Since adobe is not a strong building material, the door was the only opening in the otherwise solid walls, making the house dark inside.

Doña Otilia learned pottery making from her mother, who taught her the same techniques she had learned from her own mother. For most of her life Doña Otilia made cooking pots and stubby round pitchers in the same way her grandmother had in the 1800s. She also made "toy" figures in ceramics, which she regarded as unimportant, throw-off pieces. But later in life she realized that she could use her modeling skill to make ceramics of religious imagery.

She is from the *vereda* (rural district) of Mirque, but when she married she moved with her husband, Anselmo Jerez, to Resguardo Occidental (in

English, "western reservation"), a name that records the indigenous origins of the people. Along with her two sisters, she inherited her parents' farm in Mirque, and she continues to plant corn and potatoes there with the aid of her husband and children. They eat what they plant and rarely have any surplus to sell from the farm. Her husband also plants his land in Resguardo, works as a day laborer for others, and collects sisal for the making of bags and other objects. They inherited the house where they live from his parents, and they still do not have running water or electricity. Doña Otilia, or her daughter Graciela, collects water every day from a nearby creek, and they wash the clothes in the same place. She cooks over an open fire in the kitchen in traditional Boyacá fashion. Although she has begun the new practice of using aluminum pots, she also continues to use ceramic ones. On cool, rainy days this is a favorite place to visit, where people sit on stools made from sectioned tree trunks that have become polished smooth with age and use.

Doña Otilia has relatives scattered throughout Resguardo, which is one of the rural areas most important for ceramics. It is more than an hour's walk up the steep incline of the mountain from the town to her house, where she lives in a world of rural tranquility in which she can envision churches that she has never seen and dream about the Virgin Mary, Christ on the cross, the flight to Egypt, the Resurrection, the Last Supper, or the nativity scene and convert them into hard ceramic reality. An altar in her house contains several images of the Sacred Heart of Jesus, a couple of crosses, the Virgin of Fatima, and angels. She goes to mass on Sunday in Ráquira and attends the annual religious festivals, but her favorite religious event of the year is Easter Week. When she was young, she wanted to become a nun and pursue a life of religious devotion (Fiori 1990:20). As a nun, she would have had a life of spiritual and intellectual pursuits, far from the rigors of farm life, but her father arranged a marriage for her, and instead she has lived as a rural farm woman and potter.

Doña Otilia is always working with her hands. At home she usually works with clay, making nativity scenes, Christ figures, churches, and other religious imagery, and sometimes she makes figures of the farm life that reflect her daily life. When she leaves home to walk to town or visit a friend, she takes along her portable work, which is esparto grass from which she weaves strainer baskets. Following the pattern in Andean indigenous communities, she is also a midwife, assisting with births in the neighborhood, and she is an herbal curer and knows how to treat body pains and stomach problems, among other ailments.

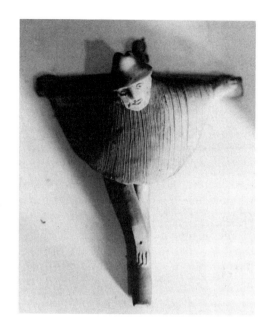

Campesino on the cross. This cru-cifixion figure made by Doña Otilia Ruiz de Jerez shows a Ráquira-area *campesino* (peasant farmer) nailed to a cross in a Christ image. A parallel is being drawn between the hard life of the *campesino* and the suffering portrayed in the crucifixion.

She frequently works outside or under the covered porch of her house, but when it is raining she moves to the workroom, where she stores clay that is ready to use and pots that are drying. Pieces that have been fired may be found in various corners of the house or a storage closet off the workroom. When she needs help, she gets it from her husband, one of her four daughters, her son, or another relative. Her husband mines the clay from her land in Mirque, and he cuts the wood for the firing from his land in Resguardo. Two daughters, Rosa María and Graciela, learned ceramics from her and are recognized potters in their own right, making religious images and country scenes that are typical of Ráquira. Rosa María makes churches and country houses that lean and twist with flowing lines that owe more to the organic world of Resguardo than the straight-lined rigid-ity of Spanish architecture.

As Doña Otilia recreates the Christian iconography in her rural images, Christ on the cross may wear a Boyacá *ruana* and the nativity figures may look like local farmers. She is celebrating the life that surrounds her and setting a standard by which her daughters and grandchildren will remem-ber her. In spite of the weight of seven decades of hard physical work on the farm, her mind is alive with imagination, and a smile wrinkles her face as she talks about her work. Although officially called mestizo, she is from an Indian tradition that cultivates the esthetics and spirituality of craft. Her face registers the genes of her indigenous heritage, and her knowledge of ceramics is a heritage from the precolumbian past. Her religious figures show the syncretism with the European ways that arrived to her ancestors in Ráquira, and she seems to be as comfortable with her past as with the present.

Doña Otilia is heir to a rich ceramics tradition, which she has changed because she believes that ceramists should enjoy their imaginations. She passed on a repertoire of forms to her daughters that is different from the one she received from her mother and grandmother. Along with that, she handed down to them an attitude of respect toward the esthetics and traditions of clay that will survive into the twenty-first century.

The women and men potters of Ráquira, like Doña Otilia, take inert, shapeless clay and give it the life of pottery and design. Although some may possess the eagerly awkward fingers of a child and others the skillful but tired fingers of the septuagenarian, the passion for ceramics can burn in one as strongly as in the other. Through this medium the isolated woman potter can create objects that transcend social and economic barriers and inspire the appreciation of the urban executive who includes the warmth and earthiness of this pottery in his or her corporate suite. As with the other arts, crafts breach the social gulfs that separate people and give them a common element to share. The pot that is for cooking potatoes for lunch in the country becomes a planter in front of an elegant apartment in Bogotá or an object of study for the anthropologist, and that pot links ways of life that are otherwise socially distant and sometimes unintelligible to one another. This book is what we have understood from what the people of Ráquira told us with their actions and words.

1

Gender and Economic Expansion

In Ráquira, two ceramics working styles coexist: the prehispanic, indigenous-based craft of domestic pottery that is produced by women and the Spanish-based commodity production run by men. This division between two contrasting and gender-based orientations to craft work is common in the Andes in both weaving and ceramics. Usually, women are the primary craftspeople in Andean groups, a characteristic they share with women of most other nonindustrial societies (Bradley 1989:117; Lewenhak 1980:96; Murdock and Provost 1973:207). Andean women are also the ones who perpetuate the precolumbian-derived working styles, which has led to indigenous ethnicity being identified primarily with them (Miles and Buechler 1997:8). Women incorporate pottery making into their daily round of household activities, making the domestic pots used in their houses for cooking, water, storage, and serving food.

Men started making pottery in Ráquira after mass-production techniques were introduced in the 1950s and occupational specialization gave the work commercial importance in the 1960s. They followed patterns of male appropriation of women's work similar to those observed in other contexts of economic development (Bradley 1989:117). As they established their own workshops, men began making pottery that could be sold in wider regional markets. As a result, economic development has occurred almost exclusively in men's-style workshops, and they have consistently made commercially oriented choices about forms and techniques of production.

Gender and Capitalism

The capitalist reorganization of ceramics making in recent decades has been the most significant cultural change to affect Ráquira since the Spanish Conquest. Capitalism is understood to be a private ownership of the means of production, which is directed toward maximizing profits through con-

The valley of Ráquira. The town of Ráquira is located in the center of the photograph on the valley floor. The largest planter factory is located on the lower reaches of the opposite mountainside. Although there are clusters of trees, most of the mountainsides have no tree cover.

trol of costs and of the distribution system. Capitalism in Ráquira is a low-investment, low-profit entrepreneurial version that bears little resemblance to high-investment corporate capitalism. The limited resources of this form of capitalism have led to abuses within the labor system, such as the exclusion or marginalization of women workers and the exploitation of hired workers, especially the contract laborers in town who work under sweatshop terms of minimum pay, a demanding pace, and harsh physical conditions.

Making pottery for commercial purposes is not new in Ráquira because historically people sold their pottery, and even the most traditional women potters say that their primary purpose for making pots is to sell them. However, the reorganization of pottery production in favor of capitalist and industrial values has gone beyond commercialization and led to structural changes in the society and culture. As in other craft communities (Annis 1987:140), this change has meant a decline in the status of women and an increased differentiation between families based on wealth and social status. The changes resulting from the capitalist-style economic expansion of Ráquira ceramics have shifted the focus of production from the rural areas to the town and from women to men.

Women are marginalized because their role has changed from being primary producers to being assistants to their husbands. Younger men have become proletarian workers performing a single specialized task in a production system that emphasizes efficiency and speed. Older men are excluded when they are no longer able to maintain the physically demanding pace of mass production, although if they have sufficient capital they can become owners of their own workshop and hire younger men to work for them.

The cultural construction of gender leads to contrasting behavioral expectations for men and women in Ráquira today, and as could be expected they have reacted differently to the economic changes of recent decades. Men have been at the forefront in creating the nontraditional ceramics oriented to the market economy, while women master potters have preserved traditional design values and styles in the country domestic pottery. Although men and their pottery dominate the ceramics market today, women maintain the cultural integrity of the country pottery style identified with Ráquira.

Symmetry and Asymmetry in Gender Relations

Gender relations in the Andes reflect the two primary cultural layers of the national societies, the Spanish (hierarchical and patriarchal) and the indigenous (more symmetrical). Gender roles among indigenous people in the Andes have traditionally been constructed symmetrically, with both men's and women's work seen as vitally important for the family (Miles and Buechler 1997:2). Men and women are assigned distinct but interdependent tasks in collaborative family work. The result is complementary gender patterns with each being essential and valued; for example, men plow and women sow (McKee 1997:14). In Ráquira ceramics, women make the pots and men fire them. Within the indigenous tradition women are the primary producers of certain crafts and, in some cases, the owners of land and animals, which gives them importance within the family economy. This balanced control of each gender over productive resources results in a partnership that empowers both men and women. The power that each has is to pursue goals rather than to exercise domination over others (ibid.:16). This gender complementarity does not necessarily result in equality or sameness, but it does permit a balanced valuation of work and access to control of the resources of the family (ibid.).

The Spanish pattern of gender relations in the Andes emphasizes inequality between men and women, with the men being the breadwinners and dominating public activities (Miles and Buechler 1997:2). The role of women in the Spanish model is primarily limited to the social reproduction of the family with little public or family authority. The income-producing work of men is publicly visible and valued, whereas the domestic work of women is invisible, does not produce income, and is undervalued. This cultural construction of gender is reinforced and compounded by capitalism, which emphasizes income-producing skills. As subsistence workers enter capitalist markets, the contribution of women to the household economy is devalued (ibid.:3).

The capitalist economy forces the family to adopt a multiple resource strategy in which one partner produces a stable income while the other pursues a diversified work pattern (McKee 1997:21). Historically, in the subsistence agriculture of rural Ráquira, men provided the stable wealth in the form of food for the family, and women carried out the diversified production of crafts. However, as capitalist markets and consumer goods have gained economic importance, the steady income produced by the rural women potters has grown and has become for many families the source of cash needed to buy the new consumer goods. Although both men and women still carry out their traditional work (agriculture for men and pottery for women), the larger economy has reversed their economic roles, making women more important today in the production of stable wealth for the rural family.

In contrast, in the Spanish-derived model of family organization followed in town households, men control the production of ceramics, and the role of women is marginal. Although it is the unremunerated work of the women that permits the men to work full time, their work is not seen as important. The patriarchal emphasis on men's work even leads to significant errors in official statistics and by implication errors in the social planning that is based on those figures. Magdalena León and María Viveros (1983:9) found that official Colombian statistics showed only 4 percent employment by women whereas their research indicated that 44 to 56 percent of women were employed. In the patriarchal model of family organization in town, the family does not collaboratively pursue multiple strategies of income production because men are the primary producers of income, and the women work to sustain his income.

Factors That Lead to Capitalism

The change in traditional crafts from domestic to capitalist production is directly linked to asymmetry in gender relations and this process of change is primarily shaped by four factors, according to June Nash (1993:131f): (1) culture-based gender ideology; (2) the way capital and labor requirements differentiate craftspeople into owners and workers; (3) the way n ket relations affect men and women differently; and (4) the interventior state agencies. Each of these factors can be traced in Ráquira, and they ha ve had a major effect on the men's-style, commodity-oriented workshops. The following discussion describes the impact of these four factors in Ráquira.

Gender Ideology in Capitalist Expansion in Crafts

Gender ideology is the first factor shaping the change from domestic to capitalist production. In the gender ideology of Ráquira, the man is the primary breadwinner in the family, and the woman has the responsibility for basic life-maintenance tasks, such as food preparation and child rearing. The public world of markets, hired laborers, and ceramics distribution belongs to men while the private world inside the house belongs to women, and the cultural constraints on women limit their work largely to the house.

This division between *casa y calle* (house and street) has existed in Latin America since the colonial period (Safa 1996:150). The Andalusian Spanish tradition assigned women to the house to protect their virginity and the family honor so that they could marry well. For this reason it was important that the Spanish colonial woman not work, or at least that her work be carried out inside the house and remain invisible to the community. In contrast, indigenous women could be required to work publicly during the colonial period because of the forced-labor requirement, and they commonly worked as servants or cooks for Spanish families. Indigenous women were also the makers of ceramics, baskets, and woven clothing, and they helped their husbands in agricultural work as well. So there was no taboo on the visibility of the work of indigenous women. This division continues today in Ráquira, in that women whose work in ceramics is clearly visible to the community are considered to have lower status. Usually these are women from rural families or poor town families who maintain more indigenous practices. In contrast, the work of town women in ceramics is less visible to the community because their husbands act as the workshop managers, following the Spanish model.

Since the man is expected to be the primary breadwinner in the patriarchal, Latin American gender ideology, the woman's income has always been classified as supplemental (Safa 1996:150), which also renders her work invisible. Since women's craft work at home is interspersed with domestic work, it is seen as a leisure-time activity and therefore not "real" work (Mies 1982:54). In contrast, the man's work is considered real because time and spatial divisions separate his "work" from his family obligations. His work is performed in a specialized workshop that is physically differentiated from the house, and it claims his full attention during working hours.

In the capitalist system, work is validated by income, so if women have little or no income, their work has less validity or visibility. The "invisibility" of the woman's work is reinforced when she does not complete it herself (Mies 1982:59), as is the case in Ráquira. Since there are taboos against women firing the kiln, this step is done by men. Without being fired, the pottery is worthless, but once the man fires it, it is considered to be as much his pottery as that of the woman who shaped it. The man usually sells the pottery, and he keeps most or all of the proceeds as the breadwinner and financial manager of the household. A woman will not normally protest that the man takes all of the money because her work is for the family and not for herself, and she may not expect any personal benefit from the income. Some men, acting as brokers, buy unfired pottery from widows, which they then fire and sell. Thus the firing done by the man makes the pottery his and renders even less visible the work of the woman who fabricated it.

Although gender behavior in Ráquira is changing, the understanding of women's roles and rights continues to reflect colonial-era rules. Many men still use physical and verbal abuse to reinforce their authority over their wives, similar to the practices in other rural areas of Colombia (Reinhardt 1988:216). In town, where the patriarchal authority is more marked, men do not allow their wives to engage in income-producing activity unless it is performed in the house under their own supervision, thereby rendering it "invisible" or not valid work. In contrast, the work of the more indigenous rural women is publicly visible, but as a result they are assigned a lower social status in the Spanish-influenced town concept. However, in fact, they have higher status within their families than do the town women.

Capital and Labor Requirements

Capital and labor requirements constitute the second factor affecting the change from domestic to capitalist production (Nash 1993:131f) Since the gender ideology permits men to control most if not all of the money for the family, they have greater access to capital to invest in expansion. Men have used that opportunity to build commodity-oriented workshops in town, and through these they now control the largest share of production in Ráquira. In contrast, women have retained traditional techniques in part because they have no access to the family capital. If the woman is a potter and the man invests to expand the workshop, then he will come into the business; and following the cultural expectation, he will assume the management of the workshop, which marginalizes the woman. The end result is that in the commodity-oriented workshop, the man is the principal owner and manager and the woman is, in practice, an unpaid assistant to the husband. Only in the rural-style, family-based workshop can the woman remain the master potter and principal producer.

Gender and Market Relations

Market relations are the third factor affecting the change from domestic to capitalist-style production, according to Nash (1993:131f). Global economic trends are affecting ceramics in Ráquira, and men have taken advantage of the new opportunities. As men in town workshops have expanded their production through investment in equipment and facilities, they are in a good position to respond to the subcontracting system that has come to characterize international markets (Safa 1996:136). Since they contract their own workers, they can expand or shrink the workforce as necessary according to orders.

Men control more capital and have more contacts outside of the local community than do women, and as a result men are in a better position to become intermediaries, buying from local producers and reselling in Bogotá and other urban areas. Men have the capital to buy or contract the trucks that are necessary for this business, and they can easily travel alone to the cities on selling trips. Women do not have that freedom of mobility because of their responsibilities for child care and food preparation and the cultural taboos against women of child-bearing age appearing in public without a family escort.

Intervention of State Agencies

The intervention of the state is the fourth factor affecting the change from domestic to capitalist-style production, according to Nash (1993:131f). In Ráquira state agencies have stimulated the economic expansion in ceramics production. The establishment of the state ceramics school in Ráquira in the 1940s contributed to introducing mold-based mass production to the men of the town, and the semi-autonomous state agency Artesanías de Colombia (Crafts of Colombia) has played an important role since the early 1970s. The latter taught men to throw on the production-style potter's wheel, to make glazed tableware, and to fire in electric kilns. The agency also arranged favorable economic terms for the purchase of molds, wheels, and electric kilns. These factors led to the establishment of workshops oriented toward commodity production, which benefited men. State agencies have been ready to support programs seen as leading to economic development, which is primarily associated with men's work. Although Artesanías de Colombia has supported the marketing of women's traditional ware, as a whole women have benefited less from state support because their work is not seen as having the same potential for quantity production and job creation.

While gender ideology, capital and labor, market relations, and state agencies have each influenced the changes in Ráquira, gender has been the central factor. Gender differences in ideology and social status have become even more marked in the younger generations, which have been most affected by economic change, and these differences are the basis of the culturally opposite gender responses to economic expansion and technological innovation.

Gender Strategies and Capitalism

Women and men have developed gender-specific strategies for dealing with the economic changes that have accompanied the capitalist-style economic expansion of craft making in Colombia. In the rural areas, people have modified their traditional strategies by increasing production to meet demand. They still work in both agriculture and pottery, but the latter is more important now than it was previously. Rural men assist their wives today, as they have done historically, but their primary job has always been agriculture.

Most rural women still make pottery with the idea of supplementing the husband's subsistence production in agriculture. Women continue to balance craftwork with their domestic tasks, using a craft technology that impinges only minimally on the family and household; they negotiate the collaboration of their husbands or other male relatives when they need help. Their primary change in strategy has been to increase production with the increased involvement of their husbands. Among rural families, the strategy of both women and men is to increase the woman's production.

In the town, in contrast, the strategy of both men and women is to increase the production of the man. The dominant strategy of men in town workshops can be summarized in four points: (1) maximization of productivity through technology and labor specialization; (2) full-time profit-oriented production based on labor as a commodity; (3) expansion of marketing to include local tourism as well as national and international markets;

and (4) establishment of a hierarchical control structure to direct work. The strategy of women in the capitalist town workshops is to assist their husbands and increase his income.

Since men's workshops have the economic advantage, the domestic working style that has historically characterized women's workshops in Ráquira has become less important. Ehlers's observation among women weavers in Guatemala is that economic development weakens and devalues craft-type production, which is primarily done by women, in favor of the commodity-oriented wage labor, which is primarily done by men; and as a result women lose power and significance within the economy (1990:20). Both of these observations hold true for Ráquira, where women have lost social and economic status in the transition from the woman-based craft workshop to the man-based commodity production system. Men have assumed the primary responsibility of supporting the family in the new system, which means that economic development has led to increased dependency for women.

According to Ehlers (1990:160), the shift from a local domestic economy to a capitalist economy diminishes the status and authority of women within the family and community. The mechanisms by which this occurs are: (1) the market for homemade items is undermined by industrial products and consumer goods; (2) women substitute contracted piecemeal work for traditional craft production, losing control of their own production goals and purposes; and (3) the number of daughters entering the craft decreases. As the daughters enter new, noncraft employments, their mothers and grandmothers cannot train or supervise them in their new occupations, which undermines the position of the older generations as role models. As women lose control over production, they become economically dependent on men, a change that coincides with increased female seclusion, especially in upwardly mobile families. Their role in the family shifts from being primary producers to serving as symbols of affluence whose consumption and productive invisibility emphasize the success of their husbands (ibid.:163).

Craft and Capitalism

The introduction of capitalism in the town workshops in Ráquira has occurred at the expense of the economic significance and independence that women potters traditionally had in the rural areas. There is a trade-off in that they move into the more "honored" position of women who have the luxury of apparently not working and whose status is determined by their husband's work rather than their own, which is the historic position of the high-status Spanish colonial women.

A similar shift occurred in Europe in the late Middle Ages, when labor specialization led to the marginalization of women as workers. There is a parallel between Ráquira and Europe of that period in that each experienced a transition from a domestic economy to incipient capitalism. According to David Herlihy (1990:xi), women had important roles in Europe in crafts, health care, and administration during the twelfth and thirteenth centuries, but they had lost their "visibility" and apparently their importance in these areas of work by the fifteenth century. By the close of the Middle Ages, home-based production dominated the industrial economy in Europe, based on a "putting out" system in which a merchant entrepreneur distributed work to women working in many domestic units under the supervision of the male head of household (ibid.:186).

According to Herlihy, five factors are responsible for the transformation of women from independent, recognized workers to individuals who were subservient within the household and whose work became invisible (1990:187). These same five structural factors can also be observed in the transition from the traditional craft production of rural women in Ráquira to the semi-industrialized workshops developed by men. The first factor is the confinement of women's work to the house. The independent workshops run by women disappear, and women become home-based workers separated into individual households, which leads to their losing recognition and collective influence. Second is the urbanization of the work. Craft work moves into towns, making it more accessible to the urban markets run by men. Third is specialization of labor. Mass-production techniques require greater labor specialization, which favors men; they are able to dedicate their time to working in one specialized task, while women must divide their time between public and domestic work and thus cannot specialize. At this point, women become the assistants to the husbands.

The fourth factor leading to the subservience of women is capitalism. As part-time workers, women do not accumulate capital, nor can they attract it easily. Men, as full-time workers, can obtain capital more readily, and, as a result, they are able to acquire the more technologically complex production equipment and increase their productivity. The fifth reason that women fall behind men as workers is the monopolization of the craft employment by men, which occurred in the Middle Ages as guilds were established as male-only units. In Ráquira it has occurred because the working conditions of the semi-industrial workshops have effectively eliminated women workers. As in the European transition to incipient capitalism, these five factors have been barriers blocking women from working as equal partners with men in the new economic order in Ráquira. The question is then raised why one-half of the potential workforce would be culturally disempowered.

There are two primary explanations, according to Karin Tice (1995:13), for this marginalization of women workers. One attributes it to patriarchal authority; the other argues that the system of capitalism, which requires full-time specialized labor, favors men and structurally discriminates against women. It can also be suggested that these two explanations are integrally linked and that patriarchal authority figures use capitalism to control women's labor and guarantee a favored position for men. Tice suggests (ibid.:15) that the gender division of labor, which assigns women responsibility for the social reproduction of the labor force, including child care, preparation of food, cleaning, and other domestic chores, leaves them at a disadvantage for competing for the important positions in the society and workforce.

Lisa Leghorn and Katherine Parker carry this idea further to suggest that men assign basic life-maintenance tasks to women out of a concept of entitlement or natural right to the subservience of women (1981:284–85). Assigning life-maintenance tasks to women eliminates them as equal participants in capitalist labor markets. Patriarchy and capitalism have been intertwined in the mass production workshops of Ráquira to create a system in which the labor of women is subsumed and disappears from public view under the husband's leadership of the family business.

Gender and Innovation

During the twentieth century, the kind of pottery made in Ráquira changed in response to larger events affecting the town, such as the opening of roads that facilitated the transportation of goods and increased contact with urban buyers and global capitalism. Leading the changes were the people who first understood the new opportunities for the craft and led other people to them. This pattern of a small number of individuals introducing innovation in traditional pottery communities has been mentioned by researchers in other communities (Hendry 1992:127; Foster 1967:294). Sometimes, the community reacts negatively to innovation and obligates the creative person to conform to traditional pottery styles (Reina 1963:24). Although change has many causes, Dean Arnold argues that social status is the engine that drives innovation, with the high-status people innovating to establish leadership and maintain their distinctiveness, whereas low-status people innovate in an effort to improve their social and economic conditions (1985:220).

The leaders of change in Ráquira in the last half century have been men, especially Reyes Suárez and Aurelio Varela. Both were producers, and neither was a teacher or formal economic change agent. They provided leadership by instituting changes in their own workshops; as other potters observed their successes, they emulated the innovators. The changes introduced by Suárez and Varela were economic and production oriented, and as a result the new ceramics shapes and work procedures frequently had little or no reference to the earlier practices of the community's women producers. Change in the men's workshops during recent decades has been oriented to increase speed in production, and careful finishing has been deemphasized. Men's town workshops have taken definitive steps toward industrial ceramics, and the production of planters has symbolized this process. Colombian economic planners have encouraged this economic transformation of crafts in recent decades, and the changes in Ráquira are only one manifestation of that policy.

Economic Expansion and Men in the Crafts

As politicians and economists in Latin America debate the economic future of the individual nations, crafts are mentioned for their potential for job development and economic growth (Lauer 1984:58ff; Urrutia and Villalba 1971:1–3). Since craft is one of the most important sources of work in the mestizo and indigenous countries of Latin America, including Colombia (Duncan 1983, 1986), it is a target for change. Artesanías de Colombia records suggest that there are a million and a half craftspeople located in 458 of the country's one thousand townships (Montoya 1990:15). In a survey of craft production in Latin America in the early 1980s, Mirko Lauer (1984:40) also documented one and a half million craftspeople in Colombia out of an economically active population of just over eleven million (11,067,000), representing 13.55 percent of all workers. Ecuador and Peru also had 13 percent of their workforces in crafts, and these three countries have the highest percentage of people in the crafts in South America. Most Andean craftspeople have traditionally been farmers or small-town dwellers living within subsistence-based economies, and this noncommercial sector of the economy has been a difficult target for development planners to reach.

In a study of crafts and economics in Colombia, Miguel Urrutia and Clara Elsa Villalba (1971:2) suggest that if the purpose of economic development is to increase the income level of the population, official policy should focus on shifting the traditional sectors of the economy to modern industrial production. This implies moving people from traditional occupations to "modern" ones or transforming traditional craft production to increase productivity and income levels.

By focusing on industrializing traditional sectors of the economy, development theory has essentially supported the transfer of village crafts from women to men. In male hierarchical communities like Ráquira, men assume control of crafts production when market expansion occurs (Ehlers 1990:20; Tice 1995:13). Even though women may have been the traditional potters, they are marginalized when men assume control of production because of the cultural construction of gender and work. So, there is a gender differential in the benefits of economic expansion when communities exchange the gender complementarity of craft production for the male domination of production, markets, and capital in semi-industrialized workshops.

Néstor García Canclini juxtaposes the issues of tradition and development by defining Latin America as a place where traditional culture has not disappeared and modernity has not completely arrived, and he questions whether modernization should be the primary objective for countries in the region (1990:13). As Latin America moves into the twenty-first century, he suggests that traditional crafts will coexist with satellite transmission, video, and other forms of electronic communication (ibid.:200). This suggests that traditional cultures are developing along with the larger nation of which they are a part, but in the process the economic expansion transforms them.

Ceramics as Craft or Industry

In Colombia country earthenwares have historically been made by craft techniques, but in recent decades that has changed with the introduction of proletarianized working patterns to meet the increased market demand for pottery that symbolizes the "authenticity" of rural culture. Ironically, potters in town have reacted to the expanding market for symbolic cultural goods by adopting mass-production techniques that virtually eliminate the traditional craft that their pottery symbolizes.

Although rural ceramic forms were limited to traditional cooking and storage pots until the 1930s, industrial products now meet this need, and rural ceramics have shifted to a new symbolic role representing the nostalgia for country life. The functional role of earthenware pottery has changed dramatically with the introduction of new materials for the manufacture of cooking and food-storage containers, the expanded accessibility

of aqueducts, and changes in food preservation, such as canning and re-
frigeration. Although earthenware pottery is no longer needed for most
traditional functional purposes, it continues to be made. Today, traditional
pottery may be found in the corner of a peasant farmer's adobe house as
chicha (corn beer) ferments inside, or it may serve as a decorative high-
light in an elegant urban apartment, placed next to a computer and international design magazines. These seeming contrasts are part of the unique
mosaic of tradition and modernity that characterizes Colombia at the end
of the twentieth century.

Although crafts were historically made in Colombia for domestic use
and for local trade, in recent decades crafts have become commodities in
national and international markets, and the economy associated with them
now entails large-scale contracts, trading of futures, and brokers. However, the majority of craftspeople still produce just to survive and have
little opportunity for renovation of their forms and little time for issues of
symbolism and significance (García Canclini 1990:228).

The increased leisure time of Colombia's urban professional classes in
recent decades has led to a growth in tourism, which frequently involves
searching for authentic cultural roots in village crafts. Although this interest has coincided with the decline in the functional uses of earthenware
pottery, many village potters continue to produce pots that are perceived
as autochthonous and culturally correct because they conform to the expectations of the urban tourist in search of "cultural roots." More than
pots, craftspeople are selling ethnicity and cultural memory. The Colombian anthropologist Nina S. de Friedemann suggests that this tourism-driven
commerce is as destructive to the traditional values of village ceramics as
was the Spanish Conquest (1993:151).

Traditional village and indigenous ceramics have not disappeared, but
they are in the process of a radical transformation. In some cases nontraditional workers are now making village earthenware, and totally new
forms have appeared as potters have adapted to the demands of urban
markets. Although many potters from the older generations continue
making traditional country earthenwares, the younger generations regard
ceramics as a source of employment and income, and in the town of Ráquira
young men potters have completely turned to industrial mass-production
techniques to augment yields and income.

Potters are concerned with what will produce more income for the family, and they make the pots that sell the best. The new commodity-type
production in town represents an attempt to take advantage of the market
possibilities of the national and international economies. After many cen-

turies as a rural domestic women's craft, Ráquira ceramics have been discovered by men interested in their potential as a medium of capitalist production, and they are leading the next generation in that direction.

Craft and Change

Ráquira is a study of social and economic change from a local domestic craft to incipient industrialism, fueled by the expansion of national and global capitalism. For Ráquira potters the balance between tradition and economic change has gradually shifted toward commodity production as the number of men potters has grown over the past few decades. As the people of Ráquira begin their second millennium as potters, the men's style is leading toward industrial production, but the women's style continues as a strong representation of tradition and cultural memory. The contrasts in the cultural construction of gender between rural and town people lead to women being the conservators of tradition and men the perpetuators of capitalist-style economic expansion.

Out of the tension between gender, ethnicity, and economics over the last five centuries, the people of Ráquira have constructed the social organization and ceramics styles that characterize them today. The two ceramics styles are the result of contrasting systems of cultural assumptions between the rural and town populations which are reflected in gender ideology and economics. The roots of these gender and economic systems can be traced from the period of colonial history to the twentieth century.

2

Ráquira and Colombian Ceramics History

Colombia's indigenous groups had a five-thousand-year history of making earthenware pottery before the arrival of the Spanish, and prehispanic potters in Ráquira formed part of that tradition. As a *mestizo* ceramics community today, Ráquira draws from both the indigenous and Spanish traditions, and these form the basis of the division between women's and men's styles of ceramics. The contemporary gender-linked styles in Ráquira began to take shape in the dynamic between gender, ethnicity, and social change during the colonial period. As occurred in other areas of the Americas, indigenous men adapted readily to the public culture of the Spanish, borrowing the tools and technology of the newcomers, which led to new work styles in agriculture and building. Since there were fewer demands for change in the domestic sphere, women were able to retain their indigenous work styles in such areas as child rearing, food preparation, and crafts. The department of Boyacá was the heartland of Muisca culture, and much of that heritage survived the Spanish colonial period, which has contributed to the continuation of indigenous work styles.

Muisca Period: Indigenous Crafts

Ráquira was described by the earliest Spanish chroniclers as a center of pottery making, and archaeologists have also documented prehispanic ceramics workshops near the present-day town (Falchetti 1975). Writing in the early 1600s, Fray Pedro Simón ([1627] 1981:305) mentions that when the Spanish first passed through the area of Ráquira in 1537 (they actually were in the neighboring town of Tinjacá), they were surprised at the abundant production of good ceramics there. They called the town "el pueblo de los olleros" or "the town of the potters," confirming that this was an established ceramics region before the arrival of the Spanish. Although it was not an important center for pottery before the Conquest, nor during the colonial period, it did survive and maintain its tradition.

The Muiscas were the indigenous inhabitants of Ráquira, and their ceramics were limited to utilitarian rustic ware (Falchetti 1975:198). Their settlement pattern consisted of houses dispersed on agricultural plots, with a few dwellings clustered around a chief's house (Villamarin and Villamarin 1979:37, 39). Ráquira was an isolated community during this period, as it has continued to be until today, and was not involved in the production of elaborate luxury ceramics. Indeed, the Muiscas devoted their creative energies more to politics and social organization than to material culture. They were known for a complex chiefdomship political organization and for economic wealth based on the production of salt and emeralds. In fact, one of the first references to Ráquira in colonial documents is to its Chief Suaya (Orbell 1995:40). Before the Spanish Conquest the Muiscas dominated the present states of Boyacá and Cundinamarca politically, economically, and culturally. Although they were productive weavers, goldworkers, and potters, their craft work was poorly finished. Carl Henrik Langebaek (1987:93f) has shown that they carried on an active commerce in ceramics between towns that made pottery and those that did not.

The form for which the Muiscas are most known is the *múcura,* or bottle. It has a spherical body about 15 centimeters in diameter and a vertical spout that is 10 to 12 centimeters long. A *múcura* is usually decorated with slip designs, with human and frog forms sometimes modeled onto the spout, and it would normally hold one liter or more of liquid. In addition to the bottle, the Muiscas also made a pitcher with a broad, spherical body, a short wide neck, and a handle; it would hold approximately two liters of liquid. There are also large storage bottles for liquids, as well as cooking pots and bowls.

The decoration of Muisca pottery was not carefully applied and in many cases seems to have been rushed and irregular. They used geometric designs including the circle, the sunburst, the chevron, the cross, and the scroll, among others. The human figure was highly stylized with a flat face, angular nose, and coffee-bean eyes. Only a few pieces were well modeled, suggesting that the potters were not specialists but were probably engaged in agriculture in addition to pottery making.

Ráquira was never an important center during the prehispanic or colonial periods; moreover, finer ceramics were produced in other regions of Colombia (Duncan 1996b, 1992; Duncan et al. 1993). Indeed, the fact of its economic marginality was probably the major factor contributing to the survival of ceramics production in Ráquira. The reason is that country pottery is economically viable only where agriculture is marginal and must be supplemented by craft production. Ráquira has always been a small town in an arid, agriculturally poor valley of the central Andes of Colombia, and that fact forced its people to make pottery to supplement their incomes. Prehispanic indigenous production techniques and styles continued virtually intact throughout the colonial era and are still in use today.

Spanish Ceramics

The Spanish were also heirs to a rich ceramics tradition, which Charles Fairbanks (1972:143) attributed to the deforestation of the Iberian peninsula by agriculture and animal herding. With little wood or other materials for making containers, the Spanish specialized in ceramics. Iberian potters were introduced to all of the major influences in ceramic technology and style from the Greco-Roman Mediterranean world, but the most profound and long-lasting influence came from Muslim ceramics (especially during the Moorish occupation of A.D. 711–1492). It was the Mediterranean heritage that most influenced Spanish ceramics, and it was especially important in the pottery traditions of the southern region of Andalusia (Rosselló 1992:97), which reached the Americas.

In the first two hundred years of Colombian colonial history, the Spanish law that controlled the American colonies was rigid and restrictive and did not permit trade with any nation other than the mother country. Even trade between the colonies was restricted, so that majolica ware made in Spanish-built workshops in Puebla, Mexico, could not be traded to Colombia. Glazed ceramics could be brought to Colombia only from Spain, and even Chinese porcelains had to be imported through Spain.

Shipping records from the Archivo General de Indias (General Archive of the Indies) indicate that during the sixteenth century most of the Spanish ceramics entering Colombia were majolica ware and shipping jars from two ceramic centers: Seville and Talavera de la Reina. As one of the most important cities in southern Spain, Seville had been an important Moorish administrative, economic, and cultural center, and it continued to be so after the Christian reconquest of that city in 1248. It was a major ceramics-producing center during the Moorish period, and Hispano-Moresque (*mudéjar*) ceramics continued to be made there until the sixteenth century. *Mudéjar* ceramics followed Moorish design principles and technology but frequently incorporated Christian symbols or decorative elements into the finished pots. The Moorish ceramics quarter, called Triana, was located on the west bank of the Guadalquivir River and continued as the center of ceramics making after the reconquest, and Moorish potters made ceramics for the new Christian rulers as they had previously for the Muslim rulers. Most of the common functional pottery that arrived in the Americas from Spain was from this tradition.

Talavera de la Reina is located in central Spain, removed from the *mudéjar* influences of the south and more oriented toward European ceramics. During the sixteenth century Talavera potters produced blue or white wares with decoration influenced by designs on imported Chinese porcelains. Designs incorporated stylized floral and animal figures, such as butterflies and deer. Plates and vases were significant forms, but wall tiles were also important. The outstanding manifestation of Talavera de la Reina ceramics was in murals made of wall tiles and placed in churches, convents, and public buildings. While some were historical, frequently they had strong religious themes, which gave them an identity as "Christian" ceramics, an identification that was reinforced by a tradition of expert monk potters who lived and worked in the community and in the neighboring pottery town of Puente del Arzobispo (Giral 1993:57). Some priests in Colombia taught Spanish-style pottery making as one aspect of the evangelization efforts (Romero 1984:355f.), but the Talavera de la Reina style was never established in the country.

Seville was the primary port city for exportation to the Americas during the sixteenth century, and through it passed shiploads of wine and food packed in ceramic shipping jars and many thousands of vases, bowls, plates, wall murals, and other ceramic objects primarily from the workshops of Seville and Talavera de la Reina. Spanish ceramics were shipped to Colombia throughout the 1500s, largely as containers for wine and other foodstuffs, such as olives, olive oil, and capers. However, other kinds of ceramics were also sent. For example, in 1534 a potter from Seville, Fernando Omedo, sold two large glazed baptismal fonts to the bishop of Tierra Firme (as Colombia was known in the early sixteenth century), Father Luis de Berlanga (Gestoso y Pérez 1903:428). In 1542 a shipment of 5,000 roof tiles went from Seville to Tierra Firme, along with 20 empty storage jars for each of 35 casks of wine, in total 700 storage jars (Archivo General de Indias [hereafter AGI]: Protocolos). In 1546 another 70 storage jars were sent with 10 casks of wine. In 1572, 5,400 ceramic shipping jars filled with wine and foodstuffs were sent. In 1580 a similar shipment of 905 jars of wine and foodstuffs was made (ibid.).

A government-controlled price list of 355 imported items in Cartagena in 1575 includes Talavera-style majolica and other ceramics from Pisa and Seville, including vases, fruit bowls, and other forms, along with the hundreds of items required for the colonial lifestyle, ranging from clothes and shoes to saddles and tools (AGI: Audiencia de Santafé, Legajo 187). In 1583 a shipment of Spanish majolica included 36 bowls (*escudillas*), 204 pieces of blue and white dinnerware (*loza*), 108 additional pieces of dinnerware with unspecified decoration, and 96 juglike pitchers (*jarros*) (Lister and Lister 1987:317). These kinds of shipments continued throughout the colonial period, so these ceramics styles were well known at least in Spanish households in Colombia.

Today there are examples of colonial-era shipping jars in the collection of the Casa Juan de Vargas, a museum in Tunja, which is near Ráquira, and these jars are also mentioned in accounts of colonial life in Bogotá. The glazed versions of these shipping jars (called *botijuelas*) were used for wine and liquids, and the unglazed versions were for oils or solids such as tar or lard. Capers, lima beans, and chickpeas were also shipped in the unglazed versions, which were sealed with natural cork. These shipping jars were later reused as water jars, and when broken, the sherds were used as fill in construction. The Spanish versions probably were made near Seville and Cádiz (Goggin 1970:3f). Diego Velázquez's painting "The Waterseller of Seville" (ca. 1620) shows the waterseller using a shipping jar like the ones in the Casa Juan de Vargas to carry water (Clarke 1996:153), which documents the use of that type of pot in Seville.

The Spanish majolica tradition of painted ceramics, derived from Muslim sources, was never introduced into Colombia, although it was practiced for a few decades in Panama. In fact, no Spanish potters came to the Americas in the first hundred years following contact (1492–1592) (Rubio y Moreno 1917:49). Passenger lists were kept for all ships leaving Spain for the Americas, and the occupations of passengers were recorded, but there were no potters. Several things are indicated by the absence of Spanish ceramists in the Americas in the early colonial period. One is that local indigenous potters were supplying everyday domestic needs. Also, the policy of the Crown was to export Spanish goods to the colonies in exchange for precious metals and other natural resources rather than to develop industries in the colonies. Finally, the small Spanish populations in the individual colonies did not constitute a market large enough to support separate ceramic industries, and only in Mexico was a permanent Spanish-style majolica industry established. The result in Colombia was the uninterrupted development of the local village ceramics traditions of strong forms and undecorated, monochrome surfaces, such as the one in Ráquira. This tradition of village ceramics has dominated all regions of mestizo ceramics in Colombia, from the Conquest to the present day.

The most important contributions made by the Spanish to ceramics in Colombia were in architectural ceramics, most notably bricks, roof tiles, floor tiles, and water and sewage pipes (Herrera 1976:108). The availability of this new set of building materials gradually transformed architecture in the country. During the first years after contact, thousands of bricks and roof tiles were shipped to the Americas from Spain, frequently as ballast in ships (Lister and Lister 1987:204). As the Spanish influence grew, brickyards and roof-tile workshops were established locally, and indigenous laborers were assigned to work in them. Brick was used primarily in urban areas, especially for official buildings, church architecture, and the residences of the Spanish elite. The indigenous practices of *tapia pisada* (packed adobe walls), stone walls, and thatched roofs continued to be used in rural architecture, including houses and churches. The making of brick and tile became one of the most significant Spanish influences that transformed precolumbian ceramics into mestizo ceramics. Another Spanish contribution to ceramics was the introduction of the Mediterranean kiln (Therrien 1991:71), which began to replace the indigenous practice of open-air firings.

Missionaries played an important role in the introduction of Spanish ceramic techniques to indigenous people, although there is no documented evidence of their direct influence on Ráquira ceramics. During the 1500s and especially the 1600s, Jesuits were active in the eastern plains region of Colombia, evangelizing and developing European-style crafts among indigenous groups while emphasizing the use of local materials such as natural fibers, resins, leather, cloth, cotton, and ceramics. The Jesuits produced pots, water-storage jars, and other "unusual" vases that were sold in Bogotá and elsewhere (Romero 1984:355f). In addition to their work among indigenous groups, they established a pottery next to the parish church in the Barrio de Belén (Bethlehem Barrio) in Bogotá, which later became the site of the first ceramic industry in Colombia. Germán Colmenares confirms that the Jesuit model of missionary work combined the development of productive industries in textiles and ceramics with education and evangelism (1969).

Although the history of Colombian ceramics after the arrival of the Spanish is one of gradual indigenous adaptation to Iberian designs, there were always pockets of resistance to the foreign influences, and many communities retained their traditional styles. Since the American colonies were to be consumers of Spanish goods, Spanish ceramic technology was not transferred to Colombia until the late eighteenth century, and then only storage jars for gunpowder were made there. The more expensive Hispano-

Moresque ware for the table was never made in the country and was instead imported throughout the colonial period.

Types of Ceramics in Colombia during the Colonial Period

Six types of ceramics were used in Colombia during the colonial period (Duncan 1985b:53), and most were imported wares used for shipping. However, the imported ceramics also included display ceramics and tableware. Architectural ceramics and domestic cooking pottery were made locally. The six types are as follows:

1. Porcelain. As early as the sixteenth century, Chinese porcelains were brought to Colombia from Spain, and by the late 1700s porcelains made in the new English and French factories were reaching Colombia as well. Porcelain dinnerware, vases, and sculptural pieces became collector's items in Colombia, as in Europe, but they were not produced locally.

2. Hispano-Moresque. This majolica style of ceramics from Seville was brought to Colombia throughout the colonial period. It is based on the Islamic tradition of tin-glazed earthenware with a painted decoration over a white background. The related Talavera style was also popular in Colombia, and today Talavera-style plaques can still be seen on the sides of houses in the colonial section of Bogotá, identifying street names. Hispano-Moresque ware is similar to what is called majolica in Italy, faience in France, and delft in the Netherlands.

3. Creamware. This was an English development designed to simulate the appearance of porcelain in more common, industrially produced ware. In 1765 Josiah Wedgwood began the industrial production of dinnerware and other household items in creamware, making "fine ceramics" available to the public at a modest price. It was imported to Colombia shortly after it appeared in European markets, and by 1832 it was being produced in Colombia (Perdomo 1965:5).

4. Common glazed earthenware. The Spanish produced a low-fire glazed utilitarian ware without decoration that was used to store and transport wine, olive oil, and even gunpowder. This pottery performed the role of today's tin cans and glass or plastic jars in packing foodstuffs for shipment. A common form was the wine or olive-oil jar (*botijuela*), which contained approximately twenty liters and had

a small, five-centimeter mouth that could be corked and sealed. Common colors resulting from the lead glaze used on this ware ranged from deep olive green to yellowish cream. The wheel-thrown, lead-glazed ceramics made by village craftsmen in various parts of Colombia today are an adaptation of this Spanish tradition, and the same glaze colors are still produced.

5. Unglazed earthenware pottery. This was by far the most common type of ceramics available during the colonial period, and it consisted primarily of the simple, rustic, unglazed earthenware pots used for cooking and storage. These were made throughout Colombia by local indigenous potters, responding to the need for containers for food and drink. The traditional pottery produced today in Ráquira is similar to the cooking and storage pottery from the colonial time (Cardale 1989:57).

Common domestic earthenware pottery used for food preparation and storage in the rural areas and small towns of Colombia forms part of a cross-cultural earthenware style that exists in many agricultural societies in the world. Its origins probably lie with the first pottery developed during the agricultural revolution of several thousand years ago. The food-preparation pots (*ollas*) have a round, globular shape and a mouth that is sufficiently open to permit easy stirring and serving. The shape produces a strong, seamless profile capable of resisting the repeated thermal shock of rapid heating and cooling associated with open-fire cooking, and the same profile permits easy balancing on the stones used to build a fire. Water pots also have a globular or oval profile, but the ones used for carrying water have a narrow, elongated neck to prevent the water from spilling.

6. Floor and roof tiles. Spanish architecture required fired brick roof and floor tiles. As discussed earlier, they were originally imported from Spain, but local production was set up in the early years to meet the construction needs for houses for the landed elite, churches, and official buildings. These tiles were unglazed and made with red earthenware clays, similar to ones used today.

Conquest and Early Colonial Period (1537–1620): Spanish Feudalism

In March 1537 Gonzalo Jiménez de Quesada reached the highland plateau of the Muiscas with an army of two hundred men, having traveled overland for eleven months from Santa Marta on the Atlantic coast. They defeated the Muiscas and collected a considerable amount of gold (Bushnell 1993:9). The area was called El Nuevo Reino de Granada (The New Kingdom of Granada) in honor of the final Spanish defeat of the Moors in Granada in 1492, but the name was commonly shortened to Nueva Granada during the colonial period.

In 1550 Santa Fé de Bogotá, as the city was known during the colonial period, was made the administrative seat for the royal representatives in the colony, and in 1564 a president was named for the colony, raising its status in the hierarchy of colonial administration. During this period New Granada was of secondary importance among the Spanish colonies, following New Spain (Mexico), and New Castille (Peru), areas that produced greater wealth in precious metals and other valuables. New Granada's most important city, Bogotá, was located in an intermontane valley in the interior of the country, accessible from the coasts only by a month-long trip up the Magdalena River, followed by a difficult climb up the eastern range of the Andes onto the central plateau, located 2,600 meters above sea level. Its geography made New Granada the most isolated of the major seats of Spanish rule in the Americas.

The early colonial period was a time of conquest, mercenaries, and transient representatives of the Spanish Crown. The first "Spanish" towns were established during this period, but they were Spanish primarily in name because their architecture, agriculture, material culture, and inhabitants were largely indigenous. For much of this period, the Spanish were fighting outbreaks of armed resistance from indigenous groups, and their military and political control was tenuous. There was little or no attempt to establish Spanish industry because all of the Spanish efforts were directed toward conquest and consolidation.

Although Iberian towns do not generally have central plazas, virtually all Latin American towns have one, including Ráquira. Towns in the Americas were built as Spanish strongholds, and the central plaza became an important architectural feature for displaying and defending their power. The town was the locus of Spanish people, institutions, and political power: the wealthy (*encomenderos*), the powerful (representatives of the Crown), the military, and the clergy. The four sides of the main plaza (or *plaza mayor*) were lined by the buildings of the municipal government, the church, important commercial establishments, the military garrison, and the houses of the wealthy. The *plaza mayor* could easily be defended in times of conflict, while in times of peace major public events and ceremonies were held there to impress the indigenous people with the power and wealth of the Spanish. The design of the central plaza made a political statement, affirming the preeminence of the rulers over the subjugated populace (Rojas 1978:347–54). The organization of towns became the principal tool for the consolidation of Spanish control over public culture during the colonial period.

Early Colonial Ceramics

Indigenous functional pottery continued to be made during this period (Herrera 1976:108), including domestic earthenware for cooking, eating, and drinking. As the Spaniards asked for the bottles, pitchers, and covered containers that were familiar to them, the indigenous potters produced them along with the cooking pots and bowls that they made for themselves. The result was the gradual development of a new mestizo style of pottery that combined precolumbian cooking pots and bowls with Spanish amphoras and pitchers. The ceramics made in Colombia during this time included toasting pans, cooking and storage pots, fermentation pots for *chicha* (corn beer), water storage jars, and water bottles (Cardale 1989:57).

The wealthiest Spaniards imported highly valued European and Chinese glazed and painted ceramics for use in their homes, including pitchers, wash basins, bottles, pharmacy jars, and jars for wine and olive oil. The presence of imported porcelains and ceramics in a house served as an identifier of social class, which was inherently linked to European ethnicity. Display ceramics were of foreign origin, while the disposable pots of daily kitchen use were of local, indigenous manufacture. The fine display ceramics of Muisca design, such as stemmed goblet/bowls and complexly painted water bottles (*múcuras*), gradually disappeared from use during the first century of the colonial period (Cardale 1989:57).

The precolumbian design features and symbols related to indigenous religions also began to disappear from ceramics decorations during this period (Herrera 1976:108; Duncan 1992:14–17), as did the ceramic icons of shamans and mythical beings (Duncan 1993:24–25). Today some isolated Indian groups still retain those motifs in their craft designs, but generally mestizo communities do not use them. When potters stopped making the prehispanic ceramic figures of chiefs and shamans, they started making Spanish-inspired figures of horses and chickens in their place, transforming and continuing the tradition of figure making.

Although the history of Colombian ceramics after the arrival of the Spanish is one of gradual indigenous adaptation to Iberian designs, there were always pockets of resistance to the foreign influences and many communities retained their traditional styles. As a result, indigenous, prehispanic production techniques and stylistic elements continued throughout the colonial era and are still used in mestizo and indigenous communities today (Cardale 1989:57). In many areas of Colombia, the local indigenous village ceramics traditions of strong forms and undecorated, monochrome surfaces still exist, traditions that have dominated mestizo ceramics in Colombia from the Conquest to the present.

The Mixing of Cultures (Mestizaje)

Starting from the indigenous basis of Colombian culture and ceramics at the time of the arrival of the Spanish, some sectors of the population remained almost completely indigenous while others adopted Iberian cultural influences. The Spanish presence was small in the province of Tunja, the name of the administrative district that covered the region around Ráquira during the colonial period. During the last half of the sixteenth century there were only two hundred Spanish residents to seventy thousand tribute-paying Indians in the province, and in the next century the number of Spanish residents rose only to six hundred (Gómez 1984:172–73).

Colombia was never "Spanish" culturally in part because there were few Iberian women to raise children with Spanish values and behaviors. Between 1550 and 1750 men constituted 90 percent of the migrants from Spain to the Americas; women made up just 10 percent, and most of them arrived only in the last decades of that period (Céspedes del Castillo 1992:183). During the first century, most Spanish men took indigenous wives or mistresses, which led to the biological mixing of the two groups. However, the indigenous mothers raised their mestizo children with their own indigenous values because, of course, they could not raise them with Spanish values. Since women are the primary cultural influence in the training of new generations, Colombia's biologically mestizo society was largely indigenous culturally, and the people and the traditional ceramics of Ráquira reflect that pattern of mixture.

Early Colonial Ceramics in Ráquira

The Colombian archaeologist Monika Therrien Johannesson excavated the waster pile of a colonial-era ceramics workshop in the area of Ráquira that had been a reservation for tribute-paying Indians, and she documented the types of ceramics made during that period. Among the shapes she found are the water bottle, bowl, cooking or storage pot, toasting pan, and footed bowl. All are still made in Ráquira except for the footed bowl, although it was made until recently in the neighboring township of Sutamarchán (1991:88).

Burial ceramics continued to be made in the Muisca style at least until 1580. This included coiled serpents modeled in relief on pots and bowls and water symbols painted on the surfaces (Therrien 1991:98), which indicates that the Spanish influence in this kind of ceramics seems to have been negligible during the first fifty years after contact. The water and serpent symbolism is associated with the Muisca origin myth of Bachué and Bochica, who are said to have emerged from a sacred lake in the region at the beginning of time. After having children and populating the world and teaching them the arts of cultured living (agriculture, weaving, and other crafts), they transformed themselves into serpents and returned to the lake. The Muisca-style ritual burial ceramics do seem to disappear by the beginning of the seventeenth century.

The basic design elements of prehispanic ceramics continued uninterrupted in the daily domestic wares of Ráquira during the colonial period (Therrien 1991:100). Therrien found *múcuras* (water bottles), *copas* (footed drinking bowls), and *cuencos* (round serving bowls) in large quantities, and she postulated that these were commercially produced for trade. She also found reduced quantities of the *olla* (cooking pot), *arepero* (toasting pan), and a smaller version of the *cuenco*, suggesting they may have been made for domestic use (ibid.:91).

The commercial production of *múcuras, copas*, and large *cuencos* may have been for use in the *chicherías* (bars for home-brewed corn beer), which were common during that time. In fact, large numbers of *chicherías* existed during the colonial period in this region, and they were known for the social disorder associated with them (Villamarin 1972:81). These *chicherías* continued to exist well into the twentieth century and were eventually replaced by the beer stores of today, which are still the primary gathering places for men on weekends. Many families still brew *chicha* and *guarapo* (slightly fermented sugar cane) at home for their own consumption, following the indigenous pattern.

In excavations in the *veredas* (rural districts) around Ráquira, Falchetti (1975:240) found two different styles of ceramics dating from the colonial period. She found newer ceramic forms in the area of Pueblo Viejo (the old townsite of Ráquira), in contrast to the ceramics found in four "rural" areas distant from Pueblo Viejo. This coexistence of contrasting ceramics styles continues to be important today.

Encomienda and Church

In 1562 Ráquira was mentioned for the first time as a town in Spanish colonial records when it was referred to as an *encomienda* with Indian tribute payers (Orbell 1995:38). The *encomendero* was an individual who had been given land with the charge (or *encomienda*) of pacifying or conquering the people on it and collecting tribute from them for the Crown. Ráquira, Tinjacá, and the neighboring towns were made into *encomiendas* as early as 1540, following the same political divisions used by the Muiscas (Villamarin and Villamarin 1979:34).

A 1565 list showed 189 Indian inhabitants under the Spanish *encomendero* Diego Alfonso, and his tenure continued at least until 1601 (AGI: Sección de Contaduría). His wife, Eugenia Alfonso, succeeded him in 1606 (AGI: Audiencia de Santafé, Legajo 164). The names of other *encomenderos* of Ráquira include Juan de Uzquieta y Valdés in 1651 (AGI: Audiencia de Santafé, Legajo 370), Juan Martínez de Santoyo in 1666 (AGI: Audiencia de Santafé, Legajo 769), and Luisa Teresa de Villela in 1692 (AGI: Audiencia de Santafé, Legajo 370). This system ensured that tribute could be collected from the indigenous population and that they could be evangelized. As tribute was collected for the Crown, the *encomendero* was permitted to collect additional tribute for himself or herself. Since the Crown had no effective control over these *encomenderos,* this practice frequently led to the uncontrolled exploitation of indigenous communities, which was strongly protested by Bartolomé de Las Casas ([1552] 1992) and others (Orbell 1995:37–39).

Under the *encomienda* system, indigenous people were also required to perform unpaid labor for the Spanish, called the *mita* or *concierto,* which included building churches, public buildings, or houses, constructing and maintaining roads, cleaning toilets, mining, domestic service, and other such jobs. The *mita* was based on the indigenous practice of *minga,* or communal labor done for the larger community, but the Spanish converted it into a tribute labor for public and private projects. Spanish law required that people be paid for this work, but in practice they rarely were. In 1584 Don Diego de Torres (the Hispanicized name of a Muisca village chief in the province of Tunja, today Boyacá) denounced that Spanish townsmen were paying the Indians with broken pieces of lamp bases and other metal that had no value (AGI: Patronato 196). Since the local people had seen so few coins, they could not distinguish genuine Spanish currency from similar Spanish metalwork and could be easily defrauded.

Under the Spanish, Ráquira was restructured from a dispersed rural community into a nucleated town to facilitate tax collection, political control, and evangelical activity. Like other small indigenous settlements, Ráquira was officially recognized by the colonial government in 1580 as a distinct economic entity. Father Francisco de Orjuela of the Order of Saint Augustine was the priest then (F. Bonilla 1989:12), and he is identified as the founder of the town. Priests played important roles in the organization of nucleated towns because that process facilitated their evangelical efforts.

A permanent priest was assigned to Ráquira at the beginning of the 1600s, and a church was built in 1613. The church was said to have been beautifully decorated (Mora 1974:10). The original church was built with the same thick adobe walls as the colonial churches in the neighboring towns of Sáchica, Cucaita, and Sutatausa, which still exist today (Orbell 1995:144–45). The church in Ráquira was a *templo doctrinero,* an architectural style built in small, colonial towns that featured an outer porch where indigenous people could stand and observe the mass. This outer porch was originally intended to facilitate evangelization since it permitted the person of indigenous descent to hear the service without having to enter the church. However, this architectural style also communicated the difference in social status between the Spaniards and acculturated mestizos sitting inside the church and the illiterate, unbelieving Indians standing outside.

Reservations and Indians

In 1592 reservations were established for Indians, whereby they were guaranteed land that could not be taken from them by the Spanish or mestizos, who were even prohibited from living or working on reservation lands. In exchange for the land, Indians were required to pay tribute to the Crown and contribute *mita* labor for the *encomenderos.* However, much of the land in the reservations (*resguardos*) was arid and barren mountainside not conducive agriculture (Moreno y Escandón 1985:329). Many Indians, however, rejected the offer of reservation land, simultaneously rejecting the obligation to pay tribute and perform *mita.* They either moved to more remote areas not controlled by the Spanish, or they stayed and became acculturated into the mestizo group.

In May 1598 there was a concentrated effort on the part of the Spanish to round up the dispersed Indians, but they had little success because of Indian resistance (Colmenares 1970:70). All of the towns near Ráquira were losing population, and the Spanish responded by consolidating smaller communities in an attempt to maintain nucleated towns. In 1602 the Crown inspector, Luis Henríquez, ordered the Indian inhabitants of the neighboring areas of Tijo, Chivatá, and Urancha to be consolidated into Ráquira (ibid.:112). The resistance of indigenous people to the Spanish was manifest throughout the colonial period in the fact that they continually returned to dispersed settlement patterns that gave them greater independence, even though the Spanish insisted on grouping them into towns (Villamarin and Villamarin 1979:47).

The order of the Crown to consolidate indigenous groups into towns was intended to accelerate their acculturation and teach them European-style cultural patterns (Mora 1974:13). It also complied with the recommendations of the Church to form nucleated urban settlements to facilitate the teaching of Christianity. Merchants favored the formation of towns, which created centralized markets for the buying and selling of goods, and the military preferred towns because it was easier to control the populations. But indigenous people also saw the implications of town living under the Spanish, and many avoided it. Thirty-four years later, in 1636, Juan de Valverde found that Indian resistance to living in towns was so strong that many houses in the region where Ráquira is located were empty and covered with grass (Colmenares 1970:74). This process of resistance seems to have continued in Ráquira, as indicated by the continual decline of indigenous inhabitants until 1690.

Even today the traditional people living in the scattered rural communities surrounding Ráquira are considered Indianized mestizos by the town dwellers. When they engage in "countrified" behaviors, such as urinating in public, they are called *indio* (Indian) by the town dwellers, and the expression "No sea indio" (Don't be an Indian) serves to reprimand anyone who acts in a socially unacceptable manner. Although everyone is considered mestizo now, the colonial pattern continues of Hispanicized mestizos living in town and indigenous-like mestizos living in the rural areas.

Death in Ráquira

Spanish colonial records show high rates of population loss among the indigenous people of Ráquira during the first two centuries of contact, rates similar to those in other parts of the Americas. The first census in Ráquira was not made until 1565, twenty-eight years after contact with the Spanish. At that point, there were 188 tribute-paying indigenous people, but that figure had dropped to 37 by 1690, a fifth of the size of the first count (Ruiz Rivera 1975:209, 358). After 1690 the indigenous population began to increase. Because of the population loss in those first two centuries after contact, much technical information and design skill in ceramics, weaving, and basketry must have been lost.

Table 2.1. Decline of tribute-paying population in seventeenth-century Ráquira and neighboring towns

Towns	1602	1636	1690	Percentage remaining
Ráquira	96	49	37	38.54
Sutamarchán	169	100	68	40.23
Sáchica	299	142	74	24.75
Tinjacá	378	246	158	41.80
Tijo-Chivatá	141	95	34	24.11
Cucaita	183	107	61	33.33

Source: Ruiz Rivera 1975:355–59

This decline in the tribute-paying indigenous population was due to a number of causes. First was the violence used in the Conquest itself. The Spanish used armed force, and when the indigenous people resisted, many paid with their lives. Even in recent decades, ranchers along Colombia's cattle frontier in the Eastern Plains region have continued the practice of killing entire bands of Indians over land conflicts. One example that was successfully prosecuted occurred on December 27, 1967, when a rancher in La Ribiera, Arauca (300 or more kilometers to the east of Ráquira), invited a band of Cuiba Indians to dinner and with the help of others killed eighteen of them. During the trial, which the author attended as an observer, the ranchers argued in their defense that it was a common cultural practice to kill Indians, and they did not know it was wrong. At the conclusion of the trial they were acquitted. The national government, however, was able to retry them later in a different venue and win a conviction.

It was the large number of incidents of this type that led to the protests of the Spanish priest Bartolomé de Las Casas in the early sixteenth century ([1552] 1992:116ff), in the midst of the Conquest. His writings make it clear that there was an abnormally high death rate among the indigenous population, resulting from torture and systematic killings by the *conquistadores*. He protested the inhumane treatment given to Indians, whereby many were put in life-threatening work situations, especially in mines, and allowed to die. The Spanish showed little concern for the well-being of Indian laborers because they could be easily replaced by others working under the *mita* obligation. In some cases, people were killed as political examples to intimidate the population. High mortality rates also resulted from the introduction of European diseases, adding to the conditions that combined to create a de facto genocide.

A second reason for the declining numbers of indigenous people in colonial-era records was that many migrated from their lands to avoid the
Spanish requirements of forced labor and payment of tribute. Juan Friede
(1969:60) suggests that many became fugitives from the *encomienda* system and took up essentially homeless lifestyles. Spanish control was concentrated in a few towns in certain regions of New Granada, and Indians
could avoid their control by moving to remote rural areas or regions with
little Spanish presence. Indigenous people resisted Spanish control by hid-
ing from the census takers, tribute collectors, and *mita* enforcers.

The third cause of the declining indigenous population was the fact
that Spanish men took indigenous women as wives or mistresses, and their
mixed-blood children were called *mestizo* and not Indian. As this process
of *mestizaje* grew, the Indian population shrank. Discrimination against
Indians must have led many indigenous women to a strategy of consciously
choosing to have mestizo children so they could avoid the onerous obligations of paying tribute and performing forced labor like other Indians.

The first generation of mestizos after the Conquest were directly linked
to the *conquistadores,* and they were well accepted by the Spanish. However, with time the mestizo population grew to be the largest segment of
the population, and they began to challenge the Spanish more directly
than the Indians did. A number of attempts were made to formally segre-
gate the Spanish inhabitants from the Indians, mestizos, and mulattos,
and complaints were written into legal documents to the effect that the
population had become so mixed that it was impossible to distinguish between the racial groups (Archivo Histórico Nacional de Bogotá, vol. 63,
folio 1035 [hereafter AHNB]). This suggests a merging of the Indian population of tribute payers with the mestizo population. The decline in the
number of Indians partially undermined the colonial economic system,
which depended on their tribute and labor.

Fourth, some indigenous people must have "passed" as mestizos, changing their social identity to avoid the racist treatment afforded to Indians.
Today many people of European, mestizo, and African descent in Colombia continue to hold patronizing and negative attitudes toward Indians,
similar to the racism Native Americans and African Americans still experience in the United States. By learning Spanish, becoming Christians, aban-
doning their lands, and moving into town, indigenous people in colonial
Ráquira could blend with the mestizo population and lose their status as
Indians. By acculturating to Spanish ways and identifying themselves as
mestizo, indigenous people could avoid both racism and the obligations of

tribute and *la mita*. Indigenous political leaders were encouraged to acculturate by using Spanish language and dress, as well as being rewarded with certain privileges reserved for the Spanish (Orbell 1995:41).

Finally, the Spanish historian Juan Friede (1969:42) suggests that the colonial government never effectively counted the indigenous population, so that the real decline in population during the early colonial period cannot be known exactly. He indicates, for example, that in 1551, 100,900 tribute-paying Indians were officially registered in the province of Tunja (now called Boyacá) out of a total indigenous population that was probably closer to half a million. So he suggests that the Spanish probably registered no more than 20 percent of the Indian population in the censuses during the early colonial period, which means their numbers were not reliably tabulated and that the population decline may have been greater than was officially represented.

Many indigenous people probably survived and functioned outside of the realm of Spanish control, where they were able to preserve indigenous craft traditions, such as those found in Ráquira today. The fact that the designs and working styles of rural ceramics in Ráquira still follow prehispanic indigenous patterns is because many of the Muiscas survived, became mestizos, and continued making pottery. Their descendants are the inhabitants of Ráquira today.

Middle and Late Colonial Period (1620–1810): Cultural Consolidation as Muisca/Boyacá Ceramics

By the early 1600s, the Conquest had been completed, and the Spanish had political and military control of Colombia. The *encomienda* system had achieved its purpose of establishing an administrative and taxation network, and churches were being built in most towns to further the evangelization of the indigenous populations. More Spanish influences were introduced in ceramics, and majolica ware was produced at the beginning of this period on the coast of Panama, which was then a part of Colombia.

Spanish Influences

Panamá Viejo was a town established on the coast of Panama in 1619 and continued as a center of trade, transportation, and ceramics production until 1671, when it was sacked by Sir Henry Morgan. Charles Fairbanks estimates that the ceramics production began in the early 1600s and continued until the town was sacked (1972:150). The Panamá Viejo majolicas were traded northward into Central America and southward into Colombia, Ecuador, and Peru (Deagan 1987:90). Very little Spanish majolica has been found in Colombia, but there are some examples from Bogotá and Cartagena (Goggin 1968:47).

The kiln used at Panamá Viejo had a circular, updraft design, similar to traditional kilns used in Ráquira today. It was about two and a half meters in diameter and made of brick; it had four stokeholes, and it showed evidence of several decades of use, perhaps sixty to seventy years. The kiln furniture consisted of three-legged trivets used to support bowls and saggers for plates. The latter included openings for triangular pins to support the plates. This was kiln furniture for glaze firings, and it was similar to that in English delftware kilns (Fairbanks 1972:150).

Ráquira and the Spanish

During this period, the colonial social structure in Colombia was paralleled by the material culture, with the peninsular Spanish having the highest status (corresponding to Spanish majolica), followed by American-born Spanish (and Panamá Viejo or Mexican majolica), mestizos (local earthenwares with Spanish influence), and at the bottom indigenous people and crafts (traditional indigenous earthenware). The ceramics of this period tended to be heavy, functional, rustic, and undecorated, and they included indigenous cooking and storage pots similar to those produced today in Ráquira. They also included shipping jars, bottles, pharmacy jars, pitchers, basins, and other forms from the European tradition (Duncan 1985b:55f; Martínez Carreño 1985:21). Fine decorative ceramics and dinnerware sets were not introduced until the late colonial period. As the wealth of the colonial population grew, there was greater unrest over the Spanish prohibition of the importation of luxury goods, such as glazed ceramics, from Europe.

The Spanish presence continued to be small in Ráquira, whose population in the 1750s consisted of 681 mestizos (70 percent), 210 Indians (22 percent), and only 80 Spaniards (8 percent) (Mora 1974:15). The overwhelming majority (92 percent) were of indigenous and mestizo descent, indicating the continued importance of indigenous culture. Thus, at the height of the Spanish presence in Colombia in the 1750s, less than 10 percent of the population of Ráquira was of Spanish descent. Since the town was located in the geographic center of the Spanish-controlled heartland of Nueva Granada, this is also an indication of the marginal presence of the Spanish in the remainder of the country.

During the last half of the eighteenth century a number of reforms were instituted to ameliorate some of the onerous colonial obligations and racial distinctions. In 1756 a number of towns in this region were reclassified from *pueblos de indios* (Indian towns) to *parroquias de españoles* (Spanish parishes), and Mora suggests that Ráquira was probably declared a parish at that time (1974:15). In 1770 Viceroy Pedro Messia de la Cerda ended all but six private *encomiendas* in Colombia, converting them to Crown obligations (Friede 1969:51).

In 1778 Ráquira was visited by a representative of the Crown, who discovered that the reservation that had been assigned to the indigenous inhabitants was a rocky mountainside with little good land to cultivate. People were planting wheat, but their harvests were so poor that they had to pay the tribute and their debts with pottery (Moreno y Escandón 1985:329). Annis mentions that in Guatemala tribute was also paid with crafts, making it one of the most important means of wealth extraction during the colonial period (1987:125). Although earlier production of ceramics is documented archaeologically (Falchetti 1975; Therrien 1991), this is the first official record of ceramics actually being produced within the present-day township. By 1791 pottery making was the principal occupation of the land-owning Indians in Ráquira (Falchetti 1975:41), but by 1803 there were only five tribute-paying Indians left on reservation land in Ráquira. While those five were permitted to retain the land they were using, the remainder of the reservation was sold to Spanish inhabitants. Chibcha, the language of the Muiscas, also disappeared about that time (Mora 1974:15), marking the end of the independent, indigenous culture. The evolution from the prehispanic culture to the Boyacá mestizo culture had taken almost three hundred years.

Synthesis Culture

Indigenous working styles and shapes were used throughout the colonial period, perpetuating the prehispanic indigenous tradition in Ráquira. When the Spanish arrived in the mid-1500s, women potters added new shapes to their repertoire of cooking pots and bowls. As the newcomers requested Spanish-style bottles, pitchers, and jars, the Ráquira potters produced them along with their own indigenous forms. The result was a mestizo pottery that synthesized the style of the Muiscas with the Iberian-Moorish tradition of Spain, especially Andalusia. Potters in the departments of Boyacá and Nariño and along the Caribbean coast also adopted elements of Spanish ceramics during this period.

The Spanish culture that was brought to the Americas during the early, formative periods of colonial American culture was a mosaic of influences, and in the realm of material culture (ceramics, architecture, woodwork-

Sidesaddle kickwheel. This is the Muslim-type kickwheel used in Andalusia and brought to Boyacá in the colonial period. The potter sits on the right side of the wheel and throws to his left. Only men use this traditional potter's wheel.

ing, leather design), *mudéjar* (mixed Spanish and Moorish) influences were particularly strong. The Spanish ceramics adopted in Colombia carried strong influences from the Muslim tradition that had become well established in Andalusia, the southernmost region of Spain, during the Moorish occupation of almost eight hundred years. The male-dominated, commercial town potteries in that region still reflect the Muslim presence today (Lister and Lister 1987:270–79). This pottery tradition accompanied the Andalusians, whose numbers (40 percent) were more than twice as large as any other regional group of Spaniards coming to the Americas during the early colonial period. With slight regional variations, Andalusian immigrants predominated for most of the first century of the colonial era (Gutiérrez Escudero 1992:234–36). Although Ferdinand and Isabella had conquered al-Andalus, the kingdom of Granada, in 1492, the population of Andalusia remained predominantly Moorish culturally throughout much of the sixteenth century, the period of the primary migration to the Americas, and that fact contributed to the Muslim influences in the Spanish pottery that came to Colombia and eventually reached Ráquira.

The Morocco/Andalusia/Ráquira parallels in ceramics include similar donkey sidesaddles for carrying clay and pots, the practice of throwing pots from the left side of the potter's wheel, horse-powered mills for ceramic materials, the Mediterranean-style kiln, and Arabic terminology for ceramics (Lister and Lister 1987:259f). For the potter to throw to the left of the throwing head is characteristic of the potters' wheels in Latin America, Spain, and the Muslim world (ibid.:51). The Moroccan version of the sidesaddle kickwheel is set in a pit with the potter sitting at ground level, and in fact, the pit model has also been used in Andalusia, especially in Granada, Cuellar de Baza, Ugijar, and Guadix, each areas of historically strong Muslim influence. The practice of placing the kickwheel at table height was introduced into Andalusia in the mid-1500s, and it was this model that was taken to the Americas (ibid.:258).

Many of the Spanish technical terms for pottery making are of Arabic origin, and several forms of traditional pottery made in Ráquira and other parts of Boyacá today have names that are Arabic in origin (such as *cántaro, cazuela, jícara, jarra, jarrón, múcura,* and *tinaja*). Other words of Arabic origin used in Ráquira include *alfarero* (potter) and *azulejo* (colored tiles). Although the same shapes existed there during the prehispanic period, after the Conquest, Spanish/Arabic names were given to them. This Andalusian tradition of ceramics making was adopted in the towns by men potters while women in the countryside continued using prehispanic techniques. Spanish techniques were introduced into rural pottery making by the men who assisted their potter wives. Although the women shaped pots with indigenous techniques, men used Spanish technology to transport clay and fire the finished pots. The facts that ceramics of precolumbian design were given Arabic names and that indigenous and mestizo women made pots with prehispanic techniques and their husbands fired them in Spanish-style kilns reveal the complexity of the cultural synthesis that occurred.

This synthesized mestizo pottery, which can be called the Muisca/Boyacá tradition, became the functional ceramics that lasted in a more or less stable way from the mid-1500s to the mid-1900s. Although men may have become potters in other Boyacá towns during this period, women continued as the potters in Ráquira, with men working as farmers and suppliers of pottery, agricultural products, and wood for the wealthier settlements of Villa de Leyva, Tunja, and Chiquinquirá.

At the close of the colonial period, a wide range of ceramics were available to the wealthy, but the common people would have relied primarily on earthenware pots similar to those from Ráquira and other towns in Boyacá today. The focus of the Spanish during this period was more toward importing ceramics from the mother country than on developing

Spanish technology in Colombia, which permitted the local pottery traditions to continue without competition. That changed only slightly during the republican period.

Nineteenth-Century Republican Period (1810–1900): Isolated Mestizo Village

When the independence movement started in Colombia in 1810, functional earthenware pots were being produced throughout Colombia for domestic use, but over the course of the nineteenth and twentieth centuries local pottery communities gradually turned toward commercial production oriented to regional and national markets. During this period there was an evolution in forms from the utilitarian ware, mostly pots and bottles, based on indigenous traditions to the twentieth-century production of tableware and planters. Although there is a basic continuity in Colombian village ceramics over the last four hundred years (Méndez 1993:156), the craft has evolved as the country has changed.

The independence movement led to the Spanish being driven out and the Republic of Colombia being established in 1819. No significant changes are recorded in Ráquira during this period, which was a time of consolidation as a mestizo town of agriculturalists and craftspeople. The social changes, political realignments, and economic difficulties associated with the early republic affected the urban populations more than this remote town. About this time the town was moved to its present location after the old location was badly damaged by fire. From the mid-1500s until 1800, it had been located in what is known today as "Old Town" (Pueblo Viejo), which is somewhat higher than the present site of the town. By 1810 the indigenous population of Ráquira had been transformed into a mestizo population, although it retained a genetic and cultural heritage from the indigenous past.

Potters continued the Muisca/Boyacá style of simple, utilitarian pots with little or no decoration (Ancízar 1956:319f). Commercial trade ceramics continued to be made along with domestic pottery for local use. The commercial ceramics were traded in a radius of fifty kilometers or more to Tunja, Ubaté, and Chiquinquirá, and people made the trip to the markets in those towns carrying the pottery on their backs (Triana 1972:149), or they used oxen or horses. There were 150,000 people working in crafts in the department of Boyacá in 1830 (Herrera 1976:135), which indicates that crafts were an important factor in the economic and cultural life of the period.

In Bogotá the first attempts at setting up a national ceramics industry were being made. In 1830 the Compañia Bogotana de Industrias established a ceramics factory to make creamware for the table. It was located on the site of the old Jesuit pottery, behind the monastery of the parish church in the Barrio Belén. The local potters, however, lacked the background for an industrial operation, and in 1832 the company contracted two English industrial potters, John and Robert Peake, to install English production techniques. By 1834 the factory was operating with the technology introduced by the Peake brothers, and by 1837 it was producing enough to satisfy the needs of the entire country. It had seven kilns, sixty-one Colombian workers, four foreign workers, and an administrative staff (Perdomo 1965:5). It continued in operation for the next three decades, but by 1866 only twenty people were producing ceramics in the factory (Vergara y Vergara 1866:358), and it ceased production shortly after that because of competition from foreign imports. Since the domestic pottery of Ráquira did not compete with tableware, this factory had little impact on the largely rural clientele of these country potters.

Early Twentieth Century (1900–1930): Country Pottery

During the first three decades of this century, pottery was made in the rural areas of Ráquira (Orbell 1995:27–28), and marketing was largely limited to other small towns in the region. People were making Boyacá traditional pottery, miniatures, and figurative pieces, such as the horse. Women made domestic pottery for food preparation and storage, and men made figures and other decorative pieces. Animal figures were typical forms associated with village ceramics, and the Ráquira pony (*caballito de Ráquira*) became a symbol of the town's ceramics.

Since there were no roads into Ráquira, potters had to travel by horse trail to take their pieces to neighboring towns, as they had done in the previous period. They would leave home the day before the market and spend the night along the way, arriving by 7:00 A.M. or so. In the 1960s, Mora's informants still vividly remembered making these trips (1974:50). During this period Father Segura arrived to serve as Ráquira's priest, and he began actively supporting the craft of ceramics (Solano 1974). At the same time, potters in the other traditional pottery-making towns of the area, including Tinjacá and Sutamarchán, began to abandon the craft in favor of more lucrative farming activities. These towns were located in richer agricultural lands, which gave them more economic alternatives than Ráquira enjoyed.

Mid-Twentieth Century (1930–1968):
The Infrastructure for Capitalism

This period began with the building of the road to Ráquira and the arrival of electricity, structural changes that brought the village into closer contact with the national society. These changes, combined with exposure to mass-production techniques, laid the foundation for men to develop workshops designed to produce for urban markets. During this period, the craft production by women of traditional domestic pots for cooking and food storage was gradually supplemented and then virtually replaced by the industrialized production of inexpensive metal cooking pots. As men became full-time potters, they adopted new production techniques such as plaster molds, the potter's wheel, and improved kilns. The volume of production increased significantly, and Ráquira ceramics were sold by the truckload instead of the traditional horseload, and they were sold throughout central Colombia.

In the late 1930s, the first small industry was established in Ráquira by a family named Cárdenas from Bogotá. The purpose was to make ashtrays and other small decorative objects to be used in the living rooms of the growing urban communities in Bogotá and Tunja. They set up a mass-production workshop using molds and the potter's wheel, and they hired local workers who learned the new techniques. Reyes Suárez, who was to become one of the most important innovators of Ráquira of the twentieth century, was an employee in this workshop. The Cárdenas family's venture was short lived, and after they left, Suárez established his own production-style workshop (Solano 1974).

During the same period, another local potter, Aurelio Varela, went to Carmen de Viboral, a town in Antioquia famous for its industrially produced tableware, and he observed mass production in molds. After returning to Ráquira, he also set up a workshop using molds (Mora 1974:33). Thus the two innovators who started the men's town workshops oriented toward urban markets had the same idea at approximately the same time. As other men saw that the new mass-production workshops were economically successful, they opened similar workshops. Design changed from the traditional cooking pots and figurines to the new forms of ashtrays, planters, and piggy banks ordered by intermediaries.

In 1936 the department of Boyacá authorized the creation of a school of ceramics in Ráquira, although the school did not actually function until the 1940s (Mora 1974:32). It was equipped with all of the necessary facilities, including a complete water system, slip tanks, mixing machines, electric wheels, and test kilns. The teacher, Pablo Rodríguez, demonstrated the use of molds and potters' wheels in ceramics production, but some townspeople complained that he did not know ceramics. The problem may have been that Rodríguez taught slip casting, which no one in Ráquira used. Even today, almost a half century later, there is little slip casting in Ráquira. In about 1950 Rodríguez left, and the school closed. Within a short time, townspeople dismantled the installations and moved the equipment to their houses. One potter took over the building and used it for the next ten years (ibid.:32). So the first official effort to stimulate the development of Ráquira ceramics ended in failure.

A number of problems beset the Ráquira school from the beginning, and the first was underestimating the gender division of labor. Although women were the potters, they were not expected to be educated or technically trained, so no females were enrolled in the school. The techniques taught in the school (use of molds and wheel throwing) were considered to be "men's" techniques because they involved machinery and heavy equipment (molds), and a group of boys in their mid-teens were enrolled in classes, but they gradually dropped out. Thus, the school was teaching a production system for men at a time when pottery making was still a woman's occupation.

The second problem was that the school did not utilize the authority of men in the community to validate the legitimacy of the school. In the Ráquira family, the father is the unquestioned authority, and the behavioral logic of that system requires his validation when important cultural changes are being introduced. The fact that the school trained the sons and not the fathers undermined the fathers' authority. If males were to be trained, it would have been more effective to include the fathers. Since children could go to classes only with their fathers' permission, the opposition of the latter contributed to the closing of the school. Other studies among Colombian families have shown that social change is adopted most readily in closely knit families when the person with the most authority (usually the oldest male) is taught the new information first and uses that authority to teach the rest of the family (Duncan 1975b).

The third problem was that the pottery-making techniques taught at the school did not build on local experience but rather introduced a completely new technology that required considerable capital investment to adopt. The traditional system was based on hand building with solid clay, while the school taught slip casting and wheel throwing, methods that

Table 2.2. Suárez family generational styles in ceramics

Generation/Years		Person	Style of ceramics
First	1920s–1940s	Father of Reyes and Miguel	Corn kernel souvenir ware
Second	1950s–1970s	Reyes Suárez Salinas	Craft figures and decorative pieces
		Miguel Suárez Salinas	Dinnerware and planters
Third	1970s–1980s	José Suárez Florez*	Glazed dinnerware
		Manuel Suárez Florez*	Decorative ware
Fourth	1990–present	Reyes Suárez, younger**	Sculptural figures

*Sons of Reyes Suárez Salinas
**Son of José Suárez Florez

were radically different in concept, motor behavior, and technology from what the people of Ráquira knew.

The fourth problem was the cynicism of *boyacenses* (residents of Boyacá) toward the government and official projects. Many did not accept that a nonproducing ceramics teacher could teach them how to become production potters. Finally, during the years that the school was open, a turbulent political period known as *La Violencia* began in Colombia, and it led to migrations and upset regular government functioning. As a result, a number of families moved from Ráquira to larger cities for protection, and government operations were disrupted, which may have affected the funding of the school and contributed to its closing.

During the 1950s, another major step away from the woman-centered craft production occurred when a second attempt was made by an outside group to open a factory in Ráquira, this time to produce tableware and floor tiles. The owner was a man named Gallo, who, with other associates, came from the neighboring state of Antioquia. They were considered intruders by the local people, and in less than six months they were forced to abandon their investment and leave town (Mora 1974:33).

In spite of these failures, the school and the factories exposed some people in the community to industrial production techniques. In the 1950s, other men in addition to Suárez and Varela began establishing workshops in town based on mold production, and these workshops were set up as family businesses to earn money, in contrast to women's traditional work in pottery to earn a supplemental income. Men already knew how to prepare the clay and fire the kilns, and once they crossed the barrier of gender ideology to realize that they could also make ceramics using molds and potters' wheels, many men became potters.

By the end of this period, small, family-based production shops using press molds were firmly established in Ráquira. The school and the factory also introduced new ceramic forms, some of which people have continued producing to the present time, including an ashtray with an Indian head, planters in the form of a stylized Indian with headdress, and tea and coffee sets. The adoption of molds in the 1950s was a profound change in Ráquira, marking the transition from traditional craft to mass production.

The Reyes Suárez Family of Ceramists

The Reyes Suárez family has been important in this transition to mass-production workshops, and the generational changes in work style within that family are representative of the process that occurred in the town. Reyes Suárez Salinas has been one of the most widely respected ceramists in Ráquira in the last half of the twentieth century, and he was one of the creative leaders of the 1950s generation. His father also had a long career in ceramics, and he made country-style, corn-kernel-sized souvenir pottery. Reyes has said that he admires the fact that his father could work in a single tradition all of his life, but the new market reality demanded continual innovation and change from his own generation.

Reyes Suárez was one of the first male ceramists to move from the countryside into the town in the 1950s, and as mentioned earlier, his was one of the forerunners of the town workshops oriented toward the urban, commercial market. He adopted new designs, such as animal figures, and mass-production techniques, such as the use of plaster molds. Over the years his repertoire included hand-modeled and decorated pieces, such as whistles, turtle and armadillo banks, basins for holy water in the church, and human figures, while his wife made traditional earthenware pitchers, or *chorotes,* similar to those made in the rural areas. Like other potters in Ráquira, he prepared his own clay and learned to combine clays to obtain special colors.

For many years, the patio of the Suárez house was the workshop for the extended family, including the sons, José and Manuel, and their wives, and they produced many of the same pieces as the mother and father. Although the husbands and wives work together in this extended family, all see the husbands' roles as most important. The new generation eventually opened their own workshops and built their own kilns. José also worked many years for Artesanías de Colombia, making the glazed dinnerware sets that are his specialty. The fourth Suárez generation is now active in Ráquira ceramics. A grandson, also named Reyes (a son of José), is one of the current generation of figurative ceramists in the town. In

1994 he completed a commission for the town, the figure of a small country boy that was placed on top of the fountain in the center of the town plaza. A daughter of José, Teresa Suárez, is the manager of Todo Ráquira, the largest crafts store in town.

A brother of the elder Reyes, Miguel, also a ceramist, owned an industrial press-mold machine for making small planters, so he was one of the group that first began making mass-produced planters. He also made dinnerware sets, but later he returned to agriculture and only occasionally worked in ceramics. These four generations of ceramists in the Suárez family represent the generational changes that occurred from the 1950s to the present in Ráquira, and they arguably have been the most important family in town ceramics in recent decades.

Late Twentieth Century (1968 to present):
Technological Change and Economic Expansion

The Centro de Artesanías de Colombia was opened in Ráquira in 1971, and the programs of the center have had a continuing impact in training and marketing, and in facilitating technological and economic change. The center has electric, production-type, stand-up wheels, and it has trained many potters in production throwing. The center has also encouraged the use of molds by making them and giving them to potters. By the 1980s the electric wheel was commonplace, and by the early 1990s some families were specializing in wheel production of small planters, bells, candleholders, and other small items. A few women, such as Agripa Sierra (in Resguardo Occidental), have become expert throwers, but in other cases, such as the Néstor Reyes family, the man is the primary thrower, and the woman's job is to trim the pieces on the wheel afterwards.

Center training programs taught potters about the dangers of lead glazes and about the use of nonlead glazes, and by 1973 the use of raw lead glazes had been largely abandoned in local workshops. The center also introduced the use of electric kilns, especially for glazed ware, and diesel kilns to reduce the reliance on wood for firing kilns. Neither has had wide acceptance, but firing kilns with coal has become popular. The center also offers technical consulting on common problems and periodically offers continuing-education classes on subjects of interest to the local potters. Its technical assistance is primarily oriented toward the men's town workshops, although the center does support the marketing of women's traditional pottery.

The gender ideology that equates men with economic success has blinded many to the fact that women have been economically and culturally marginalized in this process. Even Mora's study of Ráquira in the late 1960s did not distinguish between the rural tradition of women's ceramics and the newer town workshops run by men. She said that she did not differentiate between them because she considered them to be culturally equal (1974:22). But in doing so, she overlooked important differences in the historical experience of the two genders, including differences in social status, cultural practices, technology, and economics. She did not realize that she was observing incipient capitalism and the resulting gender transformation of traditional domestic craft production, in which differences based on gender were of profound importance.

Ráquira and National Symbolism

Since the 1960s, people from the larger cities, such as Bogotá, have begun to buy village ceramics for decoration as well as for their symbolic representation of autochthonous Colombian culture. Traditional potters and figure makers have also experienced a resurgence of interest from museum and crafts professionals, as well as consumers, and that has guaranteed a market for their work. In recent decades, Ráquira ceramics has come to include traditional domestic pottery made by women, traditional figure makers (both men and women), and the mass-market production of planters and other forms. As Ráquira expanded in importance as a pottery center, the number of potters grew and sales increased. Today Ráquira is an important center of village ceramics and, in fact, it has come to symbolize the pottery tradition of the entire state of Boyacá.

3

A Town of Potters

Ráquira is a town of peasant farmers and potters located at the upper end of a small valley in the central Andes of Colombia. The arid mountains are ill suited for agriculture, and for this reason women have long supplemented the income of the family farms by making ceramics. Along that tenuous thread of subsistence production, the Muisca/Boyacá domestic pottery tradition passed from mother to daughter for centuries. During the last half of the twentieth century Ráquira ceramics have been marked by a plurality of styles and working patterns. Not only have Artesanías de Colombia and the Museo de Artes y Tradiciones Populares been active in promoting innovation and marketing, but Peace Corps volunteers introduced new American-style mold-made forms and a Japanese potter visiting on a cultural exchange has introduced Japanese elements. After a long history of traditional ceramics, Ráquira has evolved in recent decades toward the incipient industrialization of ceramics.

Since the Spanish colonial period, Ráquira has always been a source of goods and labor for the larger society. During the colonial period, it paid tribute to the Crown, gave *mita* labor to the local *encomendero,* and supplied trade goods to the larger colony. Since independence, it has continued to provide domestic pottery and pilgrimage ceramics to neighboring towns along with firewood and food crops. In recent decades, pilgrimage souvenirs have become tourist souvenirs, and domestic pottery has changed from being functional to being largely symbolic. Ráquira's role as a source town supplying goods to the larger society continues, but today the goods are increasingly decorative or symbolic ceramics for urban markets and tourists.

One's first glimpse of Ráquira pottery occurs at the turnoff from the main highway, where pots are stacked for sale in front of a small store. The recently paved road leads along the narrow valley of the Ráquira River, with pastures and the mountain on the right and planted fields on the left. Just before entering the town, the road curves around a hillside and passes one of the factories that represents the new role of capital and the proletarianization of Ráquira pottery. The road crosses the river, and one branch veers left toward the *veredas* (rural districts) that make up the eastern side of the township, such as Candelaria Oriental and Occidental.

Entering the town, one passes through two blocks of houses and small crafts stores before reaching the plaza. The houses are typical of small-town Colombia with plastered walls and tile roofs. During the week there is little daytime activity in the streets, unless some family is preparing a shipment for an intermediary to pick up; then stacks of planters spill out of the house onto the sidewalk and even into the street. These mini-mountains of planters demonstrate the productivity of the family and their economic well-being. During the weekends, visitors arrive from Bogotá and other cities to explore and buy the production of Ráquira, which represents cultural patrimony linking the present with the colonial and prehispanic periods. But much of what they buy is now imported or made in molds by the new mass-production workshops in town. The rural women who produce the traditional pots that are the cultural patrimony are rarely seen and gradually becoming more invisible, hidden behind the economic success of the men's workshops in town.

The people of Ráquira (Raquireños) are proud of their town's recognition as the most important traditional ceramics center in Boyacá. Craft-made pottery is economically successful, and the house-front shops along the street entering the town sell every kind of locally made ceramics. As they stand displayed for sale, the curvilinear profiles of the cooking pots and water jars handmade by women in the rural areas contrast with the rigidly straight walls of the planters made by men in town.

The Boyacá Region

Ráquira is located in the department of Boyacá in the central Andes of Colombia, a region known for the richness of its craft traditions. Since most communities in Boyacá are located at altitudes of 1,800 to 2,750 meters, the climate is cool all year long, and the nights can be cold. Much of Boyacá has good rainfall and is good for agriculture and cattle, but the Villa de Leyva and Ráquira area is characterized by dry, desert valleys where rainfall is rare. In this region, one is constantly surrounded by mountain peaks marked by the quilt-work patterns of the small farm fields that stretch up the mountainsides. Boyacá is known for the excellence of its craft pro-

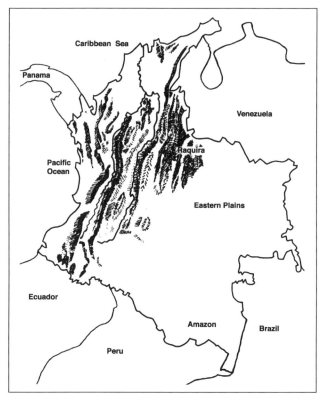

Colombia is the link between Central and South America. Ráquira is located in the easternmost range of the Andes.

duction, not only in ceramics but also in weaving, basketry, and wood working. This was one of the most important areas of Colombia during the Spanish colonial period, and it is still known for its colonial churches and towns. The small farmers and craftspeople of this region tend to be religious as well as socially and politically conservative.

Although the ceramics of Boyacá are characterized and dominated by the work of Ráquira, ceramics production occurs throughout the region, including in the towns of Sogamoso, Tutazá, Tuaté, Morca, La Capilla, Belén, and Chita. Many communities have one or more families dedicated to the making of planters, traditional pottery, or figurative ceramics. In the smaller towns and rural areas women make traditional cooking pots, water jugs, and other vessels used in food preparation. In the urban center of Sogamoso, men potters make commercial ware, such as tableware and planters, on the Spanish-style sidesaddle kickwheel. They use the Mediterranean-type updraft kiln introduced by the Spanish in the colonial period.

Other potters from Chiquinquirá, Tausa, and Nemocón in neighboring Cundinamarca make tall, thin cylindrical pots called *moyos,* which were used traditionally to boil and refine rock salt that comes from mines in the region (Villegas and Villegas 1992:55). In Chibcha, the language of the Muiscas, these pots were called *gachas* (Langebaek 1987:93). They are approximately two meters tall and seventy centimeters in diameter. A large (two-meter-long) spoon-shaped implement carved from a single piece of wood is used to stir the contents of these *moyos,* which are among the largest ceramic vessels made in Colombia.

There is also a tradition of playful figurative ceramics that reflects local society. In Chiquinquirá, for example, a larger town to the south of Ráquira, there has been a long tradition of making figures finished with the yellow-green lead glaze of rural ceramics. One of the most popular subjects has been the bullfight, which is made in a circle of ten to thirty centimeters in diameter, with spectators standing at the fence watching the *toreador* confront the bull. Potters from this region also make manger scenes, domestic animals, dancing couples, musicians, rural houses, and other scenes from daily life. The shrine of the patron saint of Colombia is located in Chiquinquirá, and the large and beautifully decorated basilica dedicated to the Virgin of Chiquinquirá is the most important pilgrimage site for the entire country. Many of the people who make this pilgrimage carry home souvenirs of village crafts from the region.

The Ecology of Ráquira

Ráquira is located in the upper end of a small U-shaped valley, surrounded by mountains on three sides. In some places, the mountainsides erode into gullies, exposing clay deposits and minerals that are excavated by local potters for use in ceramics. From the crest of the mountains, one can see far below the corrugated metal roofs of the pottery workshops, the clay roof tiles of the older houses, and the steeple of the church rising above them all. Black smoke from the coal-fired kilns can usually be seen rising from several points in town.

Since there is little cloud cover in this area, the sun is intense and the rain is sparse. It is a temperate region with an average daily temperature of eighteen degrees centigrade. Much of the land in the Ráquira township is located on mountainsides, and there is little good agricultural land in comparison to neighboring townships located on flatter valley land. Poor land combined with sparse rainfall means that farming is not very productive.

The two valley floors of the Ráquira and the Candelaria Rivers are narrow and have little arable land, and the streams flow rapidly, straight off the steep mountainside watersheds. The Ráquira River, which is a small stream as it passes through town, runs down the valley, spreading the green of vegetation along its banks in this dry mountainscape. The Candelaria River joins it below the town, and the two kilometers of the narrow valley floor below the town is the best land for agriculture in the township. Corn and potatoes are the staple crops, but wheat, barley, peas, and other vegetables are also grown.

Ecology is often a factor of critical importance for ceramics production (Matson 1965; Kolb 1989; Kolb and Lackey 1988; Kramer 1997), as it has been in Ráquira, a town of marginal agriculture, arid environment, and clay deposits. Dean Arnold (1985, 1993) and Louana Lackey (1982) have demonstrated through research in Latin America how clay deposits, environmental conditions, roads, markets, and other such factors affect the expression of ceramics in each locale. Village ceramics communities tend to exist in areas of marginal agriculture, and craft making usually becomes a viable economic choice only when agriculture does not provide an acceptable standard of living for the people. Pottery making also impacts the environment as people fell trees to fire kilns and dig craters to mine clay.

The arid and eroded land around Ráquira speaks of a fragile environment and improper land use over several millennia of human occupation. Two different explanations for this barren landscape have been suggested by Colombian archaeologists who have worked in the area. Ana María Falchetti (1975:19) says that the erosion started with the cutting of wood associated with the intensive production of ceramics in the area from A.D. 1,000 to the present. Wood has been used for centuries not only to fire kilns but also to cook; and in recent centuries, trees were also cut for firewood and charcoal to be sold in Chiquinquirá and Tunja, the capital of Boyacá, further depleting the tree cover. Given the combination of high altitude and aridity, both of which retard tree growth, the native forests could not reproduce themselves at this rate of depletion.

Monika Therrien Johannesson (1991:20) suggests that practices introduced by the Spanish may also have contributed to environmental degradation. In agriculture, the Spanish introduced the plow-and-furrow style of monocrop cultivation, which causes loss of moisture and minerals in the soil and leads to erosion in arid environments like Ráquira's. The Spanish style contrasts with the traditional Andean practice of multicrop cultivation, which entails the use of digging sticks and planting in individually formed hills. This approach conserves water, replenishes minerals, and controls erosion. Although not mentioned by Therrien, another Spanish innovation that would have contributed to environmental depletion was the heavy Mediterranean kiln. It requires much larger amounts of wood than the indigenous open-air firing practice, and this would have accentuated the process of environmental degradation.

As Falchetti and Therrien indicate, human intervention has disrupted the natural balance, creating barren mountainsides with eroded soils. Thus many local farmers are limited to subsistence agriculture, and rural families often depend on crafts—either ceramics, baskets, or mats, which are mostly made by women—to provide cash income for clothing, health care, additional food, and other necessities. Dean Arnold (1985:179) mentions this interplay between subsistence farming and ceramics, explaining that as a general rule pottery making becomes important only when the soil is too poor for agriculture.

Population, Agriculture, and Ceramics

The population of the township (which includes the town itself and the surrounding county) has fluctuated widely during the twentieth century, according to the economic and political conditions of the time. The population declined markedly in the years between 1951 (7,932) and 1964 (5,970), during the political violence (La Violencia) that swept Colombia in the 1950s and set off a massive migration out of small towns and rural areas to cities. In contrast, the rapid growth from 5,714 in 1985 to 10,375 in 1993 coincides with the economic success of the mass-production workshops and planter factories. Most of the population increase in recent years has resulted from natural growth, but there has also been some immigration into the town of Ráquira because of its reputation as an important ceramics center. Within the township, the rural population outnumbers the town population eight to one, but the town households are slightly larger (3.43 persons) than the rural ones (3.13 persons).

Although the production of ceramics is carried out in several rural areas surrounding the town, as well as in the town itself, the economy of the township is overwhelmingly agricultural. Of the 1,811 families in the township of Ráquira in 1985 (F. Bonilla 1989:2ff), most worked exclusively in agriculture (1,455 or 80 percent of the population), 120 (7 percent) worked in both ceramics and agriculture, and 81 (4 percent) of the families worked exclusively in ceramics. Most of the families that work only in ceramics are located in the town. In recent years, the commerce

Table 3.1. Family and gender in the workshop

	Rural				Town			
	Man		Woman		Man		Woman	
Relationship	No.	Percent	No.	Percent	No.	Percent	No.	Percent
Family worker	45	72.58	48	90.57	47	47.96	41	83.67
Hired worker	17	27.42	5	9.43	51	52.04	8	16.33
Totals	62	100.00	53	100.00	98	100.00	49	100.00

Source: Rojas 1983:9

and service sector has grown rapidly as the number of families that are dedicated to supplying raw materials to potters, to selling and exporting pottery, and to providing services to tourists has increased to 155 (9 percent). Three-fourths or more of the families located in the town now work in some phase of the ceramics business, either supplying, producing, or marketing ceramics (ibid.). So, people in the town are primarily dedicated to ceramics while people in the rural areas are primarily dedicated to agriculture. There is also a small elite in the town that controls the church, business, government, and schools for the township.

Records from Artesanías de Colombia indicate that there were 281 workers in 76 urban ceramics workshops in 1992, an average of 3.7 workers per workshop (Bonilla et al. 1992:26). A majority of these are actually husband-and-wife workshops with no hired workers, but a few large ones account for most of the employees. Although there has been no recent census of potters in the rural areas, in 1983 Gumercindo Rojas did a sample of ten *veredas* and identified 90 pottery workshops (1983:3). His survey also indicated that men and women workers were almost equally divided in the rural area but that twice as many men as women worked in town workshops. Almost all women workers are family members in both the rural and town workshops (ibid.:9). Based on estimates by Artisanías de Colombia, in 1995 there were 125 rural workshops with 250 workers, an average of two workers. That suggests the rural workshops are generally smaller than the urban ones, which corresponds to our observations.

The Town of Ráquira

Ráquira was an isolated, indigenous community that evolved into a mestizo town, and its architecture reflects that past. There were no rich colonial landlords and no viceroys to build mansions as in Villa de Leyva or Tunja. There are no chapels with carved and gilded altars, no public foun-

Ráquira church. The church in Ráquira was built in the 1800s in a country republican style after a fire damaged the original colonial-style church.

tains, no carved stone doorways, no evidence of the luxury of a landed gentry. The traditional architecture of the town has adobe walls and Spanish-style tile roofs, but today's houses are usually built with brick. The town is also laid out in a Spanish grid pattern with an open central plaza.

The church stands on the higher south end of the plaza and dominates the houses and stores that surround it. Built of brick and stone in the blockish, republican style of the 1800s, it is a rather austere country church without finery. The buildings around the plaza include the town hall (*alcaldía*), a small hotel, small food stores, and the largest houses in town. During the period of political violence in Colombia in the 1950s, the local landed elite left Ráquira and emigrated to the relative safety of larger towns and cities in the region or to Bogotá, selling or renting their houses to people moving in from the countryside. Some of those houses are still used as residences today, but many have been converted to commerce.

Having the Andalusian belief in the "evil eye," townspeople build walls around their patios to shut out the prying eyes of neighbors and passersby. The evil eye is a spell cast by an envious glance, which can cause

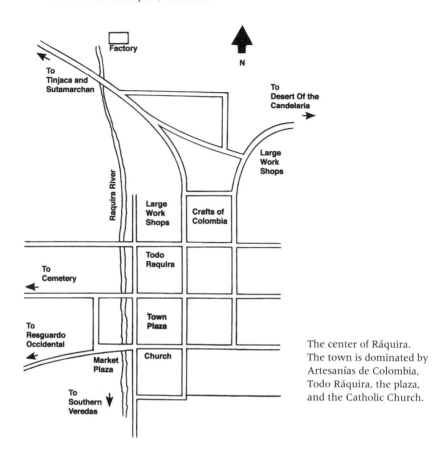

The center of Ráquira. The town is dominated by Artesanías de Colombia, Todo Ráquira, the plaza, and the Catholic Church.

problems ranging from illness to broken pots in the kiln. Rural houses, in contrast, are dispersed in the open countryside in the prehispanic indigenous pattern, and they are never surrounded by walls.

The houses of potters in Ráquira organize space according to a rural, pre-industrial style, with the house itself being the workplace. This contrasts with the pattern in urban Colombia, whereby the nonworking house is dominated by resting and entertaining areas like living and dining rooms. Town potters normally work just outside of the house, either on a roofed porch or in the open patio, and their houses are frequently filled with their production. If molds are used, a large covered area has to be built for them because they are big and bulky and they cannot get wet. The kiln occupies more space, and when wood or coal is brought for the firings, space is needed to store it. The fired pots ready to sell may be stored in the house or outside on the patio. When a family accumulates a backlog of unsold work, it may fill rooms so that the family can barely enter them. The working kitchen space may be limited to a corner that does not interfere with the ceramics production, and even the resting and sleeping areas may be invaded by pots that have not yet been sold or shipped out. The interior of the house is used only for cooking, eating, sleeping, and perhaps watching television. If someone comes by to visit, socializing normally occurs outside on the porch or in the work area.

Fourteen craft stores as well as Artesanías de Colombia are located in the two blocks near the entrance to the town. In the 1970s and 1980s, there were only five or six stores along this street, and they primarily sold Ráquira ceramics along with baskets and textiles from other crafts towns in the state of Boyacá. But by the mid-1990s, a significant change had occurred as a result of the promotion of tourism by the town's mayor, the hotel owner, and other business people. In 1995 the stores were selling textiles from various parts of Colombia, as well as from other countries such as Guatemala and Ecuador, in addition to Ráquira ceramics. This change from relying exclusively on Boyacá crafts to selling imported ones indicates a shift in attitude and marketing approaches, so that shop owners now treat local ceramics no differently from merchandise from any other town or nation.

In October 1993 the mayor initiated a campaign urging the townspeople to paint their houses with lively decorator colors (purple, yellow, green, blue) in place of the traditional white-washed walls and dark green wood trim. By the end of 1994 all of the houses in the center of town had new paint, and the Fondo Mixto de Turismo de Boyacá (Boyacá Tourism Council) selected Ráquira as the most beautiful town in Boyacá, an award that provided a major boost for tourism. The painting of Ráquira correlates with the shift from a domestic craft orientation to a capitalist orientation in town ceramics, and it signifies the increased role of the noncraft elite in the town and their interest in exploiting the commercial possibilities of tourism.

Administrative Organization and Services

Like all towns in Colombia, Ráquira is organized as a township, an administrative unit that includes the town itself and the surrounding rural areas. The town is the administrative, religious, and commercial center, and the township is organized into twenty rural districts (veredas) covering over 204 square kilometers. The veredas extend for approximately 10 kilometers to the east and west of the town and 30 kilometers into the mountains to the south. Two kilometers to the north of the town itself is the township limit with the neighboring town of Tinjacá. Crafts are produced in fourteen of the twenty veredas, and ceramics are produced in ten of them, including Candelaria Occidental, Candelaria Oriental, Carapacho,

Mirque, Resguardo Occidental, Resguardo Oriental, Ollerías, Torres, Pueblo Viejo, and Roa.

As a small and relatively isolated town, Ráquira offers few community services. Although the houses in town have electricity and running water, most houses in the rural areas have the former but not the latter. Telephone service has only recently become available in town, and it is limited to the public telephone office and a few wealthy establishments, such as the hotel and Artesanías de Colombia. In at least one rural housing cluster, the Desierto de la Candelaria (Candlemas Desert), there is a small telephone office with two telephones where people can make and receive calls during working hours.

Ráquira also has a health center with a nurse who can treat minor ailments, but all serious cases are referred to the Hospital de San Francisco in Villa de Leyva, which is thirty kilometers away. A high percentage of health problems in Ráquira stem from the air contamination produced by the concentration of ninety-six coal- and wood-fired kilns within a few blocks of each other. Between January and August of 1991, 390 patients were referred to the hospital from Ráquira. Of those 102 (26 percent) had acute respiratory infections, which are associated with the coal- and salt-firing practices used today. Most people with respiratory infections are treated locally, so the number of people affected is actually larger (Bonilla et al. 1992:6).

The *alcalde* (mayor) and *consejo municipal* (town council) are elected every two years, and they are responsible for local ordinances and water, and for serving as liaison with the national agencies that provide the remaining services. The police, schools, roads, electricity, telephone, and health services are provided by the national government, so the local government serves as the ombudsman for the local community to the ministries of the central government in Bogotá. The police and schoolteachers are hired by the appropriate ministry in Bogotá and assigned to Ráquira, so the municipal government has little authority in these matters. The *veredas* also have a Junta de Acción Comunal (Community Action Council), which organizes projects for the community and serves as an advocate for public services.

Religion and Recreation

On Sundays potters and farmers come into the town from the hillside communities to attend the open-air market, go to church, play *tejo* (a Colombian game), drink beer, and socialize. Mostly agricultural products are sold in the market, and depending on the harvest, there may be potatoes, beans, corn, onions, or other crops. A few women are usually selling traditional domestic pottery, including cooking pots, bowls, and small pitchers and jugs. People meet at the market to visit and share news even if they are not buying or selling anything.

Some people also attend mass as part of their Sunday market-day activities; mostly these are women accompanied by their small children or adolescent daughters. While women are the regular, weekly supporters of the church and its activities, adolescent boys and adult men attend the church occasionally for baptisms, weddings, and funerals. Men, however, play a central role in supporting the religious festivals that are celebrated during the year as street activities. These festivals are among the most important annual events in Ráquira, and they bring large numbers of people together in the streets, the plaza, and the cafés. Family members and friends who have moved away to other towns come back to join the celebrations.

Special church services are held, and pilgrimages may be made to shrines in the area dedicated to the patron saints. The three major public religious events are Easter week and the patron saint festivals, San Antonio de la Pared (in the town of Ráquira) on June 13 and Nuestra Señora de la Candelaria (in the *veredas* of Candelaria Oriental and Occidental) on February 2. The street celebrations of these events are paid for by a man in the community as a demonstration of his dedication to the Church. Men compete for the honor of sponsoring a religious festival, and the right of sponsorship for each festival has traditionally been reserved three or four years in advance.

Men may devote a significant part of the family income to the festival as a matter of personal and family prestige. Since sponsoring a festival can cost a thousand U.S. dollars or more, which is a year's salary for most people, the sponsors are usually men with a good income, such as the owners of the larger ceramics workshops. However, if necessary, the man may borrow money from relatives or friends to cover the costs of the festival. It is understood locally that supporting religious festivals is a way of expressing identity with the community. Although there is little community-wide cooperation in matters of ceramics production or marketing, it is expected that men will cooperate in spending what they have earned for the celebration of religious events.

In addition to religious events, community activities include the sport of *tejo* (a game similar to horseshoes), which men play for hours on the weekends while they drink beer, *guarapo,* or *aguardiente* (an anise-flavored drink) and discuss the prices of ceramics and agricultural crops. Beer drinking can be especially heavy, and some men spend a significant part of their week's income on it, much to the displeasure of their wives. As a result, Monday hangovers are notorious and production is usually low. Monday absenteeism is a tradition among craftspeople in Colombia that can be traced throughout the last two centuries (Sowell 1992:13). The expression *el lunes de los zapateros* (cobbler's Monday) is still commonly used to refer to this absenteeism among potters and other independent craftspeople.

Radio and television provide the primary contact with the national society. Since many people are functionally illiterate or minimally literate, newspapers and magazines are not important sources of information. However, people listen to the radio continually from the time they wake up until they go to sleep; it is common to hear a radio playing in the background in a ceramics workshop while people work. Although they listen mostly to popular music programs, they also hear the news, and in the late afternoon and early evening those who have television may watch it.

Marriage, Work, and Income

Gender and family are important in determining work relationships, and over 95 percent of families are headed by men (Bonilla et al. 1992:6). Although most families have a male head, the work strategies in pottery are quite different if the woman (who is subordinate) is the potter, or if the man is (with the power of his position). By their late twenties, most adults in Ráquira are married. The nuclear family is stable, as evidenced by the fact that few people are separated or divorced (1 percent). There is also a small widowed population (4 percent) (ibid.); typically they live with other family members.

Marriage is ambilocal, which means that newly married couples may live near either family. However, among potters in town there is a tendency toward patrilocal residence since the workshop is managed primarily by men and the son is frequently employed in the father's workshop. In the rural areas, living and working with the man's family means working in agriculture, but daughters continue to collaborate with their mothers if they live close enough. Although most workshops include only family workers, this does not result in the closely knit residential clusters found in some other areas of rural Colombia (Duncan 1985a).

In both town and rural families, the man controls the family's money, and surplus income is first spent on him, even if it is from pottery made by the woman. This is partly because he has first decision over how to spend it and also because his position in the community determines the prestige of the family. Consequently, the man has the best clothes and pays for frequent drinking sessions with the other men, and he will buy luxury consumption items, such as a watch or gold jewelry for his own use, even though his wife does not have comparable clothes or luxury items. If the woman needs a dress or some other personal item, the man may give her the money for it or he may buy it for her.

Dean Arnold found a similar situation in Ticul, Mexico, and he suggests that since pottery making is a low-status occupation, surpluses are frequently used to increase personal status (1985:228) rather than to improve the infrastructure of production. Although men may use the income of the family to sponsor prestigious religious rituals or show hospitality to friends, some men do invest surplus capital generated by ceramics to expand the family business. The first step is usually to build a kiln and invest in molds; however, some potters use capital to get out of the day-to-day business of pottery making and become intermediaries buying and selling ceramics, which is a higher status occupation. Recently some families have begun to use part of their surplus for the education of their children, which is described in more detail below.

Except for ceramics, women normally sell their craft production, including handspun wool, finger-woven sisal purses, reed strainers, and plaited cane mats, all of which are items used by the people of this region. These crafts are usually secondary activities that women do on their own time, while walking down the road, while talking with a relative or close friend (frequently a *comadre,* the godmother for one of her children), or while waiting for a bus. She may make strainers while she is in town on Sunday for the market day, and as she finishes them, she stacks them, one on top of the other, over her hat. It is not uncommon to see a woman in the street with four or five strainers on her head. When she has completed a group, she will sell them in the Sunday market.

Formal Education

Formal education has not been highly valued historically in Ráquira because children were expected to learn to make ceramics or work in the fields from an early age. The father decides how many years of schooling his children should receive, and he is frequently more interested in their work than in their educations. Especially during periods of peak production, it may be more important for a child to be working at home than to be in school. Today, however, there are more schools in the township, and many parents are giving attention to the formal education of their children, which is considered an avenue of mobility out of pottery making.

A mother and daughter weave basket strainers while they wait for a bus in Ráquira. The money they earn from these is personal money, which they do not have to share with the husband/father.

There are fifteen schools throughout the township (twelve elementary and three secondary schools), with one elementary and one high school located in the town itself. The eleven rural elementary schools are distributed throughout the twenty *veredas* or rural districts, each of which is large, approximately ten square kilometers. Since there is no public school-bus system in Colombia, children have to walk to school. Most walk a minimum of two or three kilometers to their local school, but others may walk five kilometers or more. The rural schools are so widely separated that some students arrange to live with a family near the school to be able to attend. Given that inconvenience, families who have the economic resources may send a son to high school in a city such as Tunja, Chiquinquirá, or Bogotá, where the schools are better. In 1976 the first high school was established in Ráquira, and by the 1990s graduation from high school was not uncommon.

Although most children are enrolled in school at the beginning of the year, their attendance is irregular, and normal progress is impeded by their family work obligations. By the time the children complete elementary school they are twelve or thirteen years old, and since they can begin to work full time in ceramics, they drop out of school. As a result, the illiteracy rate is high. For example, in the 1985 census, one-third of the people in the township were illiterate (Bonilla et al. 1992:5). People consider the schools to be for academic subjects, such as math and history, while vocational skills, such as agriculture and ceramics, are taught at home by the family.

Learning Ceramics

Learning pottery making is the vocational side of education in Ráquira, and many children learn to work in ceramics with their parents or other relatives. There are two common patterns by which people learn ceramics, according to their gender and whether or not their parents are ceramists.

The children of potters will learn ceramics by playing with clay when they are small. When the children are old enough to begin wanting to do what the others are doing, the adults will give them clay or broken pieces of pottery and let them imitate those who are working. So children play at ceramics, making small pieces and pretending to fire them. Between the ages of seven and twelve years old, they gradually assume more and more tasks in the workshop. Children primarily accompany their parents and help them with minor tasks, such as bringing a tool, moving pieces that are drying, or loading the kiln. They may also help dig clay and bring it to the house.

When they begin to make simple pieces, normally the mother will help finish them so that they will be acceptable to fire and sell. By the time a child is fourteen or fifteen years old, he or she should be able to assume adult responsibilities in the production process. A boy may stay and eventually take over the father's workshop, but more probably he will set up his own shop when he is older and married. A daughter's continued work in ceramics as she gets older will depend on whom she marries and where she lives. If she lives in town and her husband sets up a household pottery production, she will work with him in the family business. However, if she lives in the rural area, she will work independently in the woman's pottery style.

An apprenticeship is the second way to learn ceramics, which a twelve- to fourteen-year-old boy may do if his own parents do not work in ceramics. Sometimes, boys from rural families whose mothers make domestic pottery come to work in one of the town workshops to learn commercial-style production. Once these boys have learned the craft, they may stay as hired workers in the same workshop and eventually set up their own shop.

A young woman in town who marries a potter may begin working much like an apprentice, performing simple tasks and gradually assuming more and more responsibilities until she is an experienced worker.

Not everyone becomes a potter, and not everyone has the same ability to work clay. Some people believe that the Virgin Mary can help one develop his or her abilities as a ceramist, and they say that if the person will wash their hands in holy water at the church, then he or she will be able to make pieces more quickly. Many believe that God gives a special gift to certain people so that they have the facility to make pottery and decorate it successfully.

Some of the older potters are concerned that young people are not interested in learning and preserving the ceramics heritage of Ráquira. They complain that the young only want to make pieces quickly in molds or on the wheel, and that they do not have the patience to make the hand-crafted coiled pots or to perform the craft-intensive work that is required in the traditional pieces. They are concerned that the hand-craft techniques and shapes for which Ráquira pottery is known will be lost.

Traditional Beliefs

A number of beliefs are important in shaping how the people of Ráquira think about working in ceramics, especially beliefs about the evil eye, women and kilns, hot and cold, and *malicia indígena*. These beliefs are used to explain bad firings, illnesses, and other unpredictable occurrences. Not every person from Ráquira holds these beliefs with equal firmness, but most take precautions to protect themselves from them.

Evil Eye (Mal de Ojo)

The evil eye is a belief with roots in both the Christian and Muslim cultures of the Mediterranean. According to this belief, the evil of envy can damage a person's health or well-being. Ill will arising from one person's envy of another's good fortune can actually pass through the gaze and harm the person being observed. Children are particularly susceptible to the harmful effects of admiring looks from other people, and in Boyacá people hang amulets, such as jet (*azabache*) and coral beads, around their necks to protect them. The beauty of the beads is supposed to divert the gaze of the envious person and ward off the evil eye. George Foster found that mothers in Tzintzuntzan, Mexico, would even leave their children dirty and dress them poorly to discourage the admiration that might provoke the evil eye (1967:160).

Ráquira potters believe the evil eye can make a kiln fire unevenly with hot and cold spots, leaving some pieces underfired. Townspeople believe that the danger comes from local competitors, and most dangerous are women potters from the countryside. Some say that their glance can lead to an entire kiln load coming out broken, and it can affect the kiln over a period of time, causing unusually high breakage rates in successive firings. The belief that the women potters, who are the most indigenous, are especially dangerous reflects the traditional fears of the more "Spanish" town culture toward the more Indian country dwellers. This belief is also part of a cultural undercurrent that discourages neighborly visits to the workshop by nonfamily competitors. People who are not from Ráquira are less likely to produce the evil eye because they are not competitors and are not expected to be envious of what they see. One preventive measure against the evil eye is to keep the gate to the kiln patio closed.

If the kiln comes under an evil-eye spell, the expression is that the kiln "gets into the habit" (*coge la maña*) of breaking the pottery or firing unevenly. The cure is to gather certain plants from the countryside (*artemisa*, *jarilla*, and *hayuelo*) and spread them out over the pots in the kiln before the firing; then they are sprinkled with coal dust and holy water. This should ritually cleanse the kiln, protect the firing, and break the spell on the kiln. In 1970 production in the town came to a complete halt because everyone was experiencing unusually high breakage rates, and many local potters felt that they were being affected by bad luck and needed a general exorcism for all the kilns in town. After the ritual cleansing was performed, production resumed, apparently more successfully (Mora 1974:42).

Women and the Kiln Taboo

In the gender ideology of Ráquira, many observe a taboo that prohibits women from approaching a kiln when it is hot and prohibits menstruating women from the kiln either hot or cold. In other groups in the Americas, the woman is also prohibited from doing any work with clay during her menstrual period (Patiño 1990:118), when the woman is said to be *enferma* (sick). This belief suggests that the condition of menstruation can contaminate the kiln and cause pieces to break during subsequent firings. More importantly, the health of the woman could also be seriously affected. If a menstruating woman goes near a kiln that is being fired, the heat can "cause her blood to dry up"; in other words, she can become infertile. In a culture where children and motherhood are crucially important, few women will risk testing this belief. As a result, this taboo guarantees the primary control of the man over this final step in production.

Susan Rasmussen and Alma Gottlieb also describe menstrual taboos on the management of fire among West African groups. Rasmussen's study (1991:761) among the Berber-speaking Tuareg found that they believe that fire threatens the well-being of humans, and that noble women are especially susceptible during the menstrual period to the threats of fire and the evil eye. Gottlieb (1988:57) describes the menstrual taboos on fire among the Beng of the Ivory Coast with humoral (hot and cold) theory. She found that cold is associated with fertility, health, and life, and heat is associated with sterility, sickness, and death (ibid.:70). Although the menstruating woman may use fire for cooking, her fire is not shared with other people, and certain men cannot eat the food that she has cooked. The Ráquira taboo follows a similar logic in that the woman's fertility, represented by the menstrual blood, is threatened by the force and heat of the kiln.

Humoral Theory (Hot and Cold)

In the humoral belief system, health is equated with body temperature balance, and illness is the result of a loss of balance caused by hot or cold foods or experiences. This belief system is derived from Hippocrates' theory of pathology, which held that all matter was made up of four essences, to which were attributed qualities of heat, cold, wetness, and dryness (Mathews 1983:827). Hot and cold values in humoral theory may not correspond to hot and cold thermal temperature (Foster 1988:121), and not everyone agrees on which foods and experiences are hot or cold (Boster and Weller 1990:171ff). Although this theory originated in Mediterranean culture, in the Americas it was fused with existing herbal beliefs and practices to produce the particular synthesis of belief systems that exist today in the various mestizo and indigenous countries. Humoral theory interprets and explains the experience of illness and provides a systematic framework that attempts to control it.

In Ráquira the humoral belief system establishes parameters for managing the intense heat of the kiln with the experience of working with damp, cool clay. Most people believe that it is dangerous to combine firing the kiln (hot) and working in clay (cold) at the same time, or even on the same day. Another belief is that a person should not bathe or get caught in the rain (both cold) within the first day after firing a kiln. Even the cold night air at the time of the firing can be dangerous, and the man who is firing a kiln at night will wrap up well to protect himself from the cold air, covering his face or nose with a cloth to heat the air before it enters the warm lungs. People from Boyacá fear that these hot-cold contrasts can lead to partial paralysis of the face or body, producing results like a stroke.

Malicia Indígena

Translated as "Indian shrewdness or cunning," this concept is frequently used to describe social relationships in Ráquira, and it means that each person should always be cautious about the motivations of others. Its characterization as "Indian" refers to the history of the Conquest and colonial period in Ráquira, when indigenous people were systematically exploited by the Spanish; they developed a special strategy of shrewdness to anticipate exploitation and avoid it before it happened. Today it continues to be one of the most admired skills in Ráquira, and anyone who does not have it is considered to be careless and unwise.

Malicia indígena assumes that the people with whom you interact may take unfair advantage to cheat you in commercial exchanges, love, or friendship. A person who has *malicia indígena* can perceive the true intentions of the other person, using a sixth sense to detect who is honest or dishonest. The person whose *malicia indígena* fails to work and who has been defrauded loses status in the eyes of the community and is seen as having been foolish. For this reason it is rare to see loud disputes over a bad affair; the victim does not want to announce to the entire community that he or she has been defrauded. If a fraud occurs within a relationship that should be inviolate—for example, between brothers or sisters, or parents and children—the relationship may be broken forever. *Malicia indígena* leads people to emphasize nuclear and extended family ties; few dependent or trust relationships are formed outside of the family.

This style of human relationships leads to a competitiveness that functions well in the market exchange system and capitalism, but it makes cooperative community projects virtually impossible. Groups work best when there is a clear, strong leader, usually the owner, who contracts each person individually and assigns each to clearly delineated tasks. Conflicts can occur between workers when tasks are not adequately defined, and it appears that one worker is getting the credit for another worker's production. Rigid hierarchies function to control the competitiveness and suspicion that this cultural system engenders.

Town and Country Differences

The rural and town areas of Ráquira show differences in ethnicity, gender behaviors, and generation that reflect the cultural differences between them. In the rural communities, where there is greater indigenous influence in the culture, a basic equality between men and women prevails in the ceramics workshop; but in the town of Ráquira, where Spanish values are important, men organize work hierarchically, with the male owner having primary authority. Rural Ráquira also has a greater vertical integration of generations, which leads to multigenerational households. Ráquira people understand that a move from the rural area to the town is a cultural move as well as a geographical one, so that mestizos who practice an indigenous-influenced culture in the countryside begin to adopt a more Spanish-oriented mestizo culture when they move to town, and in town women assume a more subordinated role. Although these cultural differences exist between townspeople and country people, they also have bonds of kinship and common origins that unite them.

This urban-rural distinction in Latin American towns has its roots in the policies of the colonial period, when towns were consciously constructed as bastions of Spanish presence and authority that controlled the largely indigenous rural populations. During the colonial period, the Spanish (and later mestizo) town dwellers were *vecinos* (from a *villa* or town), as distinguished from the tribute-paying, reservation Indians (Friede 1969:60) who lived in the rural areas and were called *campesinos* (from *campo*, which means "country").

Arnold also observed this pattern in the ceramic-producing town of Quinua, Peru, where Spanish colonial terminology is still used to describe town and country people (1993:32). The Quinua *vecinos* are more acculturated to the national culture in that they speak Spanish, are literate, and wear Western-style clothing. The Quinua *campesinos* use the native language and dress and are rarely literate in Spanish.

The division between town and country dwellers in Ráquira is similar to that in Peru, with the exception that the identifiers of indigenous culture are work patterns and family organization more than language or dress. In Ráquira, townspeople differ from country people by adopting the capitalist, commodity approach to ceramics. Town potters are more open to social and technological change, whereas country potters are more conservative and continue to employ traditional technologies. These differences between the men potters in town and the women potters in the countryside create the two gender styles of ceramics that define Ráquira.

Conclusion

Ráquira is a small rural town in a remote corner of the Central Andes in Colombia. Its thousand-year-old tradition of ceramics has depleted its mountainsides of trees, and only a few of its people endure the rigors and poverty of pottery making to live an entire life as potters. Yet the vigor of the markets has brought economic vitality to this old pottery town. The townspeople's cultural constructions of gender, family organization, beliefs, and social interaction continue to structure their ceramics making today as they move into the world of global markets and grope to find the balance between tradition and capitalist expansion into industrialism.

4

Gender and the Social
Organization of Work

While some division of labor by gender occurs in all societies, this is an issue with particular relevance in Latin American crafts because most potters, weavers, and basket makers are women. In the heavily indigenous areas, differences in gender ideology also coincide with the differing Indian and Spanish cultural influences. This cultural contrast can be seen in weaving and pottery, crafts in which women more frequently retain the prehispanic indigenous techniques while men usually adopt the Spanish-style working patterns. This contrast can also be observed in the adoption of European-style clothing in acculturating indigenous communities in the Andes (Colombia, Ecuador, Peru, and Bolivia) and in Guatemala and Mexico, where men adopt the new style but women retain distinctive indigenous dress.

Gender ideology in Ráquira also defines a cultural divide between people of the town and the countryside in family organization, work patterns, and design styles in ceramics. The town patterns favor the Spanish colonial practices of hierarchy and control by men (a system actively espoused by men), whose position has been reinforced in recent years by their control of the economic gains from capitalist expansion. On the other hand, rural people have maintained a more complementary pattern in gender relations, a position endorsed by women because it allows them a broader range of alternatives.

The rural-town differences in Ráquira reflect the ongoing tension between the indigenous and Spanish cultural traditions among the mestizo peoples of Colombia, because they know both cultural systems, and they can switch cultural codes to use either system depending on the circumstances. For example, people in the same family may know the cultural rules for working with either indigenous or Spanish-derived techniques of ceramics making. Although the knowledge exists for working with both systems, the economic rewards are greatest for those who adopt the Spanish-based mass production approach (almost exclusively men). The tension of rural-town differences, indigenous-Spanish differences, and female-male differences is combined in these two ceramics systems that characterize Ráquira today.

The technologies used in the rural women's workshops represent a gender-based synthesis between indigenous and Spanish influences. Women make the pots by a hand-building technique that is a standard indigenous one. On the other hand, men mix the clay with a horse-powered mill and fire the pots in a Mediterranean-style kiln, practices that originated in the Andalusian region of Spain. So gender fuses with ethnicity to shape the tasks of women and men, who work side by side using techniques that have different cultural origins.

Women's Craft Culture

Craft production is a defining feature of Colombian mestizo and indigenous communities, and it is rooted in the traditional mythologies from the mountain regions, which may explain the almost religious intensity with which crafts are made. For the last three thousand years, weaving and ceramics have contributed to the identity and cultural cohesiveness of local communities in Colombia. In fact, to be a cultured or civilized person, one had to have knowledge of craft skills that were originally introduced by the creator gods. For example, among the Muisca of the highland area surrounding Ráquira, the creator gods who brought the knowledge of crafts to people, Bochica and Bachué, also taught the moral and political precepts that became the basis of Muisca society. As the craftspeople of the Muisca world rolled out coils of clay and built up the walls of pots, they were acting out a god-given skill that defined them as cultured individuals.

Today the old mythology is gone, but the special cultural meaning of craft making persists among traditional potters, especially those from the countryside. However, crafts are also sold, and the commercial dimension of craft making has become increasingly important in recent decades, even for women potters. Some Raquireños have voiced their concern that workers were arriving from other towns to work in the planter factories and had no identification with the traditions of the town. Whether ceramics making is driven by ideology or economic considerations, in Ráquira it is characterized by a strong work ethic.

Working patterns are differentiated by gender. Men typically alternate days of intensive physical work with drinking, socializing, and game playing on market days and holidays, while women work at slower but more steady and sustainable rates. In the family house or on the farm, women rarely rest between dawn and dusk. Long hours are required to prepare farm food; all clothes are washed by hand; and women are responsible for the house, the children, and most of the farm animals. They do craft work in addition to these other chores. Little time is wasted. As Ráquira women walk down the road or wait for a bus, they may be making baskets by "finger weaving" or performing some other repetitive craft task. Sheldon Annis (1987:107f) and Tracy Ehlers (1990:45) report similar work practices among women weavers in Guatemalan indigenous communities.

Women's Work Style

In the women's tradition of ceramics in Ráquira, the hand of the maker is usually visible, and the individual reveals herself in the finishing of the hand-coiled and modeled lines of pots. The traditional forms made by women are of precolumbian origin, and oxides rather than glazes are used to finish and decorate the surface of the pots. In this tradition, the earth is thought of as mother, the body that gives life, so that even the earth from which the pot is formed has feminine qualities. In the design of traditional pottery, women work with indigenous concepts of the craft.

The women's work in ceramics is characterized by part-time production integrated with other domestic responsibilities. Part-time craft work permits a woman also to supervise her children and the cooking, and to fulfill other household and extended-family obligations. In our research no woman was observed who gave primacy to pottery making over domestic work. The woman's income from pottery supplements the basic agricultural income of the family but never replaces it. Women may require their children to help with production and will negotiate the assistance of a husband or other adult male relative for the firing and other operations understood to be male tasks. The women's hand building ceramics style exists in other regions of Colombia, but it is rare that it exists side by side with a fully developed men's mass production style, as it does in Ráquira.

Working with potters in indigenous communities in Mexico and Peru, Arnold (1985) explained pottery making by women as an adaptation to the economics of marginal agriculture, and his explanation holds true for Ráquira. He suggested six reasons why women are the primary potters in Latin America. First, the making of ceramics is easily compatible with caring for children. Second, pottery can be made at home and does not require the women to leave for any lengthy period of time. Third, the women's pottery tradition does not use dangerous materials or machinery, so it presents few hazards to children. Fourth, making repetitive forms does not require great concentration and can be done amid the interruptions of a housewife's routines. Fifth, it can be easily interspersed with other household chores like cooking. Sixth, the day-to-day attention required by pottery is no problem to women who are tied to the house by children (ibid.:101).

Arnold argues that it is more logical for women, rather than men, to make pottery in a family economy based on subsistence agriculture. Since the man is the farmer and guarantees the family's food and subsistence, the woman can assume the economic risk of making pottery, which may or may not sell. He sees craft making as a preferred economic choice for women because it can be done at home without major interruption to the experiences with pregnancy, childcare, and nursing that most women have (1985:102).

Women, Work, and Remuneration

Women's work in cottage-industry crafts is frequently viewed within the local culture as unskilled work, simply an extension of their domestic work and not something to be remunerated at wage rates used for men. In a study of men tailors and women seamstresses in rural Peru, Carmen Deere found that men charged twice as much as women for comparable work, and this was justified locally because men's work was viewed as more skilled than women's work (1990:286). Annis also found that women artisans in Guatemala were paid half or even less than half of the minimum wage for agricultural day labor for men (1987:128). This pattern of women receiving approximately half of the pay of a man worker also occurs in Ráquira because their work is not perceived to be as important as the man's.

Tracy Ehlers (1990:111) points out that the productive skills of women in cottage craft industries tend to be based on domestic tasks and do not prepare them to compete with the more specialized men workers. On the other hand, cottage industries run by men are less segregated occupationally, and they are better capitalized. These advantages combined with the greater geographical mobility of men give them a broader range of alternatives in work, and permit them to adjust more quickly to market changes than women can do.

Not only is the work of home-based women in the crafts compensated at minimal levels, but women are also forced to bear most of the risk of selling. This is true of the women potters of Ráquira, and as a result their work does not permit capitalization or any noticeable improvement in their standard of living. Even though home-based craftswomen live in a perpetual cycle of hard work and minimal compensation, crafts are still the most consistent source of income for rural women, which can give them greater respect if not independence.

Women Potters and the Rural Family Working Unit

In the communities where women have the lead role as potters, they tend to set up cooperative work groups with family members. In rural Ráquira, the cooperative group is small and consists primarily of the wife-husband team, but daughters who live nearby may also collaborate with their mother. Labor is not a commodity in the domestic pottery economies of rural Ráquira but rather a family collaboration. Men or women may dig the clay, mix it with water, and gather firewood, although these tasks are considered to be primarily men's work. Women are responsible for the other steps of production, including preparing the claybody, wedging the clay, and making pots, and the children help by doing minor tasks, such as carrying the smaller pieces to their drying place.

Rural women potters normally limit themselves to the production of domestic functional pottery, such as cooking pots and water bottles, using indigenous techniques and shapes. Women make pottery sitting on the ground in indigenous fashion, and most women employ only manual techniques (pinch pot, coiling, or modeling). Seventy percent of the rural workshops are completely manual and use only simple hand tools, but another 30 percent located near town employ elements of mass production, such as molds or the potter's wheel (Rojas Escobar 1983:19). Some women, such as Agripa Sierra of Resguardo Occidental, have begun to make certain shapes on the wheel while continuing to make others by hand. The women's workshop does not require expensive tools, and the kiln can be built with adobe from the farm, so capital is not a major issue for rural women establishing themselves as potters.

In the early 1990s Artesanías de Colombia did a study of the three *veredas* with the largest concentrations of rural potters, Pueblo Viejo, Resguardo Occidental, and Candelaria Occidental, to determine current work patterns (Bonilla et al. 1992:64ff). The first two *veredas* are close to town and are more influenced by the commercialism of the town workshops. The third, Candelaria Occidental, is the most conservative area, and women there continue to make *loza de arena* (earthenware tempered with sand), which includes cooking and storage pots, country pitchers, and water bottles. In a sample survey of rural women's workshops in the three *veredas*,

Agripa Sierra is shaping a traditional pot with the pinch-pot process. She has shaped the basic form, smoothed the rim, and is adding the second handle. Traditional earthenware ceramics continue to be an important part of Ráquira ceramics.

42 of the estimated 120 rural workshops were visited (ibid.:52). Of this sample, only three (7 percent) used techniques similar to the mass-production practices used by the men in town. Women's workshops tended to be smaller and to have lower levels of production than those of their male counterparts.

Age and Family in Women's Workshops

Work groups in the rural women's workshops are nuclear-family based and somewhat older than are the town work groups. Three-quarters of the rural workers are immediate family members as opposed to only one-third of the town workers. Few rural shops have contract workers, and the normal pattern for women's workshops is for the members of one nuclear family to work together, which is a pattern associated with indigenous work customs.

In women's workshops close to 81 percent of the workers are relatives, and of those only 7 percent are hired workers. Almost three-fourths (73 percent) are unpaid family members (Bonilla et al. 1992:65). In other words, women almost always work together on a cooperative basis. In contrast, over two-thirds (68 percent) of the workers in town workshops

Table 4.1. Age and work in ceramics

Age	Rural*		Town**	
	No.	Percent	No.	Percent
7 to 13	10	8.06	6	2.14
14 to 35	30	24.19	239	85.05
36 to 55	60	48.39	30	10.67
56 +	24	19.36	6	2.14
Totals	124	100.00	281	100.00

*This represents a sample of approximately one-third of all rural workshops. Forty-two workshops were visited in three *veredas* as follows: Resquardo Occidental (twenty-two workshops visited), Candelaria Occidental and Oriental (six workshops), and Pueblo Viejo (fourteen).
**This represents the complete population of workers in the seventy-six town workshops.
Source: Bonilla et al. 1992:29, 66

are contract employees or business partners, and only 32 percent are unpaid family members (ibid.:26). The reason for this sharp difference between women and men is that family labor in the women's domestic-style workshop is not a commodity to be bought and sold, and it is considered culturally inappropriate to hire family members.

The age distribution of rural women potters (see table 4.1) shows the importance of middle-aged and older adults in maintaining the country-style ceramics in Ráquira. This represents a graying of the rural pottery tradition, and it reflects that most of the traditional potters are of the older generation. While few rural women potters are in the teenage and young-adult group, the majority of town male workers are in that age group, many of them recruited from the rural areas. Most pottery was produced in the rural areas until the 1950s, and even in the 1990s there are still more rural workshops that town ones. However, as the economic momentum of men's workshops in town makes good incomes possible for young men workers, fewer young women are obligated to learn their gender-specific version of the craft.

Women's Domestic Work

The work of women is characterized by a rhythm of many short-term tasks, collated by opportunity or necessity. Although domestic chores have the first priority for women, they work in ceramics, agriculture, or commerce as required. The income-generating work of women is seen as a supplemental activity to their basic life-maintenance tasks of food preparation, caregiving, cleaning, and helping the husband.

Food

The woman is responsible for all meal planning and preparation, and in the weekly market on Sunday, she or her husband buys the food that the family does not produce. Since there are no refrigerators, they rely on foods that can be safely stored. Milk and meat have to be consumed quickly and are not a part of the daily diet unless the family owns a milk cow. The woman is responsible for cooking and cleaning with the help of her daughters. Women also transport the drinking, cooking, and washing water for households that do not have running water, which may mean carrying water from a kilometer or more away. By the time girls are ten to twelve years old they start carrying water to the house.

If the family has a farm, the woman is responsible for preparing a large lunch for all of the farm laborers during the peak planting and harvesting periods. Lunch consists of potatoes and meat or a heavy stew containing meat, potatoes, corn, and cracked wheat; other vegetables may be added. Traditionally the meal is cooked over an open fire in large country-style cooking pots. The preparation takes several hours because everything is made from scratch, and her daughters or daughters-in-law will help the woman with the preparation and serving of this field lunch.

Caregiving

Women are expected to *criar a los hijos* (raise the children) and provide *cariño* (care or love) for them. The father has responsibility for disciplining them, but he does not have to attend to their day-to-day care. If a child falls and hurts itself or needs a drink or any other small attention, the woman is expected to respond to its needs. The man would probably send the child to its mother rather than give it the needed attention himself. The woman is also expected to give day-to-day attentions to her husband as she does to the children.

Helper to the Husband

Women are expected to help husbands complete their chores, but the reverse does not occur. According to Lisa Leghorn and Katherine Parker, this concept of nonreciprocal entitlement constitutes a male right to female subservience (1981:285). If, for example, the man is responsible for gathering potatoes for dinner or firewood for cooking and he has not had time to do it, the woman will do the job for him. If she does not finish making dinner or washing the clothes, however, the man will scold her, but he will not do the job for her. Even though husband and wife are working side by side, if he wants a drink, he may ask his wife to stop work and bring it to him because his work is considered to be more important and should not be interrupted. Since the man has primary responsibility for providing for the family, the woman's role is to assist him in achieving that. In this system, women's responsibilities are considered to be secondary in importance to those of men.

Cleaning

Women are also responsible for washing, ironing, and mending clothes. A man expects to have his clothes ready when he needs them, and it is important for the reputation of the woman that the family have clean, ironed clothes when they go to town. Women frequently use the days that their husbands are away from home, selling ceramics or making purchases, to catch up on domestic chores, such as washing and ironing. If she has any time free during those days, she may also work on her own personal crafts or basket weaving.

This gender system seems softer in the rural areas, where people retain values that are closer to the indigenous tradition. On one hand, men and women have two clearly separate spheres of activity (agriculture and pottery) in which they do not compete, a system that gives some leeway to women. On the other hand, daughters frequently marry within their local community and stay near their mothers, and this leads to cooperative, women-based support groups through which women help each other in the face of the powerful and discriminatory gender system.

Men Potters

When men make pottery in Boyacá, they normally have adopted the Andalusian (Spanish/Moorish) model of mass production workshop located in a town. This tradition continues today in Andalusia (Lister and Lister 1987:270f) and in Morocco, where James Jereb describes men's and women's workshops that are similar to those in Ráquira, with rural women making hand-coiled domestic pottery and men throwing commercial wares on the wheel (1995:115). In the rural areas around Ráquira, there is also a small group of men who make hand-modeled figurative ceramics, using indigenous techniques. Since figure making is an individualized craft, they do not run workshops like the men who make pottery containers. Instead they work alone or in conjunction with a wife who is a potter.

Although the Andalusian system of male pottery production was not adopted in Ráquira during the colonial period, it was in other towns in Boyacá and in other regions of Colombia. As Ráquira men began migrating to town and opening workshops in the 1950s, they adopted the Andalusian "male" style of pottery workshops used in other towns, including the potter's wheel, Mediterranean kilns, and commercial organization of the workshop. Most work is done on tables in European fashion, rather than sitting on the ground in the indigenous way still used by traditional women potters in rural areas (see table 3.1).

Men in Ráquira become potters when they can work full time at the craft, and their technically complex style of production enjoys a larger market share than does the hand-built style of the women. As a result, when the man is a potter, his wife becomes a worker in his shop, working in the men's mass-production style rather than the domestic style used by autonomous women. In the workshop, men and women do not work together as equals because men normally have the higher authority. When family workshops are transformed into small industries, men manage them, using a top-down hierarchical style in which they have authority over the wife, children, and other workers. The man who hires workers is *el dueño del trabajo* (the owner of the work), which means that he pays for the work and provides lunch. Stephen Gudeman and Alberto Rivera (1990:272) documented the same pattern among small farmers in Colombia. As the owner of the work, the employer emphasizes his control over it. The men's workshop hierarchy is based on financial and administrative control rather than superior technical skills, a situation that Leghorn and Parker say holds true cross-culturally (1981:281).

Within the pottery-making family today, the Spanish Conquest repeats itself: the man dominates by using European production techniques and design models, which effectively eliminate the indigenous coiling techniques and pottery styles used by the woman. Because the men's workshops are usually located in towns, they have ready access to regional markets beyond the town. The men's tradition of ceramics is found in the areas where the Spanish colonial influences were the strongest.

Men and Technology in Ceramics Making

Men's ceramics making usually involves the use of tools or machines, unlike the handwork of women. In addition to the potter's wheel, the Mediterranean updraft kiln, and glazes, men are also noted for using other mass production techniques, such as two-part plaster molds. This industrial style of production means that each man works at one specialized task, and that several men may work side by side doing the same tasks. June Nash also documented this pattern in Chiapas, Mexico, and she concluded that men organized themselves mechanically while women organized themselves organically (1985:70), referring to the fact that men repeat the same work side by side, each one working independently, while women organize their work in interdependent stages in which each woman takes responsibility for the task she does best.

Men Potters and the Family Working Unit in Town

In the town workshops, men set up and manage hierarchical work units; additional labor is brought in by hiring workers rather than relying on cooperative obligations. Most town workshops are headed by men, and that has been true at least since the earliest study by Mora in 1966, when she found 81 percent headed by men (Mora 1974:67). In 1983 Rojas Escobar recorded 84 percent of the town workshops headed by men (1983:39–40), and a decade later Bonilla's team counted 87 percent as men's-style workshops (1992:47). Over the last twenty-five years, the proportion of town workshops headed by men has been a virtual monopoly. In these workshops, labor is a commodity and work is contracted. Work is based on the speed and efficiency of the individual workers as they carry out separate specialized tasks using molds or machines. Since 87 percent of the town workshops now do commodity-oriented pottery production using molds or wheels, only 13 percent do rural-style *loza de arena* pottery (ibid.).

There are seventy-six ceramics workshops in the town, but five planter factories dominate the largest share of the town production. The remaining shops are mostly husband-wife operations; a few families hire one or two additional workers. In most families children also help in the workshop, but they are not considered workers by the parents. Men's workshops require capital for land in or near the town, for molds and potter's wheels, for a large covered work area, and for a kiln large enough for mass production. This large capital requirement is a barrier for young men in Ráquira, most of whom have to work for years as an employee before they can open their own workshop. In fact, 40 percent of the town workshops are rented (Rojas Escobar 1983:17), which is a way for younger pottery families to start their own workshop.

Town pottery workers are mostly teenaged or young adult males, and the current group of young men represents the second generation of in-

Town production of Indian-motif planters. This woman is trimming a leatherhard planter that has recently come out of a mold. Smoothing out the seams, she adds earrings and sets the piece out to dry with the others. It is fifty-five centimeters high and thirty-five centimeters in diameter. She is part of a husband-and-wife family workshop.

dustrial and semi-industrial workers. Since town workshops emphasize speed in production on the potter's wheel or with molds, young men, who have the greatest manual dexterity and endurance, are preferred workers. The few middle-aged (thirty-six to fifty-five) and older men (fifty-six and above) who work in production are responsible for its less physically demanding aspects, such as driving the horses for the clay mill, trimming, or firing.

Wives and the few contracted women workers perform the jobs with the lowest prestige (trimming and decorating), which do not require special strength or skills. Wives are not paid, and contracted women receive the lowest remuneration of all town workers. Women are assigned the task of finishing pieces, which is not as important in Ráquira as in other ceramics traditions in Colombia. In fact, Ráquira pottery is known for its rustic, sometimes casual finishing and for minimal decoration, so little is expected of women in the town workshop and they are not paid much. In the town family workshop, both husband and wife are usually considered the owners, even though the husband has the real authority over production. There is also work other than ceramics, which for the woman means domestic chores and for the man may include agriculture. The relative importance of each of these roles varies from time to time throughout the life span of the potter.

Sweatshop Conditions: No Benefits and Long Hours

Workers in the town workshops receive no benefits and are paid subsistence incomes, and their productivity and incomes can only be increased if they have the physical endurance to work longer hours. Salaries vary according to the skill level and physical demands of the job. Workers are either paid by the day or by the piece as a way of circumventing the liberal provisions of Colombia's labor laws, which guarantee a month's paid vacation to all employees, one month of additional pay as a bonus at Christmas, one and one-half sick days per month, health care insurance, and a retirement fund. In contracting by the day or for piecework, the workshops avoid classifying those workers as employees legally entitled to ancillary benefits. Most are paid at a rate that is somewhat higher than the minimum wage but less than the total remuneration of employees with benefits.

Young men agree to work under this system because it gives them a slightly higher cash income and they are willing to forgo health insurance and retirement pensions. Although all jobs may be paid by day wages, most throwers on the potter's wheel and press molders are paid by the piece, which keeps constant pressure on them to produce at their fastest pace. The piece-rate system rewards longer hours (sometimes up to ten or twelve hours per day), and some men prefer it because it permits flexible hours. The system converts the worker into a contracted entrepreneur, an independent contractor who is paid according to work produced.

This system has been criticized because it requires workers to push themselves to their physical limits, and it probably also contributes to occupational burnout, which may explain the dramatic drop in the number of workers in ceramics in their middle thirties. After that age, either the worker has the money to open his own shop and hire others to do the hard work, or he returns to agriculture, which has a more acceptable pace of work.

Men's Family Work Responsibilities

Men's responsibilities to the family include providing for the family, acting as its head (*representar y proteger a la familia*), and performing the heavy or physically demanding work (*el trabajo pesado*). Men are responsible for the basic subsistence of the family, and they are freed from time-consuming domestic chores to guarantee them long, uninterrupted work periods during the day to achieve that goal. The rhythm of men's work is one of concentrated periods of hours or even days of total dedication to single tasks, in contrast to women's work, which may include domestic tasks, pottery making, and/or agriculture, all on the same day.

Breadwinner

The man is obligated to provide the basic economic support for the family, including housing, food, clothes, education for the children, health care, and other needs they might have. A man who is sexually active with more than one woman assumes those obligations for her as well. The man is expected to be the primary economic provider.

Head of the Family

As head of the family, the man is expected to protect the family and stand up for its members in conflicts outside of the nuclear family. The expression "ponerse los pantalones" (put on your trousers) means the man is expected to take firm stands and defend his family before accusers. The expression "el hombre responde por la familia" means that the man is the one who stands up for the family in public. If there is a conflict with another family over land or water rights, about sales or purchases, about a problem at school, or any other subject, it is the man who should argue and talk for the family member involved.

The man is also responsible for work to be done outside of the house or involving outsiders. This "protects" the wife and daughters from undesirable attention from other men and avoids placing them in vulnerable positions around men. This means, for example, that the woman should always be accompanied in public to prevent other men from forcing their attention on her, and also that work to be done in an isolated field should be done by the man. This also means that work groups tend to be single-gender groups. If a woman needs assistance with ceramics or other chores, her husband, children, or female relatives will help her. When the man hires workers to help on the farm or in a town workshop, he hires men. In part this is to create single-gender work groups, and in part it is because only men's labor is a commodity to be bought and sold. Since it is considered inappropriate for women to be in charge of men workers, women rarely hire or supervise them.

It is also understood that "el hombre manda" (the man gives the orders) in the family. This means that his is the last word in family discussions and decisions. He may or may not ask for his wife's opinion; some families are more collaborative in this respect than others. His "last word" may affirm what the woman wants to do, but it is the man's word that validates it. In extreme cases, the man may abuse his authority and arbitrarily ignore the feelings and desires of other family members.

Heavy Work

The man is expected to do the work that requires physical strength or involves working with machinery or big tools. Men's work includes plowing the fields, managing large animals such as horses or cows, cutting and carrying wood, firing the kiln, and carrying loads of pots for marketing. Although the woman may cook over a fire, any big fire, such as that of the ceramics kiln, should be managed by the man, who is expected to be *duro* (hard) and to be able to tolerate the excessive heat involved.

Men's Rules on Work

Men's rules on the gender division of labor in ceramics start with the central premise that men cannot do the lower-status work of women, but that women may be required to help men complete their work. The specific rules are:

1. Men's work has higher status than women's work.
2. A wife is expected to help her husband with his tasks if necessary, so that it is acceptable for women to do men's work under certain circumstances.
3. Men will not do women's work.

Shared work is primarily men's work that women help complete, but the reverse rarely occurs. Women may do men's work, such as making planters in molds, but men will not make traditional women's cooking pots.

Gender and Work in Town and Rural Workshops

Men supervise the ceramics production when the family works in the town-style workshop. They are responsible for obtaining the raw materials, mixing the claybody, throwing on the wheel, forming pieces in molds, organizing the workshop space, firing the kiln, and being in charge of packing and shipping. Women are primarily involved in modeling forms, such as horses, banks, and pitchers, or making pieces with molds. They also assist with the men's activities, such as loading the kiln and selling the work. There are, however, exceptions to this general pattern. For example, some

women have begun to work on the wheel, and some are now more involved in selling.

Twice as many men as women work in ceramics in the town workshops, and hired workers are almost always men. The almost equal number of men and women family workers is due to the fact that husbands
and wives work together; there are few men who do not have a woman
family member working with them. Although the husband and wife are
partners in the business, both understand that the husband has primary
responsibility. There are over six times as many male hired workers as
female hired workers, indicating the predominant emphasis on the work
of men in the town workshops.

Since workers in the town workshops are contracted primarily for either the physically demanding or the highly skilled jobs that the owners
do not want to do (or cannot do), men are the most frequent candidates.
If a man is a widower and has no daughter or other female family member
to do the woman's tasks, another woman will be hired. The eight hired
women (14 percent of workers) correlate almost perfectly with the six
men who do not have a woman family member as a co-worker. It is generally considered inappropriate for a woman to work side by side with
male workers unless she is the wife or other relative of the owner, a relationship that affords a barrier of respect protecting her from sexual harassment. Larger workshops that have their own showrooms usually hire a
woman to be in charge of sales, but in that position she has little contact
with the male workers. In the town workshop, wives or hired women are
the support workers who free up the men to be the primary producers.

In the rural family workshops, more women than men work in ceramics, and here the woman is the primary producer while the man does the
support work to keep her supplied and working. The man is more of an
equal in the rural workshop than is the town woman, however, so that
the rural family makes a balanced cooperative working unit. He mines
and prepares the clay, obtains the fuel for the kiln and fires it, may assist
his wife by carrying clay to her while she makes pieces, and helps with the
selling. Although women in the countryside are the primary makers of
ceramics, men have become more involved as support workers over the
last half century as ceramics has become more profitable.

Shared Gender Tasks in Agriculture and Marketing

The production of ceramics is secondary to agriculture among rural families, with the man being primarily responsible for agriculture. Each gen-

der collaborates with the other in certain tasks, according to the urgency of the work. The woman is her husband's primary helper in agriculture, which she does in addition to her domestic responsibilities and ceramics. During peak planting and harvest periods, men and women in rural families temporarily abandon the production of ceramics and dedicate themselves totally to agriculture. This is especially true during the August dry season, when the people harvest beans and corn and shell the green peas that have been harvested earlier. Fields are then plowed, and wheat is sown. Since the time frames for agriculture and ceramics are both narrow and critical, the two cannot be carried out simultaneously in times of intense activity. Most of the contract workers in the town workshops come from country areas, and during August they too work on their family farms. There is a general slowdown in ceramics production in the town and countryside during this period, although the dry season could be the most productive of the year because of the fast drying rate for the clay.

Much of the agricultural production of the rural families is for their own consumption, but any excess production is sold. Many farmers borrow from the Caja Agraria (Farmer's Bank) to finance the purchase of seeds, fertilizers, and insecticides for their crops, but sometimes the profit from agriculture is insufficient to pay the bank and cover the costs of the next planting. When the bank pressures the farmers to pay their loans, they express their frustration through a play on words, changing the name of the bank to Caja Agria (*agria* means sour or bitter). When the harvest is poor, pottery provides the cash income to pay the debts at the Caja Agraria or other debts incurred in the planting. In its own way, pottery subsidizes the traditional, subsistence agriculture by providing a modest cash income that permits the farmer to continue growing the food to feed the family.

Both men and women may be involved in the marketing of ceramics. Traditionally, pots were bartered for food in Ráquira or Sutamarchán. Potters would trade for meat, bread, vegetables, potatoes, rice, spaghetti, brown sugar, chocolate, or other foods they use. The family would have an account at the store, and when they brought pots the account was credited. When they took food, it was debited. Now it is a cash economy, and the potters sell their work. Some intermediaries visit the mountainside communities to place orders with individual potters. However, the roads to the mountainside communities are difficult and potters' houses are dispersed, which means that many intermediaries prefer buying in town.

Single Gender and Shared Gender Work in Ceramics

Although work patterns differ according to whether males or females are the primary workers, both work in production. In 30 percent of the rural workshops, the woman works completely alone or with only marginal assistance from her husband (Bonilla et al. 1992:64). Many women who work alone are widows who support themselves by making ceramics; they hire a man to assist them with mixing the clay and firing the kiln. In seventy percent of the rural workshops studied by Bonilla et al., husbands and wives worked together in ceramics (ibid.), the man usually assisting the woman in her production. However, in the rural areas closest to town some workshops are organized and managed by men in the town style. The distribution of work patterns in the family workshops in town is: women as the primary potter (16 percent), men as the primary potter (84 percent) (Rojas Escobar 1983:39f). Women working alone in town make traditional pottery, hand-modeled figures, or small mold-made figures, while the husband-wife teams headed by men primarily produce mold-made figures and planters.

In summary, women potters tend to work alone with no employees, although family members may help her. These family work relationships are collaborative without hierarchical arrangements. In contrast, in family workshops managed by men, he is an administrator and may or may not actually make pottery. He directs the work of hired employees and of unpaid nuclear family members, including his wife and children. These gender patterns are not limited to Ráquira but can also be found in other parts of Latin America.

Comparison of Gender and Ceramics in Latin America

Working in Guatemala, Ruben Reina (1966) and later Reina and Robert Hill (1978) found differences between men's and women's work in ceramics production that are similar to those in Ráquira. In the earlier study in Chinautla, Reina (1966:57) found that knowledge of pottery making was an important marriage skill for women in Guatemala. A skilled and industrious woman potter could easily attract a husband because she could support the family if necessary, and the income from her craft helped offset the problem of poor and insufficient agricultural land.

Reina and Hill found that most ceramics were produced by indigenous communities using technologies of precolumbian origin, with women being the primary producers in each of the twenty-five traditional communities they studied. Moreover, women continued to dominate ceramics production in indigenous communities that had acculturated to nontraditional technologies (1978:200). Men made ceramics in only three of the twenty-five traditional communities (ibid.), and each of those had significant Spanish contact or had begun using the twentieth-century, small-industry-style working techniques associated with men's involvement in ceramics. In addition to the indigenous ceramics communities, there were three mestizo communities that used Spanish-style wheel production to make pottery, and in these communities only men were potters (ibid.:21). In another study of gender and culture in Atzompa, Mexico, Clare Hendry found that pottery making was women's work and that men only became potters when the economic prospects were good (1992:112). In that community, women make traditional domestic pottery by hand building, while men make commercial ware in the form of animals and ceramic toys by using plaster molds and the wheel in a pattern similar to Ráquira's. The Mexican, Guatemalan, and Colombian gender and ethnicity patterns coincide with the tendency of women potters in Latin America to maintain indigenous craft traditions while men adopt Spanish colonial and twentieth-century working patterns. Additional studies from Peru (Arnold 1993) and Ecuador (Whitten and Whitten 1988) confirm this pattern.

Gender and Social Change

Domestic obligations limit the range of possibilities open to Ráquira women potters, and as a result, they tend to become conservative, as indicated by their maintaining indigenous traditions in ceramics. Even though mass production working styles may be more efficient, the traditional hand-building system is well adapted to the domestic cycle of work culturally expected of the woman and the lifestyle that many women choose for themselves. It is also a system that can give women more vocational and economic independence within the nuclear family organization than is available to them in other work settings.

In contrast to the conservatism of women potters, men have been the primary innovators of new technologies in ceramics in Ráquira. It was men who adopted the Spanish elements, such as the potter's wheel, glazes, and the Mediterranean kiln, and more recently they have turned to small-industry technologies, using molds, electric potters' wheels, and coal-fired downdraft kilns. As men adopt new technologies, they also adopt new ceramic forms that can best be produced by those technologies. The authority and independence given to the men in the machismo system sanctions their actions and innovations, giving them support and credibility in cultural change.

The gender power of men can also be seen in their control of the kilns and the firing process. Even when the woman makes the pots, she depends on the man for the final critical step of firing. Both men and women accept the cultural premise that the handling of fire is primarily a man's occupation, and the metaphysical explanations of menstruation and the evil eye keep women away from kilns being fired. If a woman potter does not have a brother, husband, or son to help with firing, she must hire a man to do it. This problem is especially common among older widows who have no son living nearby.

Older women do have freedom to explore behaviors that are not open to younger women. By the time of menopause, most women have completed their child-rearing responsibilities, and they are freer to travel unchaperoned to town, to the market, or elsewhere. At that stage in their lives there is less danger of sexual abuse or harassment, and there are fewer people in the house to care for. Another factor is that men tend to die earlier than women. As widows women have more freedom than they have had at any other time in their lives; they can even take on tasks that are more associated with men's work.

Machismo and *Marianismo*

The role of women in craft work is structured by the system of machismo dominant in the larger society, which leads to unequal gender roles and allows women little opportunity for economic independence. If ceramics becomes economically profitable for the Ráquira family, the man takes over the operation and relegates the woman to a marginal role. In any case she is rarely permitted to escape the limits of her domestic responsibilities. The cultural system in Ráquira usually permits the woman to control her own ceramics making as long as it occupies a secondary role in the family economics and does not challenge the primary role of the man.

This system has been summarized by the concepts of machismo and *marianismo* (a term referring to values associated with the Virgin Mary), which were described by Evelyn Stevens (1973a, 1973b) and reevaluated by Tracy Ehlers (1990:134–35, 163–64). Machismo signifies the role of the man as the protector and authority within the family; he has greater authority and prestige than the woman. Although this typology of gender describes the behavior of many in Ráquira, not all men are dominating and harsh and not all women are submissive and quiet. Nevertheless, over 90 percent of the families have a male head (Bonilla et al. 1992:6) who has virtually unchallenged authority to make decisions for the family, and unchecked authority frequently leads to abuse (Reinhardt 1988:216). In practice, this means that the man can question and even ridicule the woman, but she cannot question him in return. He may also use physical or verbal abuse to reinforce his authority. In my own research, women reported verbal and physical abuse from their husbands, and other studies in Ráquira have documented reports of frequent wife abuse (Bonilla et al.

1992:7). Within the system of *machismo* the man is also expected to display sexual prowess, which may entail having many children or at least having extramarital affairs, to ensure that his masculinity is not called into question.

The complementary gender construct for women is *marianismo*, which refers to Mary, the mother of Christ. This prescribes that the woman should be submissive to the man's authority in marriage. Carmen Flórez and Elssy Bonilla (1991:72) report various reasons given by women to justify this attitude, including first, it is an inheritance not only from Mary but that goes all the way back to Eve; second, Colombian law sanctions the subordinate status of the woman; third, a woman has fewer problems if she obeys the man; and finally, men are aggressive and women do not know how to defend themselves. In addition to these four reasons given by Florez and Bonilla, representatives of the Church generally sanction *marianismo* as an ideal for women.

Women are expected to show superior moral rectitude and to serve as examples for their children, especially in sexual matters. This leads to the idea of "protecting" women from men because all nonfamily men are expected to be sexual predators. A version of female seclusion results from this since the woman's safe haven is her home. She generally interacts with the general public only at church or the market, and then she is accompanied by a child or another family member.

According to Evelyn Stevens, *machismo* and *marianismo* are behavioral phenomena peculiar to the Americas. Although they have roots in Spain and Italy, the fully developed complex occurs only in Latin America. Her explanation is that these ideologies developed from the attitudes of superiority of upper-class men in Spain, which were emulated and vulgarized by lower-class male braggarts who in turn migrated to the Americas as soldiers and adventurers. While they established a cruder version of the system in America, it declined in Spain and Italy (1973b:91).

A version of *marianismo* is described for Andalusia by Timothy Mitchell (1990:36–38) in which women fatalistically accept the implacable will of God in the same way that they accept the will of their male relatives. Mitchell also describes uncontrollable male sexuality as the defining principle of the *machismo* of Andalusian men, which is as fatalistic as the women's view of their condition (ibid.). According to Mitchell, fatalism is the linchpin that maintains the system of *machismo* and *marianismo* intact.

Its survival in Latin America can be explained by the inherent conservatism of colonial societies, which frequently maintain behaviors that have long since died out in the metropolitan centers of the colonizing countries. This colonializing attitude survives in the continuing importance to-day of the Conquest model of social relations in the Latin American coun-tries that have significant indigenous populations. In this model, the man's role is to dominate workers, social relationships, and the family. For the man who does not have workers to dominate, a wife and children may be the only subjects over whom he can exercise control.

This gender system has been explained through economic factors by Ehlers (1990:156–57), but it is also affected by Spanish and indigenous cultural differences. In Colombia this gender system is more pronounced in the mestizo areas, such as Boyacá, Antioquia, and some areas of Cauca, where the Spanish presence and forced acculturation were more severe during the colonial period. The male ideal of the Conquest was the tall Spaniard mounted on horseback who had won battles and accumulated wealth. This "conquistador" image of masculine identity is still widely ac-cepted by men and women in mestizo and Spanish-descent groups in Co-lombia, and it cuts across lines of social class. The strong-man image is sustained by obedience and subordination within the family. Most women reject the abuses of this system, but many perceive no other choice for having a family. The subordination and violence of the Conquest survive in cultural memory and are acted out in the microcosm of the male-fe-male relationship.

Although Ráquira fathers are respected and perhaps even feared, moth-ers are usually valued for their caring and nurturing. In return, there is a strong tradition of helping and protecting the mother in her old age. The woman's social prestige in the community comes from her being a hard worker, protecting her children, having their loyalty, being attentive to her husband, and not causing family or social problems.

The *machismo* system is recognized throughout Colombia, but it does not have the same characteristics in all regions, and in many indigenous areas, there is more equality between men and women. In other parts of the Americas gender complementarity is also found in indigenous groups. For example, Tracy Ehlers (1990:6) describes a relative equality in Mayan marriages in contrast to full-blown *machismo* in the town-based *ladino* (Spanish-oriented) marriages, and Laura Bossen (1984) reported similar findings among Mayans.

The *machismo* system gives the men preferred economic and social sta-tus, even though superior moral status is granted to the women. Magdalena León (1987:96–97) identifies the patriarchal ideology of *machismo* in Co-lombia as the primary factor barring the equal participation of rural women in the society and economy. Tracy Ehlers (1990:135) adds that the long-suffering *marianismo* of the women gives them the status of virtuous martyrs, but it also conceals the humiliation and brutalization that they experience socially and economically. The *machismo* system has favored the emergence of the men's industrial workshop system in Ráquira in recent decades. Men have social and economic credibility, and they have benefited from training and loan programs established to foment the industrialized production in which they specialize. Women are remembered for the nostalgic and symbolic value of their traditional pottery, but that leaves them in the marginal economic position that *marianismo* has assigned them.

Summary

Gender and ethnicity are interlocking cultural elements in Ráquira that produce two distinct strata of potters and pottery making. These two cultural complexes become the reference points around which decisions are made for change in pottery making. We can draw the following conclusions:

1. There are two gender-based cultural systems in Ráquira ceramics, one feminine and one masculine.
2. Gender and ethnicity are linked and critically influence culture.
3. The domestic culture of Ráquira is largely indigenous with the degree of Spanish influence greater among townspeople.
4. The two major tracks of ethnic influences in the formation of culture in Ráquira are the indigenous group (Muisca) and the Spanish/Andalusian traditions.

Gender indicates how larger cultural decisions are made in Ráquira, and it structures the relationship between work and family, the kind of production, and marketing. This system of gender differences is economically favorable to men and permits the women's tradition to survive only as a part-time activity integrated with domestic obligations. The women's tradition is the conservative one and it continues to use essentially prehispanic concepts of form and technology, while change is more apparent in the ceramics-making complex used by men.

5

Figurative Ceramics:
The Iconography of a Culture

Men have historically made figurative ceramics while women made pots to hold food and water. However, as men have moved into pottery production with planters in recent years, women have also moved into figure making, initiating a crossover pattern from traditional roles. Formerly, all figures were hand modeled, but after the adoption of mold production in the 1950s, many families began making figures in molds. Today both men and women make hand-modeled and mold-made figures. Hand-modeled figures are one-of-a-kind pieces and are considered art, but mold-made figures are considered production pieces. This is one of the few aspects of Ráquira ceramics in which men and women work in similar styles, but men are still more widely known and celebrated as figure makers than are women.

Since the 1970s the Museo de Artes y Tradiciones Populares (Museum of Popular Arts and Traditions) has promoted the development of figurative expressions in Ráquira ceramics through organized competitions and marketing, leading to a growing market for Ráquira figures among urban buyers. Although the market for hand-modeled one-of-a-kind pieces is not large, both the museum and Artesanías de Colombia (Crafts of Colombia) buy them for resale in Bogotá, and they are also sold through stores and other intermediaries in town. Figures made by the older generation tend to be modeled more rustically, but those made by younger figure makers are more frequently carefully sculpted.

Hand modeling of human and animal figures was common in the prehispanic period among the Muiscas of this area (Rojas de Perdomo 1985:157; Duncan 1996a:335, 1993:25). Although little of the specific content of that ceramics tradition remained after the Conquest, some expression of it may have survived in the idea of representing local domestic animals, one of the motifs favored by women figure makers. The differences between men's and women's imageries reflect their social experience, each gender favoring the animals with which they normally work on the farm.

Gender and Iconography

Ráquira women make figures of farm animals, especially sheep, chickens, and pigs, which are the primary responsibility of women on the farm. They are also common sources of meat and eggs in the diet of rural Ráquira, and, along with the cow, they symbolize food and well-being for people in this region. These figures are usually ten to fifteen centimeters in height. The other central theme for women is religious imagery, although some men, such as Laureano Martínez, have also made churches. The leaders in religious iconography have been Otilia Ruiz and her daughters, Graciela and Rosa María. They make churches, Christ figures, and nativity scenes, images that reflect their own personal religious feelings. While the human figures range up to twenty centimeters high, the churches are usually larger, thirty to forty centimeters.

Men also make ceramic animal figures, but in contrast to the women, they make the man's animal, the horse. The Ráquira horse is a work animal which the man uses in plowing and carrying heavy loads, and the man is primarily responsible for caring for it on the farm. Today women and children may assist the man in making the mold-made versions of the horse, but this normally occurs under his supervision.

One man, Teodolindo Ovalle, developed a genre of narrative scenes of village life that project the social tensions, foibles, and everyday activities of small-town Colombia. Narrative scenes may include only one figure, but many show clusters of people in activities. For example, he portrays a woman at the funeral of her husband, glad that he is dead, representing the conflicts that women feel in this male-dominated society. While some in the funeral procession cry in grief, others fight over the inheritance. Another piece shows a band of drunken musicians, in a comment on the issue of weekend drunkenness on the part of men. Yet other pieces portray domestic chores, with women spinning wool and men bringing home buckets of honey. There are also icons of Colombian national life, including important contemporary sports figures. Soccer matches may be shown, but most important is bicycle racing, which in Colombia is a sport of the rural mountain people. One piece shows a bicyclist, probably the racing legend Luis Herrera, in the middle of a race surrounded by television cam-

Laureano Martínez decorated bottle representing Simón Bolívar. The bottle section in the base is elaborately decorated with figures and geometric designs, like other Martínez pieces. The pouring spout emerges from the horse's head while the filling tube is just behind the rider's back. The dimensions are twenty-two centimeters high, twenty centimeters long, and fourteen centimeters wide. Collection of the Museo de Artes y Tradiciones Populares, Bogotá.

eras and helicopters. In these scenes men and women depict their daily preoccupations and interests, so their pieces reflect something of their gender roles.

Spanish Iconography

The most notable icon of Spanish culture used in Ráquira ceramics is the horse, the animal that represented the Spanish Conquest. This image of the majestic horse with its rider mounted as a conquering hero was modeled by Don Laureano Martínez into mini-sculptures (twenty-five centimeters high) that are *licorera* (liquor) bottles, which were used to hold rum or aguardiente (a distilled anise-flavored drink). His best-known *licorera* bottle portrays Simón Bolívar, who symbolizes Colombia's political independence from Spain, but the *conquistador* image also reflects the dominance of Spanish culture over the indigenous cultures. The majestic horse represented the epitome of power and wealth in the Spanish colonial world, as it still does today.

Martínez got the idea for the Bolívar bottle from a photograph of the bronze sculpture of Bolívar made by the Colombian sculptor Rodrigo Arenas Betancur for the city of Pereira, Colombia. The Bolívar bottles are functional, and the spout for pouring liquid comes from the horse's mouth. Martínez is recognized by most of the potters in the community as having had the most creative and fanciful imagination among the figure makers before he passed away.

Decorated church. This church façade by Laureano Martínez is a celebration of life. It is covered with flowers, birds, and angels, in addition to the crown of the King of Glory and crosses. Near the top of the decorated portion is a Spanish-like shield, similar to the one found on the front of the church at Monqui in Boyacá. A human face peers out from one of the bell towers. It is thirty-five centimeters high, thirty centimeters wide, and thirty centimeters deep. Collection of the Museo de Artes y Tradiciones Populares, Bogotá.

The bullfight is another quintessentially Spanish theme interpreted in ceramic figures, and the tightly defined circle of spectators around the bullring represents the Spanish fascination with fate and mortality, which is well understood in the indigenous and mestizo world of Boyacá. The ceramic representation of the bullfight is made in the rural areas between Ráquira and the neighboring township of Chiquinquirá. It typically portrays a circle of human figures sitting on a wall watching the drama of the bull and the bullfighter. In the 1960s and 1970s, the figures were roughly modeled and covered with a green lead glaze. Today there are new versions whose features and details are more carefully modeled, and the surface is covered with a beige-colored slip.

Important icons from Spanish culture are also found in Christian imagery, especially nativity scenes, Christ figures, and churches. Although most Raquireños do not attend church regularly, they do consider themselves Christians, and Christian motifs are important in their ceramics. These figures are purely decorative and are not considered to have metaphysical significance as religious objects, although the makers as well as the buyers usually treat the Christ figures respectfully.

The most striking churches were made by Laureano Martínez, and they have elaborately ornamented façades which are like a tree of life with plants and birds modeled in relief. Martínez began making decorated churches after a merchant asked him to make one based on a photograph of a ceramic church made by potters in Peru. He reported that making the first church took him several days until he worked out the technical problems. Later he dreamed that it was better to replicate churches from Colombia, and he began making representations of the basilica of the national patron saint in Chiquinquirá and of smaller churches in Villa de Leyva and Ráquira. At that point he also began placing a ceramic figure of Christ, which he also made, inside the churches. Making churches for him had no religious significance, however; he made them because they sold well.

Spanish Moresque Influences

Spanish Moresque influences can be seen in the work of Laureano Martínez, most notably in his bottles (*licoreras*) and the façades of his ceramic churches. In Spanish Moresque fashion, floral designs fill up all the available space in a celebration of nature and life, with birds, animals, and human figures intermingled with the foliage. Louana Lackey describes similarly ornate representations of nature in the ceramic tree of life made in Acatlán, Mexico, and suggests that the form is of Middle Eastern origin, that it was taken to Spain by the Moors and brought to the Americas after the Conquest (1982:104). Spanish and Moorish (and sometimes Berber) imagery meshed well with the indigenous concept of the fertility of mother earth; and the Indian figure, which Martínez frequently places in a central location on his pots, symbolizes this synthesis.

Laureano Martínez's ornate ceramic bottles are recognizable by their profuse decoration. Stamps are used to impress complex designs on the surface, which may be complemented or refined by incising. The designs follow the shape of the bottle and fill all the available surface space. Patterns of circles within circles, triangular shapes, and even faces may be modeled along with leaves and flowers. Several shapes are used for these bottles, including squares, ovals, and a round, flattened canteen shape with loop finger holes at the neck. One constant element in the design of the bottles is the need for flat spaces on which the designs can be stamped.

A source of Spanish Moresque influences on Martínez's surface designs was apparently the embossed leather-covered *licorera* bottles made until recently in the department of Antioquia. The leather covering of these bottles had embossed designs drawn from the Spanish leather-embossing tradition, which had in turn been borrowed from Moorish sources. The technique of embossing adapts well to clay, which in its "leatherhard" stage has the same consistency as leather, and Martínez exploited that characteristic more than anyone else in Ráquira. While his figures were unique, he contributed to the larger tradition of natural figurative production.

Figurative Styles

Three approaches to figure design are used in Ráquira: stylization, naturalistic figuration, and realism. Each style represents a different level of modeling skill, conceptualization of the piece, and time devoted to its execution. Stylization has been the traditional modeling style in Boyacá since the prehispanic period, while the naturalistic and realistic styles are more recent developments.

Rustic stylization is the defining type of Ráquira figuration, and it is characterized by a naive quality in the rough finishing and nonrealistic proportions in the figures. Major body parts are clearly represented and are usually hand modeled, but definitive details are never given. Faces are roughly modeled so that the species is defined, but there are no individual details. Arms and legs are clay cylinders, and the hands and feet may be no more than lumps of clay, perhaps with incised lines to show fingers. The Ráquira figuration has traditionally been a naive art in which the visual qualities are not as important as the narrative or meaning of the figure.

Stylization characterized Muisca figures in ceramics and gold before the arrival of the Spanish. Muisca ceramic figures ranged from rustic ones that appeared to have been made quickly to sophisticated ones whose faces showed carefully modeled features. Similar rustic figures continue to be made today, and they are considered the *campesino* (country) style. Teodolindo Ovalle and Otilia Ruiz make figures in the rustic style, and they are more interested in the narrative quality of the figures than their visual properties. Their figures comment on the rural life and people around them, and the two potters use a rural modeling style to reinforce the rural nature of their narrative. Although the figures of Doña Otilia Ruiz are based on Christian iconography, she represents them in local Boyacá terms; for example, Christ may be portrayed as a farmer. While the naive visual quality of the stylization suggests something a child might do, the pieces express complex social ideas. These qualities together communicate the honesty and the obliqueness of social commentary in Boyacá.

Naturalism is the second figurative style used in Ráquira, and moldmade figures normally embody this style. It evolved from the sophisticated stylization that was used for the finest Muisca figures before the Spanish, as well as from the European naturalistic figure tradition in Christian religious art. Naturalistic figuration has been used in Ráquira primarily for nativity figures, although recently it has been used for secular mythical images as well. This style of modeling uses a completely natural representation of the features of face, body, hands, and feet, but realistic individual details are not given. These figures are, in effect, mannequins intended to represent religious or other cultural ideas. The personal character of the figure is secondary to its conceptual message.

Naturalistic figures are well suited for representing religious imagery because they should portray a religious ideal or concept rather than the individual qualities of a person. Nativity figures in Ráquira have traditionally been modeled with natural but not realistic features, for example, so that the divine experience of the birth of Christ is communicated more than the personal happiness of Mary and Joseph.

Naturalism is also used to portray secular mythology, and Laureano Martínez used it to portray Bolívar as the heroic independence fighter and founder of the country. The younger generation of figure makers uses the naturalistic style extensively, as can be seen in the works of the Sierra brothers, Javier and Fabio, or the young Reyes Suárez. The fanciful mermaids of Fabio Sierra are one example of naturalistic figures, these representing the mysterious enticements of women. Reyes Suárez, the younger, also used the naturalistic style to model the mythical *campesino*-like cherub standing atop the fountain in the center of Ráquira's plaza and continuously urinating into the pool below. In this figure, he unexpectedly combines the Greco-Roman idealization of the human body with the indigenous Andean view of the naturalness of human bodily functions. Javier Sierra also used naturalism to model and idealize the Boyacá *campesino* farmer, in a separate sculpture placed in the central plaza near Suárez's cherub.

Realism is the third figurative style used in Ráquira, and it has been developed only in recent years, primarily in the portrait figures of Javier Sierra. Realistic figures are hand modeled based on European concepts, and rich visual details are given to individualized faces and bodies. Sierra achieves these visual details by technically superb modeling skill, and he works slowly to achieve the precise detail required to represent the individual. He has an excellent eye for observing the minute details that are idiosyncratic and personally defining, and the skill to be able to model those details.

To communicate the personal reality of rural life in Ráquira, Sierra may use the wrinkled intensity of the face in one sculpture or the muscular tension from years of hard agricultural work in the body of another. Realism is social and humanistic in its narration of the experiences of individuals, and it communicates the physicality of life experience rather than the metaphysics of naturalistic figures. By choosing his own grandmother for the portrait sculpture in the central plaza of Ráquira and by also choosing the *campesino* farmer as a sculptural theme, Sierra has added a new, real-life dimension to the examination and celebration of local life. Even though his themes are continuous with the social motifs of the pieces of Teodolindo Ovalle and Otilia Ruiz, his figures are more immediate and compelling than theirs.

Hand-modeled Figurative Ceramics

The men who make figurative ceramics have traditionally considered themselves to be on a level above the women potters, whom they see as incapable of making anything more sophisticated than cooking pots (Mora 1974:25). Today, however, women also make hand-modeled figures. These pieces are intended to be one of a kind, and even if a series is made of the same figure, each one will have some individual quality. Some figure makers make descriptive pieces that narrate the world around them, which requires considerable creative ability and an astute perception of their surroundings, while others create fanciful figures that suggest religious or mythical qualities.

The cooking pots made by women and the figures made by men were traditionally produced in the rural workshops, and the two kinds of production are still fired together in the same kiln loads. If women make figures, they start by making a pinch pot. A ball of clay that fits in the hand is pinched open with the thumbs making a cuplike cavity. This becomes the body, and the wall is pinched open until it is more or less uniform. Then the opening is gradually closed to form the body of the figure, such as a chicken or a pig. A smaller lump of clay is added to the body for the head, and details are modeled or incised into it for the face. When Doña Otilia Ruiz and her daughters became figure makers, they also used architecture for their subjects, hand modeling churches and houses, which were new themes for women.

Although Ráquira figure makers have been known historically for the horse, chicken, and nativity scene figures, some in the newer generation of figure makers create large sculptural works and include a wider range of human and animal subjects. These hand-modeled pieces have considerable prestige in the urban market, and they command higher prices than traditional pots or planters. The hand-modeled figures are seen as creative and innovative, and they are considered more artistic than the mass-produced, mold-made figures.

There have always been only a few figure makers, and that continues to be true today. Javier Sierra and Reyes Suárez, the younger, make hand-modeled figures, but their pieces have sculptural intentions, in contrast to the folk narrative figures of the past. Rosa María and Graciela Jerez make hand-modeled country-style figures, following the lead of their mother, Otilia Ruiz. María del Carmen Rozo makes hand-modeled animal figures (chickens, frogs, and owls, among others) into pots to create one-of-a-kind shapes not found in mold-made pieces. While most people now make figurative pieces in molds, these individuals and a few others continue to make hand-modeled figures.

Mold-made Figures

In the past piggy banks, chicken banks, and horses were hand modeled, but today these figures are primarily made in molds, and they have become the most popular ones in the market, primarily because of their modest cost. Piggy banks and nativity scenes are made in very large quantities; it is not unusual for a family workshop to receive an order for three thousand piggy banks. These mold-made figures are full-bodied forms with simple rounded lines that adapt easily to two-or three-part molds. The style of mold-made ceramics is associated with a rounded body form, a smooth molded surface texture, animal shapes, and sizes that normally range between ten and twenty centimeters. The type of workshop generally dedicated to the production of mold-made animal figures is the husband-wife family workshop in town in which the man, woman, and children work in the production. Since the molds are small, women and children can work with them as well as the man can. In fact, parents assign some delicate tasks to the older children because their small, nimble fingers permit them to do intricate work that is awkward for the thicker, more muscular fingers of the adults.

The Ráquira Pony

The horse is the figure that has most characterized Ráquira ceramics throughout the last century, and the *caballito*, literally "little horse," is a form distinctive to the town. The oldest person remembered for making the Ráquira pony was Antonino Rodríguez, a rural ceramist who specialized in animal figures at the beginning of the twentieth century. He made small horses and other figures to sell in the Ráquira market as well as in nearby Chiquinquirá, to people making a pilgrimage to the basilica of the national patron saint. Don Antonino's ponies were painted in various col-

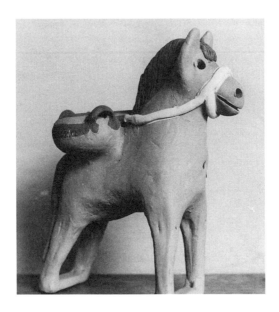

Ráquira horse. This horse is one of the forms that is most identified with Ráquira ceramics. In contrast to the imposing Spanish horse and rider, this is a humble peasant horse and beast of burden. Collection of the author.

ors, and they frequently had colonial-style saddles. After he died, another rural ceramist, Próspero Cerero, began making the pony, and he continued the tradition into midcentury. Although a traditional form, it almost died around that time. However, in the 1960s and 1970s renewed attention was given to it, and the Ráquira horse made a comeback.

The Ráquira pony has the same playful features as one in Spain that comes from the Moorish-influenced ceramics of the town of Andújar in Andalusia (Llorens and Corredor 1979:124). Bolivia also has a history of ceramic horse-and-rider figures from the Spanish colonial era with similarities to the Ráquira horse (Litto 1976:55). The Bolivian horse comes from the well-known ceramics-producing village of Huayculi, which like Ráquira has a long tradition of ceramics. By the early 1970s, the Huayculi horse had been modernized (ibid.:71), reflecting the influence of Mexican cowboy movies; its rider is portrayed as a singing cowboy wearing a rolled-brim hat and strumming a guitar. The riders on the horses from both Huayculi and Ráquira are modeled with stylized features and few anatomical details. Other Latin American versions of the horse can be found in village ceramics in Peru and Chile (ibid.:33, 82).

The saddled horse represented the prestige and wealth of the Spanish during the colonial period, just as the precolumbian mythical figures had represented supernatural power during the prehispanic period. This figure of the horse may have been the way in which the prehispanic figurative tradition was synthesized with the new reality of the post-Conquest world. The horse made during the early part of the twentieth century used a Spanish colonial-style saddle, which suggests that similar figures may have been made during the colonial and republican periods (nineteenth century), when the use or memory of the saddle still persisted. However, Mora believes that the origin of the Ráquira horse is more recent, and that it was copied from colonial-style figures made for nativity scenes, which were still available at the beginning of the twentieth century when Rodríguez was working (1974:18). Today the Ráquira pony may be made with a rider, or it may be shown carrying pots of honey or other loads. It is not a large or powerful horse, nor are expensive saddles represented; rather it is shown as a peasant workhorse, reflecting the rural way of life in Ráquira.

Chicken, Sheep, and Piggy Banks

The domestic animals that are the responsibility of women are the ones most frequently made as banks, especially chickens, sheep, and pigs. The animal shape is made, and a coin slot is cut into its back. Urban dwellers in Bogotá and other cities buy these as gifts for children to use for saving money. When the child is ready for the money, the bank is broken. The chicken is one of the traditional animal shapes made in Ráquira, and it reflects both Spanish influence and the rural nature of this genre of ceramics.

The chicken is also popular in other Andean countries, including Ecuador (Litto 1976:101), Chile (ibid.:82), and Peru (ibid.:47). Since the chicken

Chicken bank. The chicken is a form that has long been made in Ráquira, and in the last couple of decades potters have begun to make this chicken-shaped bank along with piggy banks. The dimensions are fifteen centimeters high and eighteen centimeters in diameter. Collection of the author.

is not native to the Americas and was introduced by the Spanish, it did not occur in precolumbian ceramics. However, the chicken is popular in Spanish ceramics, and Josep Llorens Artigas and J. Corredor-Matheos describe the version from Andalusia (1979:119), which is a bottle with the beak as the pouring spout. In fact, the form of the chicken has been made in Spain at least since the Greek period, including chicken-shaped liquid containers of approximately the same size as those produced in Ráquira today. An example of a Greek blackware pottery chicken is included in the collections of the National Archaeology Museum in Madrid. So the Mediterranean and Spanish chicken-shaped pot has been retained in Ráquira, but the function has changed from holding liquids to holding coins.

The piggy bank is the recent form that has gained most acceptance among city buyers, and it has become a bigger seller than the icon of Ráquira, the horse. This change from the horse icon, which represented the Spanish Conquest society, to the piggy bank, which symbolizes capitalism, suggests the new values that characterize Colombian society at the end of the twentieth century. Ceramic figures are art for the masses, and shifts in the popularity of figures are a measure of changes in the society.

Nativity Scenes

The nativity scenes are called *pesebres* and include the figures of Joseph, Mary, baby Jesus, the three wise men, and various animals. These are particularly important in Colombia because the traditional family Christmas is centered around the display of a nativity scene in the house, rather than the Christmas tree. The *pesebre* may include more than just the manger scene; the more elaborate ones may depict a small town as well as the surrounding countryside with shepherds and their animals. The figures in the nativity scene may be from five to twenty centimeters tall, and they are normally sold as a set. The official organizations that stimulate the development of crafts in Colombia (Artesanías de Colombia and the Museo de Artes y Tradiciones Populares) have sponsored contests to encourage potters to make nativity scenes in an effort to develop a market for them. Today there are as many versions of the nativity scene as there are ceramists. The bodies of the nativity figures are usually press molded, which means that they are shaped by pressing clay into a plaster mold. The faces may be made in a special kind of press mold called a sprig mold, which is used primarily for the small, delicate features of a figure. Other parts of the figure, such as arms, legs, hands, shawls, and the men's *ruana* (poncho), are hand modeled and added to the figure. Mary and Joseph are frequently shown as rural Boyacá people, Mary with a country-style shawl

Near-life-size nativity figures. Javier Sierra kneels with a full set of nativity figures that he made and fired in the family kiln. They are modeled on the lines of figures in church art. The standing figures are approximately 140 centimeters tall.

and a fedora hat, typical of country women, and Joseph with the same style of hat and a man's *ruana*. Baby Jesus is given European features with a carefully modeled Italianate face. The three wise men are usually bearded and wear robes and hats that are considered to be oriental. Visitors bringing gifts or coming to see the Christ child are frequently portrayed as Ráquira residents. Thus the nativity scenes reflect the multiple strands of influence that make up the local culture.

The Current Generation of Figurative Potters

Among the young generation of figurative potters are Javier and Fabio Sierra Rodríquez. While both make figures, they have radically different approaches to their craft. Javier hand models his figures so that each one is an original, while Fabio reproduces mold-made figures. Sometimes the two men collaborate, with Javier making the original of a figure and Fabio creating a mold of it for a mold-made series.

In contrast to the earlier figure makers, who made small pieces to sit on tables, some of the ceramists in this generation are making life-size and near-life-size figures that are intended to have sculptural value. This is especially true of the work of Javier Sierra and Reyes Suárez, the younger.

The images made by this new generation are rooted in the same rural traditions that the earlier figure makers drew upon, but today's figures explore themes never used by the previous generations.

One significant change is the making of realistic portraits of local people, such as Javier Sierra's life-size representation of his grandmother, Doña Lucía Rodríquez. This figure, located in the plaza of Ráquira, is a portrait modeled with photographic realism. The figures made by the older generation of figure makers were highly stylized and did not depict specific individuals. Sierra changed that by portraying his grandmother seated in a work position making *chorotes* (country pitchers). Although Ráquira figures have always been defined by the rustic stylization of figures, Sierra's hyperrealistic style is something one expects more in Renaissance art than in Ráquira craft.

Javier Sierra's ceramics have consisted primarily of nativity figures, in part because his knowledge of art is of religious figures and in part because there is a market for them. His largest nativity set includes six near-life-sized figures of Mary, Joseph, the three wise men, and another visitor. The largest of these are 1.4 meters tall, which is the maximum measurement permitted by his kiln. Mary and Joseph kneel while the three wise men stand holding the gifts they have brought. Facial details are realistically modeled, and the flowing robes with their luxurious folds are equal to the polychromed, wood-carved religious figures that he has seen in

Life-size sculpture that Javier Sierra made of his grandmother, Doña Lucía Rodríguez, making domestic cooking ware. It is located in the central plaza of Ráquira.

Spanish colonial churches. No one taught him to model; he learned by looking at figures and reproducing what he saw, and in the process he mastered the complexities of the Spanish tradition of church art.

Javier's brother, Fabio, represents the current generation of figure makers who work with molds. He makes plaster molds of figures that Javier has made for him, the most popular of which are nativity figures ten centimeters high. He makes three versions of these figures, one that is plain earthenware, one painted with clay slip, and one finished with polychromed water-based paints. The slip-painted version has a smooth surface, but the details of the modeling are softened and blurred by the slip. Fabio hires a young woman cousin to paint the hands, faces, and descriptive details of the clothing of figures in the polychromed sets, using commercial acrylic paints. Fabio is also one in the younger generation who is working with slip casting, breaking with the press-mold system used in Ráquira.

➤   ➤

The workshop of Javier and Fabio Sierra is an open-walled, roofed area attached to the north side of the family house. It is approximately four and one-half meters wide and six meters long. Along the wall formed by the house is a multipurpose work bench where Javier has placed smaller finished figures. Along the east side is a waist-high wall, and that side of the workshop has become a storage area with bags of raw materials to be mixed, wrapped sets of nativity figures ready for Christmas sales, and larger figures made by the brothers. Molds are stacked along the north and west sides and covered by large sheets of plastic, and the west side of the workshop is an open working area where Javier sets up his turntable to work on figures. On the north side of the workshop they have two kilns along with the piles of wood and coal to fire them. The smaller kiln is one meter in diameter and height, and it is used to fire the small figures. The larger one is one and one-half meters in diameter and height, and it is used for firing the larger figures, which are laid down in the ware chamber. The brothers also fire traditional pottery in the kilns, which may act as saggars (ceramic firing containers) for smaller figures placed inside of them. Filling out the kiln with pottery is also done to even out the firing and to make use of all the kiln space.

Javier makes his figures using photographs of a model, who poses in the position and clothes needed for the sculpture; the model is usually Fabio. The suggestion to use photographs came from a technical adviser from Artesanías de Colombia, and Javier found it useful to facilitate his memory of details such as wrinkles in the clothing. While sitting on a stool, he works on a turntable about sixty centimeters high, and he begins by laying in the base of the feet and then he *builds up the hollow legs, pinching in and modeling each layer. He covers the exposed edges with a damp cloth to prevent excessive drying during the slow modeling process as he works and reworks each detail. The figure is continued upward in the same manner to the head, which is the last part modeled, and when it is finally enclosed the hair is modeled into place. He gives attention to minute details in clothing, such as stitches, small tears in the cloth, and even the texture of the weave. His technical skills in reproducing these details creates a hyperrealism more associated with art than with country crafts. A figure that is fifty to sixty centimeters high requires one month to complete, and he can sell it for 80,000 pesos ($100.00 U.S.).*

Although Javier and Fabio first made pots as children with their grandmother, they quit making them when they became adolescents because traditional pottery is considered women's work. At that point they began making figures, which is acceptable work for men. They attended school at the Colegio de la Candelaria (Candelmas High School), which is located in the hamlet where they live, but they did not receive any formal art education. Their training consists of what their grandmother taught them, observations of religious art in the local monastery, and what they have seen in Ráquira.

Javier Sierra holds a figure representing a *campesino*, or peasant farmer. The realism of his work is expressed in carefully modeled facial features and clothing details. His studio is in the background, where life-size nativity figures can be seen.

Their visual education did include the collection of religious paintings and sculptures in the rural monastery of the Augustine fathers located just down the mountain from their family house. This isolated monastery was built in 1604 and is used today by the Padres Augustinos Recoletos (Augustine Fathers Withdrawn from the World). Exposure to this church art, as well as to the pottery made by their grandmother, has given the brothers an effective visual education, which they have parlayed into two different but vibrant styles of working with the figure.

Figures and Culture

Although contemporary Ráquira figurative ceramics do not have the ritual significance of the precolumbian figures, they do show the rich tradition and iconography of rural life. Religious beliefs (nativity scenes and crucifixions) are portrayed along with figments of the secular imagination (mermaids) and icons of rural and national life. The figures are the expressive dimension of Ráquira ceramics, and they give a more detailed insight into the society than does the cooking pot or the planter, although the latter two are much more common in the marketplace.

6

Design and Style in Pottery Vessels

Female and male potters employ different design styles for their pottery vessels and containers. Women make hand-built domestic pottery for cooking and storing food and for carrying and serving water. Men, in contrast, produce mold-made planters and other highly saleable forms that are oriented toward the urban markets of Colombia. Altogether potters in town and rural areas make over twenty different forms, and there are many different personal variations on each one. The most commonly made forms in the men's workshops in town are planters, mobiles, and banks, and they usually possess a wider repertoire of forms than the women do. The most common forms in the women's rural workshops are cooking pots, miniature pots, and banks.

A cultural system encompassing gender, residence, and family organization constitutes the unseen infrastructure of community values that shapes design styles and the ceramic subculture of the potter. Ráquira ceramics are characterized by four major styles that have developed over four centuries of documented history. Three of these (traditional pottery, playful souvenir ware, and hand-modeled figurative ceramics) have long histories, but the new style (urban market ware) only appeared in the last half of the twentieth century.

Fabrication Grammar and the Design of Pottery

To make a pot a ceramist must decide whether to work in a traditional or contemporary style, determine what form the piece will take (pot, plate, bowl, or figure), and choose among various colors, shapes, textures, and other visual elements. The potter works with this repertoire of alternatives to construct his or her particular style, which is shown in the ability to work within the known dimensions of the medium to produce a visual quality consistent with expectations. The cultural dimension of a style comes from an established repertoire of forms, such as those from Ráquira

Table 6.1. Ceramic forms by workshop in Ráquira

Form	Town No.	Town Percent	Rural No.	Rural Percent
Mold-made planters	33	43.42	9	21.43
Wheel-made planters	27	35.52	5	11.90
Planter plates	6	7.89	3	7.14
Zoomorphic banks	16	20.64	11	26.19
Traditional pots	10	13.15	23	54.76
Mobile elements	23	30.25	3	7.14
Coffee sets	6	7.89	0	0
Miniatures	12	15.78	15	35.71
Pitchers	4	5.26	4	9.52
Lamps	9	11.84	1	2.38
Flower vases	6	7.89	0	0
Candle holders	3	3.94	2	4.76
Other forms*	9	11.84	2	4.76

*Forms produced by one or two workshops, including horses, jewelry boxes, braziers, ashtrays, salt bowls, appliqués, and animal whistles.
Source: Bonilla et al. 1992:48, 76

shown in Table 6.1. This table summarizes the information on the twelve most important forms produced in the community. The pattern of forms made in the urban (male) and rural (female) workshops indicate the style.

Each style of pottery consists of a repertoire of technical and expressive elements that can be combined to make any given pottery shape. The principal elements available for making a pot are shape or line, texture, color, and reflectiveness. As new forms are introduced into the repertoire, compositional demands are placed on them, altering them to fit the preexisting visual elements (D. Arnold 1993:91). However, shape is not only a visual issue; a piece must also be functional, suited to cooking and storage needs and ease of handling. As the potter acquires a repertoire of primary visual elements for use in producing the style in which she or he is going to work, the person builds up sets of alternative elements that can also be used. This repertoire of visual elements is organized into loosely linked sets of alternatives, so that multiple and even redundant style elements can be chosen for any given design. Since the social and aesthetic context in which crafts are produced is constantly in flux, potters also change their techniques, finishing, and forms of pieces accordingly.

Women's Domestic Pottery

Ráquira's women potters produce cooking pots, water pots and pitchers, and children's toy pottery, and a few make figurative ceramics, as the previous chapter discussed. The form of the traditional Ráquira pot is defined by the profile line, which curves dramatically from the base up to the bulging midsection of the pot and then abruptly curves inward toward the mouth. Forms tend to be spherical, and small necks are used to transform even the limited profile curve of a pitcher into a near spherical shape.

Texture is the second strongest visual element of Ráquira ceramics, and one of the last steps in making traditional pots is to scrape the outside surface to smooth out irregularities in the coil-built walls. Since the claybody is heavily tempered, the scraping produces a deeply pitted surface that is associated with the rustic quality of Ráquira pottery. The reddish-beige color of Ráquira pots is simply the color of the fired claybody with some irregularities caused by flashing from the wood fire. Although this flashing is appreciated by Ráquira potters, they do not give it as much importance as it has in other traditions, such as Japanese village pottery.

In women's ceramics, pots are made with ample circular forms, consistent with the precolumbian tradition. Functionally, the circle is a strong form that eliminates the stress points that occur with angles, and this is particularly important for cooking vessels that go through thermal shock on a daily basis, as they are rapidly heated and cooled. Ample volume is preferred by women potters, and each shape is bulbous, making the pieces sufficiently open to receive liquid or solid food. Narrow forms, such as cylinders, are not made.

Women's Design Grammar

The design elements for women's pottery consist of a small set of alternative forms for the base, body, neck, lids, and handles. These design elements are combined for functional, not aesthetic, reasons to produce the recognizable forms of the cooking pot, water bottle, bowl, pitcher, and other pieces. The first design element, the rounded bottom, is a design identifier for women's traditional domestic pottery, and it represents a continuity with the precolumbian traditions of Colombia.

Various body forms are used, including an open shape (bowl), a high, slightly enclosed globular shape (cooking pot), an enclosed spherical shape (water bottle), and a low body wall with a dramatic inward curve (the *paila*). See figure 1 for these shapes. The open shape is used for soup bowls, mixing bowls, and casseroles, and in all cases the wide, open mouth is designed for ease in serving food. The globular shape of the cooking pot is widest in the middle or stomach of the pot to provide an ample capacity for the food being cooked. The low, enclosed walls of the *paila* are well adapted to the preparation of food, and the broad, open mouth permits easy access to work with the food. Some *pailas* are made with a small spout to pour off the whey from making cheese.

Although the base and body determine much of the profile of a piece, the neck is important in defining its use. The basic function of a neck is to impede water or food from spilling; the absence of a neck, such as in soup bowls, permits ease of access to the interior for serving food or drink. The three basic neck shapes are the short, slightly curved neck, the high pouring neck, and the spout. The short neck is used on cooking and storage pots; it helps prevent spillage but still permits access for stirring or dipping out the contents. This neck is usually no more than five centimeters high, and it does not significantly enclose the mouth. Ráquira pots used for fermenting *guarapo* or *chicha* have a stretched version of this neck that is slightly higher (ten centimeters) and may be straight.

An even longer neck used for pouring is fifteen centimeters or more in height and has an opening that is six to ten centimeters wide. The pouring neck may be straight or have a flaring lip that may be smoothed out into a pouring spout. This higher pouring neck is for water bottles or pitchers. The third neck is the spout, which is long (fifteen centimeters) and narrow (two centimeters), and it is used for the *múcura*. It has the functional advantage of being easily closed with a stopper, which makes it possible to carry liquids to the fields or other workplaces.

Handles are important for lifting and carrying ceramics, and all handles are usually made from coils. One is a straight grasping handle for the toasting pan or *arepero*, and it is normally a simple, thick coil, approximately fifteen centimeters long, three centimeters wide, and two centimeters thick. The second type of handle is a stirrup-shaped grasping handle used for pitchers and other pots, especially large cooking and storage pots. This tends to be a flattened strap handle a little thinner than the straight toasting-pan handle. These handles are typically fifteen to eighteen centimeters long, and they are curved to fit the shape of the closed, grasping hand. The third type of handle is the small loop made just large enough to accommodate a finger or rope. One-or two-finger versions of the loop handle are put on small *múcuras,* but three or four loop handles are put around the shoulder of large cooking or storage pots so that a rope can be passed through them and tied onto a carrying frame for purposes of transport.

Most of the rural women potters make *loza de arena,* which includes traditional country pottery and miniature pots for children and collectors.

Many different forms are made of both types of pottery. The traditional domestic pottery consists of the cooking and storage pots used in country households, including the cooking pots (*ollas*), storage pots for food or water (*tinajas*), water bottles (*múcuras, poras,* or *cántaros*), pitchers (*chorotes*), toasting pans (*areperos*), and large straining and mixing bowls (*pailas*). The miniature pots include these same shapes, but in small sizes for children's play.

The rustic pots made by women potters have clean lines adapted to practical domestic uses. The rare decoration consists of a couple of hastily painted calligraphic brush strokes of oxide wash around the neck or handle, which seem to be spontaneous and almost haphazard, in the spirit of Muisca decoration. Children are important for women potters, and they make toy pots, whistles, and piggy banks especially for them. They also make miniature pots and jugs the size of a kernel of corn that are strung together to make necklaces, and these have long been sold to tourists as souvenirs.

Each of these design elements is made slightly differently by each individual potter. For example, a strap handle may be larger or smaller according to the hand size of the potter making it, and fingers may be used to impress design lines into it. A pitcher-like *chorote* may have an almost perfectly circular profile or a broader, bulging stomach line depending on the potter. These design elements have long since been consolidated into the specific forms of traditional pottery, and they represent an integrated set of design principles. Cooking pots, water jars, or jugs made by traditional women potters from Ráquira are clearly recognizable because of the design and surface treatment associated with them. This is a design tradition that is centuries old and well adapted to its historical uses.

The Functions of Women's Pottery

Form and function in Ráquira pottery divide along gender lines, with vessels made by women following the curving lines of the human figure and focusing on human nourishment while the pottery of the men has straighter and more angular lines and primarily consists of decorative pieces. Women potters prefer full, round shapes, and their storage pots have a profile of wide shoulders on a small rounded bottom that seems to challenge gravity. Their rounded bottoms cause them to rock unsteadily on the tile floors favored by Spanish architecture, and some people build wooden stands to hold them when they are used inside houses. In contrast, they are well suited for the natural undulations in the ground. While they satisfy a domestic need, such as storing food or water, they also delight the eye.

Women make pottery that is functionally adapted to meet their needs in the preparation, serving, and storage of food and water. The design of

Table 6.2. Functions of women's domestic pottery

Form	Clean/mix	Cook/ferment	Store	Carry	Serve	Decorate
Olla		P* S**	S			S
Olla con cuello	P	S	S			S
Múcura				P	S	S
Chorote					P	S
Cántaro		S	P			S
Arepero		P			S	
Cuenco					P	
Cazuela		S			P	
Panguas				P	S	
Paila	P P				S	
Platón	P					

*P: Principal use
**S: Secondary use

this domestic cooking pottery continues prehispanic and colonial designs, and it is adapted to the traditional practice of placing the pot on three stones over a cooking fire. Pottery is also designed to conform to the lines of the human body, and, in fact, ceramic pots are frequently conceptualized in terms of the human body and described as having a mouth, lips, neck, shoulders, and belly; they may even have a soul (Nash 1985:53). The shapes of vessels in village ceramics are adjusted to the motor habits and carrying positions used by the local society (Arnold 1993:121). The primary functions of Ráquira domestic pottery have traditionally been carrying water, cooking food, serving food, and storing food and liquids.

1. Carrying water. The curves of water jars follow the curves of the human body because historically most families had to make several trips a day for water, so it was important for the water pot to rest comfortably on the bearer's hips, shoulders, or back. And since water pots are usually carried by women, the profile is fitted to the lines of a woman's body. The curved bottom of the water-carrying pot is made to rest in the hip curve of the woman, and its narrow neck is of the right length and position to cradle in the bend of her arm. This design permits the woman to walk considerable distances carrying a heavy load of water.

Water pots are designed with a narrow neck to prevent spillage as the water rocks back and forth inside the pot as it is being carried. Small versions of the Ráquira water pot hold four to eight liters and are carried by hand with a strap handle. The water bottle (*pora*) and water jug (*chorote*) are used to carry small amounts of water, and both have short necks (from two to ten centimeters). The larger ones hold twenty liters and have three finger-sized loops placed around the shoulder of the piece. A rope is passed through these loops to tie this heavy pot onto a donkey or to facilitate its being carried between two people. Large *múcuras* of this type are in the range of seventy centimeters tall, including a neck that is thirty centimeters long.

2. Cooking. Cooking is another primary function of domestic pottery, and it may be done in either enclosed, spherical pots or open, concave toasting pans, depending on the food to be cooked. The *olla* or enclosed pot is used for cooking stews and boiling potatoes and vegetables, and its full, round, bulbous shape gives it ample volume. It also has a slightly enclosed mouth, which helps prevent the contents from boiling over. The open toasting pan (*arepero*) is also made for cooking the thick, pancake-like *arepas* made of cornmeal.

3. Serving. Food—whether it is a more liquid dish like stew, or a drier meal such as meat and potatoes—has traditionally been served in a soup bowl. However, people also use the toasting pan as a plate for serving dry food. Plates are not an indigenous form to Ráquira. Some potters, however, have experimented with making the shape for urban markets in recent decades, but without much success.

4. Storing food and liquid. A version of the *olla* or cooking pot may be used for long-term storage of dry foods, such as grains, as well as temporary storage of cooked foods. Water was also traditionally stored in these pots, but that need is largely met today by manufactured containers and by piped water systems. The same kind of pot has also been used traditionally for the fermenting and storage of *chicha*, the corn beer. Usually one special pot is set aside for this purpose because it absorbs the taste of the *chicha*, rendering it less desirable for other purposes, and also because the fermentation process is considered to go better in a pot that is already cured.

In sum, women's pottery is adapted to the functional requirements for the family's food and drink, and water for utilitarian purposes. The basic pottery forms that are made to satisfy these requirements are the water

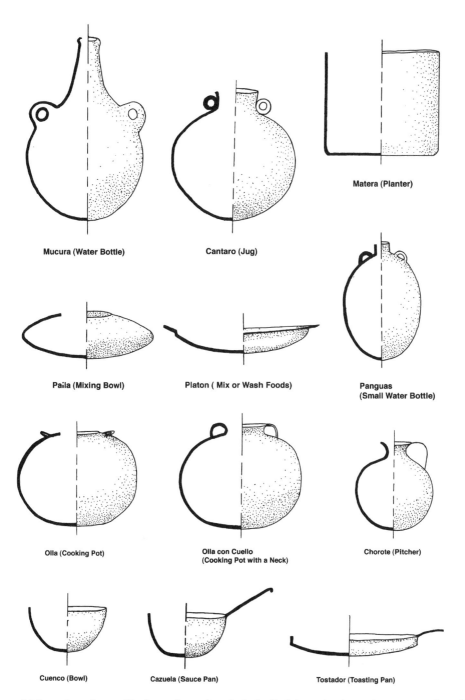

Mucura (Water Bottle)

Cantaro (Jug)

Matera (Planter)

Paila (Mixing Bowl)

Platon (Mix or Wash Foods)

**Panguas
(Small Water Bottle)**

Olla (Cooking Pot)

**Olla con Cuello
(Cooking Pot with a Neck)**

Chorote (Pitcher)

Cuenco (Bowl)

Cazuela (Sauce Pan)

Tostador (Toasting Pan)

Major pottery shapes. The forms shown here include all of the major domestic pottery made by women and the planters made by men. The split half drawing style emphasizes the profile line of the pot on the left and the form of the pot on the right. The gripping handles or finger loops that are added to the *ollas, chorote, múcura, cántaro,* and *panguas* are made with small coils of clay. More substantial handles are added to the *cazuela* and *arepero,* and they are made from thicker coils. All handles are attached to the pieces when they are at the leatherhard stage of drying.

bottle, cooking pot, toasting pan, and serving bowl. These four basic shapes are made in most women's pottery communities in Colombia with local variations in the profile of the pot, style of handles, shape and length of the neck and lip, and surface treatment. How these design elements are shaped and combined to form pots identifies the particular styles of each local pottery community.

Forms of Women's Pottery Style

The traditional pottery made by women is part of the Boyacá functional earthenware style, which includes cooking and storage pots, bowls, pitchers, and bottles. The surface is the natural claybody, which is neither glazed nor sealed by a clay slip, and this pottery is always formed by hand modeling and coil building, using heavily tempered clay. (Hence its name, *loza de arena*, which means tempered ware, or *loza de suelo*, which means earthenware.) Today, hand building is considered old-fashioned and is not highly valued among the men ceramists in town, who say the process is too slow and results in pieces that are shaped irregularly. However, rural women potters continue hand building, because they prefer the technique and because it would be difficult to make their large, bulbous pots using the press-mold system of the townspeople.

Traditional pottery is still used as functional ware in some areas of Colombia. Although aluminum cooking ware is readily available, some people believe that it is unhealthy to cook in it because of the metallic taste it imparts to the food. Seven forms of traditional functional pottery are produced today, and while some are derived from the prehispanic tradition of domestic pottery, others show marked Spanish influences. Each of these forms is made in various sizes, and the individual finishing by each potter produces some variations in shape.

1. Pots. The cooking pot, or *olla*, is the most widely used and most recognized form of traditional pottery. It is of prehispanic indigenous origin, and it seems to have been preserved with slight modifications throughout the colonial and republican periods. It is a spherical pot made by the prehispanic indigenous pinch pot and coiling technique. There are cooking and storage versions of this pot, which are differentiated by the size and shape of the mouth and lip. It may have two or more eyelet-like finger holds, or it may have grasping handles. The cooking pot is important in all of the village traditions of Colombia, although its shape changes from region to region.

The form and size of the *olla* in Ráquira change according to its functions. The storage version of the pot has a relatively narrow, flat

The traditional cooking and storage pot is the basic shape for Ráquira earthenware. In the foreground are two pots without a neck; this style is used to store corn and other grains. The three pots in the background have a short neck and flaring mouth. They are used to store liquids, such as water or *chicha* (the fermented corn drink). Today people living in cities use these pots as planters or as patio decoration. Spontaneous brush strokes of slip are added to the upper part of these pots. Photo from the Villa de Leyva market.

mouth with no neck, which makes it easier to seal or cover. These are used to store grains such as corn, wheat, and barley and to protect them from rodents, which has been one of the primary uses of ceramics in all cultures. The *olla* with a higher (ten centimeters) cylindrical neck is used for fermenting *guarapo* and *chicha*. In size the *olla* normally ranges from ten to fifty centimeters in height and fifteen to sixty centimeters in diameter. They have been made in sizes up to seventy-five centimeters tall and ninety centimeters wide, but the larger ones are rare. The cooking version of the pot has a short neck and a flaring lip and is called the *olla con cuello* (pot with a neck).

The smaller cooking pots are used to prepare soup, vegetables, or rice for a family meal. The three standard family-sized pots are the four-cup *jícara*; the *olla de media jícara* (or half-*jícara*), which makes the equivalent of two cups of food; and the six-cup size called the *tapera*. The larger sizes, called *almorceras* or "lunch pots," range in capacity from fifteen to thirty cups. In rural Colombia they are used for cooking the main noontime meal for working groups on the farm. The farm owner is expected to provide this meal for laborers hired during the planting and harvesting seasons, a practice also described by Stephen Gudeman and Alberto Rivera (1990:108). The lunch is prepared at the worksite by the women of the family using large *almorcera* pots placed over an open fire. *Guarapo,* the fermented sugar-cane drink, is also kept in a storage pot on one side of the field for the use of workers who get thirsty during the day.

2. Serving bowls. The soup-sized bowl, called the *cuenco,* is one of the forms that occurs most frequently in prehispanic sites, and in this region of Colombia rural people still commonly eat from bowls, following the indigenous tradition and the Asian traditions from which it is derived (Tsuji 1972:167ff). Ráquira potters produce many variants on the bowl shape to be used according to the food served. Three basic kinds of food are recognized, and bowls are made for serving each one as a different course during the meal. The three courses of food are soup (*sopa*), the main dish which is called the dry food (*el seco*), and dessert (*postre* or *dulce*). The main dish may also be referred to as the "salt" portion (*comida de sal*) to distinguish it from the sweet portion, or dessert. Salt and sugar are kept in small bowls and are readily available for seasoning the food during the meal.

In the countryside, as well as in town, food is not necessarily eaten at a table. Since the main meal is served in the middle of the day, workers frequently eat on the work site, seated on the ground. There it is easier to eat from a bowl because the food is less likely to spill. The *sopa* is a thick, stewlike soup of wheat germ, potatoes, green beans, and perhaps meat from the cow's tail, and the *seco* consists of rice, potatoes, fried plantain, and meat. This lunch is high in calories and carbohydrates, giving the workers energy for the hard manual work required in Colombian agriculture, which is based on working with the hoe. This heavy farmer's lunch is also popular in urban areas of Colombia, and a play on words describes its energy-giving potential. It is called ACPM (or diesel) for *arroz* (rice), *carne* (meat), *papas* (potatoes), and *maduro* (fried plantain). The soup, rice, and potatoes are each cooked in separate *almorceras.* The climate can be cool in Ráquira, and foods are served hot to help warm people. The enclosed shape of the bowl and the thick earthenware walls help preserve the heat of the food until it is eaten. In addition to the high levels of carbohydrates, sugar comes from the dessert, and the two provide energy and heat as the calories are burned off.

3. Mixing bowls. The large Ráquira mixing bowls are primarily derived from Spanish forms. Although there were precolumbian bowls that served the same functions, they were altered in such a way that the Spanish elements became dominant. The open bowl (*platón*) is a common form in Spain, and it can be found from Andalusia and Extremadura in the south to Galicia in the north (Llorens and Corredor 1979:77). In Ráquira it is used as a washing basin and a mixing bowl. It may be used to wash clothes, dishes, or green vegetables, or to prepare cornmeal dough for the thick pancake-like *arepa* that is a popular food. The sides of this bowl flare open at an oblique angle to make a wide, open container with a flat bottom.

The *paila* is different from the *platón* in that it has a rounded bottom and short, slightly enclosed walls. It may be used for washing potatoes, vegetables, or plates, and it is also used to make soft cheese. The *paila* is made in six-, ten-, and twenty-cup sizes, and as a special order it can be made with a spout, which is especially useful for pouring whey off the cheese curds. The cooking bowl (*cazuela*) is adapted from Spanish antecedents, and Llorens Artigas and Corredor-Matheos describe versions from Extremadura and Andalusia (1979:82, 109). This is a rounded bowl that may have a flattened bottom and that is used for toasting or frying over an open flame. It may have a frying pan–type handle or two grasping handles.

4. Toasting pan. The toasting pan (*arepero*) is a broad, slightly curved pan used to toast corn cakes over an open fire. Throughout the indigenous and mestizo communities of the Andes (Colombia, Ecuador, Peru, and Bolivia), it is common to toast corn kernels in similar ceramic pans, and a version of this toasting pan, the *comal*, is also made in indigenous communities in Guatemala (Reina and Hill 1978:50–51).

5. Water bottles. There are two versions of the bottle, one of which is probably of precolumbian origin (the *pora*) and the other of Spanish origin (the *pangua*). The precolumbian version is based on the *múcura*, described earlier for the Muiscas. The base of the *pora* is a sphere, and its long, narrow neck ends in a small mouth that is closed by a stopper. It has a small, finger-sized eyelet handle instead of a grasping handle. It is made by rural women in sizes ranging from one-half liter to eight liters.

The Spanish version of the water bottle, called the *pangua*, is flat and has two handles; it is similar to the Spanish *botija* made in

Loza de arena múcura or traditional country water bottle from Ráquira. The two side loops may be used as finger holds, or a rope may be passed through them to carry or hang the bottle. Dark, watery slip has been splashed across the loops and painted around the middle. The dimensions are forty-five centimeters high, thirty centimeters wide, and twenty-five centimeters deep. Collection of the Museo de Artes y Tradiciones Populares, Bogotá.

Andalusia (Llorens and Corredor 1979:133). The neck is long, the mouth small, and the body is slightly flattened like a canteen. There are two opposing handles, one on each side of the neck. The *pangua* is used to store either *guarapo* or *chicha*, and it is made in the two- to eight-liter sizes, with the small size being called the *panguitas*. Laureano Martínez made a carved, highly decorative version of the *pangua*, using the surface-relief design typical of his work.

6. Pitchers. Pitchers are made in two versions that differ from each other according to the diameter of the neck. The narrow-necked version is called a *chorote*, and it is a Boyacá symbol of personal possessions. There is a common expression, "mis chorotes," with which people refer to their "things" or "stuff." The *chorote* may be a synthesis of precolumbian forms and the Spanish *cántaro* from Extremadura (Llorens and Corredor 1979:80). The body is round, forming a sphere, which narrows into the neck and pouring spout. This narrow-mouthed pitcher is also made in the one-half- to eight-liter sizes, with the small size being used to make hot chocolate or a popular hot drink made with raw sugar called *agua de panela* and the larger sizes used to store and serve *guarapo* and *chicha*, the two fermented drinks. The wide-mouthed pitcher is called the *jarra*; it is distinguished from the *chorote* by its wider serving mouth. The primary function of

the *jarra* is serving water or *guarapo*. Its volume ranges from the size of one cup to five liters. The *jarra* is also made primarily in the country, and the form is from Extremadura in southwestern Spain (ibid.).

7. Water storage pots. The *tinajo* has been used historically to store water and other liquids, such as *chicha* or *guarapo,* and it may serve as a fermentation pot for both. The *tinajo* is a taller and narrower pot than the ones used for food preparation and storage, and the relatively tall neck serves to prevent spillage.

Traditional pottery has been adapted in some cases to produce forms for the urban market, such as planters, but it is also common for urban families to buy country cooking pots and jugs for their decorative value. These pots have symbolic value because they represent both the past and the traditional way of life that still exists in the country towns. As a result, this pottery is changing its function from cooking and storage to decoration and symbolism as it moves into the urban markets of Bogotá and other cities.

Pilgrimage Souvenir Ware

Decorative ware has always been made in Ráquira in addition to the basic functional ware. Although both types were sold outside of the local community, the functional ware tended to be more regional in distribution while decorative ware was sold over a wider area. Since Chiquinquirá is

This traditional jug or *chorote* may be used for water, *guarapo* (cane drink), or *chicha* (corn drink). It has a narrow pouring mouth and a bulging body suited for holding a sizeable volume of liquid, approximately four liters. The body was made with the pinch-pot method, and the surface is pitted from being scraped in the leatherhard stage. Dimensions are thirty-two by thirty-five centimeters. Collection of the Museo de Artes y Tradiciones Populares, Bogotá.

the site of the basilica of the patron saint of Colombia, the Virgin of Chiquin-quirá, it is one of the most frequently visited religious centers in the coun-try. Although it was a pilgrimage site during the colonial period, it became even more important during the republican period in the 1800s. At least by the mid- to late 1800s, if not before, the people of Ráquira had begun making miniature pottery for sale to Chiquinquirá pilgrims, and older in-formants indicate that by the beginning of the present century this com-merce was well established.

By the early 1900s toy pots were being sold in the patron-saint festivals of many towns throughout the region. Ráquira had long been known for its earthenware pots, but by then it also began to be known for this toy pottery. Souvenir ware is made by women using the same forms as tradi-tional pottery, and there are two categories of these playful vessels: toy pots and miniatures.

The toy pots are called *loza de dedo*, literally translated as finger pots. They include toy-sized cups, pitchers, and dessert bowls that are deco-rated by carving or impressing images on the surface. Although this toy pottery was originally made for children, adults also bought it for its deco-rative value. These pots delight people because of their small, nonfunc-tional size (three to five centimeters) and because of their decorative sur-faces.

The miniatures are even smaller and are called *maíz tostado*, which means roasted corn, and they may be literally as small as a kernel of corn. Cups, pitchers, dessert bowls, and chicken-shaped whistles are common forms, and they are strung together like beads to make a necklace. Mora (1974:49) suggests that these forms might represent the survival of a precolumbian ceremonial ceramics, especially as offerings to the supernatural to request good results from one's work. Even though they have no immediate cer-emonial meaning, the fact that these forms are associated with religious activities in the twentieth century (patron-saint festivals and the national shrine in Chiquinquirá) suggests that this interpretation could be correct.

Painted Design on Women's Pottery

The handles and borders of traditional women's pottery are painted with a dark oxide wash (*chica oscura*) to emphasize the form, and a white clay slip is used to paint designs around the edge of the dark design. The most common motifs are parallel sets of horizontal lines or semicircular lines like arches painted with a rag or feather. The semicircular lines can take on the appearance of stylized feathers or ferns. This stylized painting is the only decoration that includes even the suggestion of figuration, and there are no painted zoomorphic designs. Mora suggested that these motifs were the result of the women's daily involvement with plants and agriculture (1974:37). These designs are drawn around the neck, mouth, and handles of the water bottles (*múcuras*) and cooking pots (*ollas*), while toasting pans (*areperos*) have a simple accent line drawn around their border. Mora suggested that these designs were continuations of the indigenous heritage of the Ráquira potters (ibid.:38). Although painted designs are used by women on traditional pottery, painting is not used in the men's mass production pieces.

Decoration

Until the 1960s, toy pottery and some tableware had elaborate surface decoration, but that tradition has largely disappeared in recent decades as commercialization has led to an emphasis on speed of production, which does not permit the luxury of elaborately decorated surfaces. Various techniques of surface decoration are used according to the form and style of the piece, including impressions on the clay, additions, and carving. Impression is frequently used and may employ either found objects, such as a stick or a screw, or specially made ceramic seals. The latter are made by someone in the family who has the ability to carve an original design.

Additions are also used to decorate surfaces, and these may be hand-modeled, such as the facial features or arms for a human figure, or they may be sprig-molded additions (appliqués made in small molds) to go on the surface of a vessel. The latter may include floral designs or human features. Finger marks are used on the borders of hand-modeled pieces to give them an organic, almost floral effect, or throwing marks may be left by the fingers on wheel-made pieces. A smooth texture is produced by wet polishing the almost dried surface. Carving is not used much today, but wheel-made pieces may have a decorative horizontal line carved into the surface as they rotate on the wheelhead. Carving is also used to accentuate pressed designs or to clean up modeled additions, and to create stamps for the pressed designs.

As ceramics have become more commercialized in Ráquira, some of the finishing techniques traditionally used by women have been lost, especially those requiring a considerable investment of time. Burnishing was once used to give a hand-crafted seal to the surface, but it is not practiced now because it is slow and not economically justifiable in local terms. The more complicated designs that were traditionally drawn on the toy-sized pots (*loza de dedo*) were still commonly used in the 1960s, just as the industrialization process was starting. However, the designs were not common by the 1990s, when people had become more concerned with efficiency and volume of production. Since the 1970s some urban market ware has been decorated with a post-firing painting of bright commercial colors, in a dramatic departure from the traditional opaque, earth-toned Ráquira colors. By the mid-1990s some town potters were painting flower vases and other decorative pots with iridescent colors, a kitsch transformation of this rural craft.

Women's Ceramics, Prehispanic Roots, and Symbolism

There is an inherent contradiction in the attitudes of the larger Colombian society toward the traditional earthenware pottery produced in the small towns and rural areas. On one hand, the shapes, colors, and surfaces of traditional pots are important visual experiences for most Colombians and this pottery evokes an element of Rousseau-like nostalgia for the rural basis of national life. Colombia is a predominantly agricultural country, and urban dwellers, as well as rural people, depend on the countryside for their economic livelihood. Most urban people also look to the countryside for recreational relief from the stresses of urban life.

However, there is another side to the rural social experience: the poverty, poor education, and low socioeconomic status of the people who live there. This problem can be graphically seen in the attitudes toward precolumbian ceramics, and toward rural women potters who are the survivors of that tradition today. Although Colombia has incorporated precolumbian art into the national iconography, taking pride in that distant past, ceramics made in the same style today, by the descendants of precolumbian artisans, are considered poor rural handicrafts or tourist trinkets made by people of low social status. Helaine Silverman describes a similar problem in Peru (1993:129), an Andean country with a comparable social division between high-status mestizos and people of European descent and low-status mestizos and indigenous people.

Women potters themselves are frequently blunt in their statement of this problem. For example, Agripa Sierra of the *vereda* Resguardo Occidental told the author in 1995 that traditional country pottery is *fea* or ugly, and it puzzled her that people would buy it when the prettier mold-made and glazed ceramics are also available. Her own deprecating remarks about the pottery that she herself makes reflects the opinion of the larger society that today's remnants of the prehispanic traditions are rural, poor, and of little value. They symbolize the ambivalent attitudes of urban Colombians toward the countryside and small-town lifestyle that is the basis of Colombian society, and they are an omnipresent reminder of that cultural identity.

Men's Pottery

Men's pottery does not have a central functional purpose, comparable to the women's emphasis on food, that would promote an integrated design style. Men will make anything that can be mass produced on the potter's wheel or in molds and that is easily marketable. For the men, pottery functions to produce income, and as a result Ráquira men's ceramics have a wide range of styles and forms, including such diverse products as planters, bells, and piggy banks. This diversity is a result of their readiness to adapt to new market demands and to borrow successful ideas from other craft traditions. The industrial ceramics produced by men for the urban markets have a smooth, mold-produced surface, and people in the community like this industrial-quality texture, associating it with greater technological sophistication.

Important Forms of Men's Pottery

The men's mass-produced planters have simple, straight profile lines and flat bottoms that are adapted to the efficiency of mold and machine production. These forms are basic cylinders, and their designs are largely determined by production factors. There is little of aesthetic interest in these pieces, except for the smooth surface texture.

Most men's workshops in town produce mold-and wheel-made planters, mobiles, and animal-form banks (Bonilla et al. 1992:48), all examples of decorative ware intended for the urban markets in Bogotá and other cities. (See table 6.1.) The first two forms (mold-made and wheel-made planters) are frequently made in the same workshop, but the mobiles and animal banks are specialized products that are normally produced in separate workshops. The mobiles feature small (five centimeter), wheel-made ceramic bells that are strung together with other small pots to make strings from one meter to one and one-half meters long. The mobiles are hung in doorways or windows so that they will sound like chimes when the wind blows or someone brushes past them. The most popular of the zoomorphic bank forms is the piggy bank, but they are also made in the forms of chickens, ducks, sheep, and armadillos. In some husband-and-wife workshops in town, women continue to produce country-style ware, including miniatures and cooking pots. Since these families came originally from the countryside, they have continued their traditional production in town.

Although table 6.1 specifies only the twelve most produced forms in
Ráquira, the town workshops actually produce eighteen different forms,
which is a measure of the diversity of their production.

Design of Men's Pottery

When men established the town workshops in the 1950s, they began making tableware, planters, and other forms associated with various commercial sources. The decision to adopt a new form seems to have been determined by its adaptability to mass production and its commercial value. As
discussed earlier, tableware ceramics were introduced to Ráquira potters
when the Cárdenas family made their attempt at industrial production,
and Aurelio Varela traveled to the town of Carmen de Viboral and observed tableware production in factories there.

During the early 1970s, Artesanías de Colombia began to offer technical assistance in design and production in the community, and local potters were introduced to various tableware designs, including cups and sau-
cers, teapots, and dinnerware sets. Some potters adopted the shape of soup
bowls made in La Chamba, another pottery-making town in Colombia.
Designs for candlesticks and other small tableware items came from the
Ráquira workshop of the Museo de Artes y Tradiciones Populares.

Design for Production in Men's Pottery

Since the pottery made in the men's workshops has been adjusted to the
technologies of press molds and the potter's wheel, the pieces are round
and have straight walls or profiles with gentle curves. Their bottoms are
flat and form a sharp angle with the walls, an angle that is not well adapted
for thermal shock. Men's pots are not intended for cooking, however; they
are meant to sit on the tables and floors of urban houses and apartments.
Men's pottery consists of designs that can be made quickly with mass-
production techniques, and lips or edges may be left somewhat irregular.

Men make tableware (teapots and cups, bowls, plates, candlesticks, and
other serving ware) on the potter's wheel. The shapes are flat (plates),
variations on the cylinder (teapots and cups), or open bowls. Men's tableware also includes lidded pieces such as pitchers and teapots. Although
these pieces can be made quickly, they are limited to smaller sizes under
thirty centimeters.

In contrast to women's work, male potters in Ráquira make forms that
have little reference to the traditional pottery of the town. The hodge-
podge of forms made in men's workshops corresponds to what is commercially successful, and the repertoire of forms changes from year to year

as market tastes change. The visual identity that ties men's ceramics together comes from the smooth surface quality produced by the plaster molds that are used in mass-produced ware.

Commodity Ware for Urban Markets

When men began working in ceramics in the 1950s, Colombia's cities were growing, and the new urban middle class wanted decorative items for their living rooms. Men potters began producing such forms as coffee or tea sets (including cups, the coffee or tea pot, creamer, and sugar bowl), candlesticks, flower vases, hanging lamps, strands of bells, Indian head ashtrays, piggy banks, and mold-made animal figures. By the 1960s potters were making an Indian-motif planter or *matera*, with gentle curves and figurative features, including a face, feathered headband, and clothing. (See photograph on page 79.)

There has been controversy over some of these new forms, especially from outside of the community. People interested in authentic culture criticized the introduction of the North American forms by a Peace Corps volunteer during the late 1960s. The animal forms of the armadillo, lion, turtle, and owl appeared at that time as did the Indian head ashtray and other forms. Yolanda Mora de Jaramillo (1974) did not document these forms in her study of Ráquira made in 1968. However, we observed them in visits in 1974 and 1975, which indicates that they were introduced during the interim between her work and our first visits.

The Indian motif had existed in the community from the time of the ceramics school when the Indian planter was introduced, and Mora documented an example of it in 1968. The motif was used by a number of potters during the 1970s to elaborate designs also for ashtrays and decanters of *aguardiente*. The motif documented by Mora draws on themes from precolumbian art in Colombia of large earrings and breastplate, which would have been gold originally, and it had no headdress. In the 1970s Reyes Suárez added a precolumbian style nose ring and a sunburst headdress to pieces he designed, and other potters added the feathered headdress to the planter at that time.

These were town potters experimenting with the image of Indians. Since everyone in Ráquira had acculturated to mestizo identity by the 1800s, these pots referred to people of the past or to tribal Indians who live in other parts of Colombia. During the 1970s and 1980s indigenous activists in Colombia succeeded in raising the awareness of their culture in the larger public, and with that cultural sensitivity the Bogotá market dried up for the Indian-motif ceramics. By the 1990s these pieces had dropped out of production. By the 1980s the planter design had evolved to a plain, terra-cotta cylindrical form that is made in various sizes from fifteen to sixty centimeters high. (See photograph on page 157.)

In the 1970s and 1980s, a few family workshops began to evolve into semi-industrial workshops with hired workers. These larger workshops used mass-production techniques, especially the mold and the wheel, and they developed in response to the growing demand in the cities for village ceramics. The larger planters were made in hand-pressed molds, which became the industry standard for production of larger pieces. Smaller pieces were thrown on the potter's wheel, which is well adapted to making small orders of many different designs, the usual market pattern for Ráquira ceramics.

In the 1980s and 1990s, traditional tableware, especially earthenware bowls, became popular in the households of Bogotá and other cities. Tableware forms include the soup bowl (*taza para la sopa*), a simple rounded shape that approximates a halved sphere and comes in one- and two-cup sizes. The plate (*plato*) is a Spanish form, and it is normally made with a flat bottom and flaring edge, similar to the larger *platón* or open bowl. The cup (*pocillo*) is made for hot drinks, including chocolate, *agua de panela*, and coffee. The cup is sometimes made like a small pitcher or *chorote*, and the European-style cup made today may be derived from that shape. None of these are traditional forms except for the soup bowl.

Today's small workshops are normally run by the male master ceramist/owner, who designs the pieces and supervises the production of workers. Although the master ceramist is primarily involved in organizing and marketing the production, he may work alongside the workers, and his wife and children may also help. However, by the 1980s specialized planter factories had emerged with professional managers and hired workers. By 1995 there were five planter factories, and local people were complaining about the influx of non-Ráquira workers to take these industrialized jobs, which do not require much, if any, previous knowledge of ceramics. In part, these factories explain the rise in Ráquira's population by 1994 to its highest level in history. Although traditional ceramic production has continued, many people were concerned that the industrial development in the community might undermine the Ráquira craft tradition, one of Colombia's cultural assets.

Men and Change in Style

A comparison of the changes in design and style in women's and men's pottery in Ráquira shows that village ceramics are not static. Indeed, the essence of a strong craft tradition is its vitality and creativity in renovating itself. Although change has occurred in the pottery of both Ráquira women and men in the twentieth century, men have been more restless in their search for innovation. Over the last fifty years they have adopted ideas and forms from all the major ceramic centers in Colombia and from others in Peru, Ecuador, and Mexico. The stylistic and technological changes also correlate with gender. The shift from traditional ceramics to market ceramics is correlated with the entrance of greater numbers of men into ceramics, and they work with pottery as a commercial enterprise rather than a domestic craft. These men have not had a tradition of working in ceramics, and they are not limited by the domestic constraints that affect women, so they have developed entirely new ways of making ceramics, entirely new forms, and new attitudes toward the medium of clay.

A number of factors have influenced men in Ráquira to produce the commercial style of pottery associated with them. First was the seemingly failed ceramics school in Ráquira, which stimulated change by teaching about mold-made forms, including flower vases and ashtrays, the Indian-motif planter, and tea sets. Because none of these were used in the rural and small-town markets that Ráquira commonly served, they were exclusively made for the urban market.

A second set of influences came from foreign technical-assistance programs. When the Peace Corps volunteer introduced the armadillo, turtle, lion, and owl as mold-made banks, his idea was adapted to include the local figures of the chicken, sheep, and pig. The volunteer also suggested cutting holes into a cylinder shaped like a flower vase and hanging it mouth down for use as a lamp, an idea that did not survive long. Both the banks and the lamps were hobby ideas originating in popular crafts stores in the United States, and only the bank idea was adopted for local use. These ideas, however, did reinforce the trend toward mold-made figures. The animal forms introduced at this time related to the local idea of animals as a theme in figurative ceramics but differed in two aspects: they were mold-made rather than modeled by hand as figures were traditionally made, and they were not autochthonous themes. Whereas the earlier figures narrated local events or portrayed local animals, the lion and the owl did neither. Apart from the U.S. Peace Corps volunteer, the Japanese government sponsored a cultural-exchange potter in Ráquira during the early 1990s, and he introduced wheel-made flower vases, bowls, and other Japanese glazed tableware. He also demonstrated the use of excellent monochrome glazes, but by 1995 neither the forms nor the glazes had been adopted locally.

A third set of influences came from Artesanías de Colombia, which developed designs that could be made by wheel, such as dinnerware, candlesticks, and other tableware. Specifically, the organization contracted with artists and designers in Bogotá to develop designs that could be reproduced by workers in their Ráquira center. This has usually been glazed ware, fired in the electric or diesel-fired kilns of the center, and this program has had a major influence in introducing industrial design to Ráquira potters. Since this institution has largely followed an economic model, it has frequently emphasized productivity and industrial design more than the principles of traditional craft. The male potters of Ráquira have responded to the Artesanías de Colombia program with considerable interest, and it, in turn, has given them information on design, potters' wheels, molds, and kilns.

A fourth set of influences came from urban market forces expressed through intermediaries who communicated the desires of the buying public through their orders for pottery. By far the most important form of the urban market ceramics is the planter (*matera*), which is made in various sizes and shapes. Planters may be produced in either family or industrialized, mass-production workshops.

Gender, Design, and Style

The two ceramics subcultures represented by the women and men potters of Ráquira constitute a cross-section that represents the major patterns of village ceramics in Colombia. Ceramic design is different between the two genders, indicating the contrast in attitude toward ceramics and work and differences in design and culture. The cultural history of women's and men's pottery and their contemporary cultural contexts establish the parameters within which the potters make decisions about their craft. These ecological and historical differences in context have created two different human experiences, and reacting to that, the potters have created different styles of ceramics. A comparison of pottery forms shows that 87 percent of the town workshops produce urban-oriented decorative ware while an almost equal number of rural workshops produce traditional country wares (Bonilla et al. 1992:48, 76).

Women potters have maintained the integrity of the principles of ceramic design associated with the indigenous traditions of the region, creating cooking pots (*ollas*), bowls (*cuencos*), and water bottles (*múcuras* or *poras*). In contrast, the commodity style developed by men in recent decades has become a major element in the new definition of Ráquira as a commercially dynamic ceramics center. The people of the town of Ráquira have shifted away from the rural craft tradition to develop a commodity-oriented ceramics that relies on industrial production techniques. The people working in a craft medium form a cultural microcosm in which the individual craft makers manage a similar set of parameters, and the solutions they contribute to their craft reflect the dynamic of the culture and result in the style associated with the group. Within a culture various internal forces push toward conformity in design, resulting in the recognizable styles associated with a specific ceramics community. None of these factors alone is sufficient to produce a consistent design style, but these multivariant influences working together do produce a style. Four factors can be identified that contribute to producing a consistent style: intergenerational learning, in-group interaction, market symbolism, and materials and mechanical factors.

1. Learning from generation to generation is a powerful influence on producing the consistency of form that is style, and teaching is normally transmitted from mother to daughter and from father to son, following socially established rules for descent and postnuptial residence (Arnold 1993:188). Much of the instruction in ceramics in conservative pottery communities occurs through the intergenerational process, especially in stable communities with a functioning unilocal postnuptial residence rule. However, when rapid social change occurs, as happened in Ráquira during the last half of the twentieth century, or when residential patterns are ambilocal (newlyweds may join either parental household) or neolocal (they live with neither parental family), children may not learn ceramics from their parents. Then other models must explain how consistency of style is formed within a community.

2. Social interactions among potters also account for the similarities of design structure within a group that create a style (Arnold 1993:189). The basic design structure gives coherence and continuity, which is style, but specific design elements may be used in more individualistic ways. The effects of group interaction can be observed in Ráquira, especially in the social change process. As Aurelio Varela and Reyes Suárez started producing mold-made ceramics for the urban market, other potters saw the economic success of that approach and many adopted it, leading to a new style.

3. A ceramics style may also be shaped by the collective symbol-

ism of design elements, and in capitalistic societies that symbolism is what makes the product marketable (Bourdieu 1993:115). Today traditional pottery is sold to urban markets more for its symbolic than its functional value. Ráquira pots symbolize the rootedness in earth and place of the rural, Boyacá society, a symbolism that has particular nostalgic power amid the seeming urban chaos and corruption associated with the drug trafficking of the 1990s, and the pots are frequently placed near the doors of urban houses as unspoken symbols of stability and continuity.

4. The materials and mechanical procedures of the ceramics community also affect the expression of style, and the raw materials available to the community will determine the colors and the quality of the claybody that can be used in ceramics. The special hue of iron red with which Ráquira pottery is identified comes from the interaction between local clay, the process of preparing it, and the firing process. The shapes and surface textures of women's pots result from the pinch-pot and coil-building process that distinguish the work and could not be easily replicated on the wheel or with molds. So the shape, line, texture, and color aspects of style in a given pottery community result from the limits and influences exerted by materials and the mechanical aspects of the production process.

Gender and Innovation

Market pressures have led Ráquira's ceramists to place a higher and higher value on new designs. A potter can carve out a special market niche if he or she specializes in a form made by few others. Innovation is most important among male production potters who produce for mass markets and for the figure makers. If someone develops a new design, it is generally understood that it belongs to that person, and most potters are possessive of their designs. If another person uses the same idea, he or she must vary some of the details, at least slightly, to legitimize the claim of the copier to his or her own personalized versions of the design.

In some Latin American indigenous villages, innovation is discouraged because it is seen as a form of individualism that undermines group unity. In fact, research in various Mayan pottery communities suggests that innovation in craft making is consistently associated with people who are socially marginal. June Nash (1985:48) and Ruben Reina (1963:18ff) both reported cases in which community pressure forced potters to abandon innovative designs. In Tzintzuntzan, George Foster found that potters were innovators with only half the frequency of the general population (1967:296), and he concluded that the nature of pottery making leads potters to avoid innovation. Since pottery requires attention to detail and precise repetition of formulas for successful production, any error or change in a body shape or in the composition of a claybody can lead to greater than normal losses in the firing, which translate into economic losses. Thus change creates a risk that, according to Foster, reinforces the avoidance of change among potters (ibid.:300–301). A cultural balance is maintained within village ceramics traditions between the flexibility of individual innovation and the continuity of the community model.

The *machismo* system also influences innovation in pottery making because it controls and limits the exercise of initiative in women while it encourages and rewards initiative in men. The result has been that men are the innovators in Ráquira while women make traditional forms and shapes according to rigid rules that are centuries old. Because there is little room for imagination and innovation in cooking pots, skill is expressed in technique, and women strive for perfect finishing and clean, flowing profiles for their pieces. However, women are somewhat freed from this system after menopause, and some older women become very creative. For example, Otilia Ruiz began making imaginative religious figures later in life, after a career making traditional pots. Since then, she has challenged the system even further by encouraging her own daughters to make figurative pieces. Although the communal and cultural constraints on innovation seem to affect women most strongly, they can be superseded.

Transition and the Tension between Women's and Men's Ceramics

The forms of Ráquira ceramics have registered the various cultural influences that have affected the town, and they show how a people can renew a tradition in response to new social and economic situations while preserving its distinctive identity. The complex forms and production procedures introduced by men in the last half of the twentieth century have created a process of renovation that will project Ráquira ceramics into the twenty-first century in a position that is economically stronger than it has been at any other point in its history.

However, the women's style of ceramics has lost its utilitarian purposes, and few women other than the older generation continue to practice it. Although industry seems to be taking over, new artistic and symbolic roles for pottery have appeared, suggesting the lines of development that Ráquira design may follow in the coming decades. Some people worry that the craft tradition is dying out; however, the ceramics of Ráquira have been changing for centuries, and today they are more complex, economically stronger, and richer in visual expression than at any previous time. When the European countries industrialized, they lost their crafts traditions. It remains to be seen whether Ráquira can industrialize and still retain its craft tradition.

7

Production Techniques

In the organization of work, the contrast between the domestic orientation of women and the mass-production processes preferred by men is starkly apparent. Women potters, who are mostly of the older generation, do more hand building and hand modeling than do men, who are mostly of the younger generation. Women's techniques require few tools, and their work can be done around the house as time allows, without interrupting the flow of other domestic activities. Men, on the other hand, prefer to work with molds and potters' wheels, which require their full attention and ample working space. For this reason their workshops are frequently set up as separate covered areas outside of the house. The men's production style is a full-time activity that occupies the family's daylight hours, dominating domestic life rather than being incorporated into it.

Gender and Stages of Workshop Complexity

Most Ráquira ceramics are produced in family-run household workshops in which the gender of the primary potter defines the work organization and technology used. Neve Herrera Rubio (1976:141f) suggested a four-stage evolution of craft workshops in Colombia, which also defines the types of workshops in Ráquira, and each has a gender identity. Similar stages of artisan workshops were described by José Alonso in Mexico (1983:163) and by Dean Arnold in Peru (1985:225–27).

The first stage is *trabajo familiar* (family craft work) in which production is carried out within the household by the woman, who incorporates it into her other domestic responsibilities. There may not be a formal workshop, and the woman may work on the craft wherever she has space in the house. In Ráquira these are mostly rural workshops producing fewer than five hundred pieces per month. Usually the woman works alone with minor assistance from the husband or children. The family is the unit of production and consumption (Herrera 1976:141).

Table 7.1. Categories of workshop types

Type	Rural		Town		Description
	No.	%	No.	%	
Factory	0	0	5	6.58	Produces over 10,000 pieces per month. Hired workers. Located only next to town.
Industrialized workshop	3	7.14	16	21.05	3,000 to 10,000 pieces per month, mostly planters. Wheel and/or mold production. Hired workers.
Husband/wife	14	33.33	35	46.05	500 to 3,000 pieces per month. Wheel and/or mold production of various forms. No hired workers.
Household	22	52.38	11	14.47	Fewer than 500 pieces per month. Hand and mold production. No hired workers. Mostly women working alone or assisted by husband, making traditional earthenware.
No information	3	7.14	9	11.84	
Totals	42	99.99	76	99.99	

Source: Adapted from Bonilla et al. 1992:49, 77

The second stage is the *taller casero* (a husband-and-wife workshop), in which the husband has become the primary worker. Craft work dominates the house, which begins to look like a workshop. Production takes precedence over domestic responsibilities, and some work may be contracted. The smaller town workshops fall into this category. Alonso identified this stage as a multipersonal workshop in which one or more members of the family, usually daughters, work with the mother (1983:163).

The third stage is the *taller industrial* (industrial workshop), in which workers become the primary producers, using molds and potters' wheels, although family members do some work. In Ráquira these workshops are located in town, and they have usually grown up around the family's house. In Alonso's concept these are multipersonal workshops with multiple employees who are not family members (Alonso 1983:163).

The fourth stage is the *fábrica* (factory), which engages in large-scale industrial production using highly specialized labor. This group is represented by the planter factories located just outside of the town of Ráquira, in which the workforce consists completely of hired laborers working at single, specialized tasks. In Alonso's terms these are multipersonal workshops in which the chief artisan becomes a manager, and the production takes on a mechanized and specialized factory organization (Alonso 1983:164).

Gender Differences in Work and Kinship

The role of family members in pottery production differs in the women's and men's workshops, but both have specific expectations. In women's workshops, family members are expected to help the potter, and over 70 percent of the workers are unpaid family collaborators. Ceramics is considered a domestic task much like the woman's household duties of washing clothes and cooking; it is not viewed as a purely commercial enterprise. Sons, daughters, husbands, brothers, sisters, and grandchildren may help as needed, and their help will be reciprocated when appropriate. Lynn Stephen (1993:44) describes similar collaboration among Zapotec women weavers, who characterize their production process as a team effort involving husbands and children. Although women control the major production decisions, such as the assigning of work to children and the timing of production, they take the needs of other family members into account. Since rural women typically work at pottery part-time, adding it to their agricultural and household obligations, they have little need for hired laborers, except in some cases for a man to fire the kiln.

Table 7.2. Types of Relationships among Workers

Relationship	Rural				Urban			
	No. of workshops	%	No. of persons	%	No. of workshops	%	No. of persons	%
Family	35	83.34	91	73.39	33	43.42	91	32.38
Nonfamily employee	3	7.14	17	13.70	18	23.68	60	21.35
Associate	3	7.14	7	5.65	3	3.95	5	1.78
Mixed relationship	1	2.38	9	7.26	22	28.95	125	44.49
Totals	42	100.00	124	100.00	76	100.00	281	100.00

Source: Bonilla et al. 1992:26, 65

In men's workshops, one-third of the workers are unpaid nuclear family members and two-thirds are hired workers. Two out of three of the hired workers are other family members, so three-fourths of the workers in a workshop are either nuclear or extended family members (Bonilla et al. 1992:26). The hiring of extended family workers from rural areas creates a conduit for rural-to-town migration along family lines. In contrast to the taboo against hiring family members in the countryside, it is the preferred pattern to hire relatives in town, where the urban workshop is a commercial venture and labor is a commodity, as in any other business. Workshop owners prefer relatives as workers because the kinship bond guarantees greater loyalty and collaboration, and workers feel more closely connected to their jobs. Owners also feel more able to trust relatives not to steal, embezzle, cast the evil eye, or otherwise harm the business.

Gender and Labor as a Commodity

The gender-based division of labor defines men's work as a commodity that can be bought and sold in the community, but women's work is not a commodity. Rather, it is considered to be non-negotiated, unpaid domestic labor. On the negative side, this means that a woman potter may not receive any direct compensation for her work because her husband can legitimately keep the proceeds from the sale of the pots and use the income as he deems appropriate. It also means that women are rarely hired as paid laborers in workshops. In fact, in a survey of Ráquira workshops carried out by Artesanías de Colombia in the 1980s, only 13 of 102 women workers were hired workers (Rojas Escobar 1983:9). However, this arrangement also means that a woman can function without a male partner because she can hire men to do such jobs as firing the kiln or mining clay, as in fact happens with considerable frequency in the rural workshops of widows.

A man, however, cannot function without a woman to assist him in pottery making and to perform the household tasks of food preparation, caring for children, and cleaning. Since her labor is not a commodity, there is no labor pool from which a woman can be hired for those tasks. If a wife dies or leaves, the man must remarry, move in with other family members, or find a female relative who will assume her work for him. The fact that a woman's labor is rarely bought and sold limits her economic activity within the community, but it also makes her domestic role essential because it cannot be made a commodity.

Women's Production Techniques

The prehispanic indigenous technology used by the women of rural Ráquira is similar to that used throughout the Americas in indigenous potter communities. Hand modeling and coiling are well adapted to the requirements of household production in that they involve minimal investment and space requirements and allow flexibility in the number of forms made. Using these techniques a potter can make cooking pots, water storage jars, water bottles, serving bowls, and many other shapes, although most women working in a traditional workshop limit themselves to two or three. Although the modeling and coiling system allows potters the flexibility of easily changing shapes (D. Arnold 1993:92), Ráquira women rarely do so. The major limitation of this system is its low productivity, which means low returns for the potter.

◆   ◆

Mercedes Bautista: A Woman Potter

Doña Mercedes Bautista is a member of the older generation of rural women potters, and she is a good example of women potters. She makes country-styled earthenware called loza de arena, *and her pots are rooted in the prehispanic tradition. Her pieces include cooking pots, water bottles, pitchers, and other forms that have been used in country houses for generations. As a child, she learned to make pots from her mother by watching and imitating her techniques. She lives and works in the* vereda *Pueblo Viejo, the Old Town rural district that is an hour's walk or more above Ráquira. Several generations of the Bautista family have been potters in this same* vereda, *but Doña Mercedes is the last member of her family still making pottery.*

The house and farm belonged to her and her husband, Miguel, until he died in the mid-1980s. After that her daughter, María Lucila Bautista, and her husband, José Chacón, and their children, Diana and Freddy, came to live with her, and now they do most of the agricultural work on the farm. Both the daughter and granddaughter learned to make pottery with Doña Mercedes, but María Lucila works full-time on the farm with her husband and has no time to make pots. Twelve-year-old Diana does make pots with her grandmother, and she sells them, saving the money to buy schoolbooks.

Doña Mercedes does not work at her pottery full-time. She also tends sheep, helps carry water, and assists with the cooking, washing, and agricultural chores. The Bautista farm does not have a source of water, and family members have to carry all the drinking and cooking water from a creek one kilometer away. Two years ago they paid to have running water piped to their house through a communal project

Doña Mercedes Bautista normally works on the ground in front of her storage room. Finished cooking pots of various sizes are stacked behind her.

for their vereda, *but it has not been completed, and they are afraid the money may be lost.*

Doña Mercedes had seven children, of whom six are still living. Two reside in Tolima and two in Bogotá, but none of them became potters. When her husband was alive, he sold all of her work and usually kept the proceeds from the sales. He used the money to buy food for the house, clothes for himself or for her, and materials for the farm, but he also used some of it for drinking sessions with friends. If she complained, he would hit her with his hand, a stick, or whatever was close by. She said that when she was younger, women tolerated harsh treatment and even physical abuse from their husbands. Doña Mercedes realizes that she will probably be the last traditional potter in her family.

The indigenous techniques used by the women potters in Ráquira include the following.

1. Turntable plate. Placing the pottery on an unpivoted turning plate (*plato de bailar*) while coils are being added is common practice in indigenous communities in various parts of the Americas, from Mexico (Lackey 1982:65) to Peru (Litto 1976:29).

2. Coiling. Vessels have been made by the coiling process in Ráquira since the Muisca period, as evidenced in the two styles, "Suta finished orange" and "Ráquira compact orange," which seem to be ancestral forms of the traditional pottery of today (Falchetti 1975:146, 286).

3. Combined technique. This process, in which the basic form of a pot is made by one technique (in Ráquira, the pinch-pot technique) and completed by coils, occurs in indigenous-influenced pottery communities in both the Andean region of South America and Mesoamerica. In La Chamba, Colombia, the base of traditional cooking pots is formed with a slab over a drape mold (which is another pot); when it is firm, the upper section is completed with coils (Duncan 1985c). In Acatlán, Mexico, a similar slab-and-coil technique is the most common form of production, and Louana Lackey suggests that it may be the most ancient technique used there (1982:78). The wide distribution of this combined technique in indigenous-influenced mestizo communities in the Americas suggests that it is of indigenous origin.

4. Oxide and slip decoration. Decoration with slip or oxide wash is a prehispanic technique that was used in this region by the Muiscas (Rojas de Perdomo 1985:156).

5. Open-air firing. This style of firing is still used by many rural women potters in Colombia, and until recently some women in remote areas around Ráquira did open-air firings in the indigenous style.

These techniques have been transmitted from parent to child for generations, suggesting a continuity that survived the centuries since the arrival of the Spanish. These techniques are still used by contemporary indigenous groups and indigenous-based mestizo groups in Colombia and other Latin American countries.

Pinch Pots and Coils

Most women potters still make ceramics by hand, generally using homemade tools. For the average workshop, the only factory-made tools are the *peinilla* (a machete used to cut large chunks of clay), *garlancha* (shovel), *pica* (pick), and *azadón* (hoe), all of which are used in the excavation and preparation of the clay. The other tools are either made or gathered by the family locally, including the *mazo* (a wooden club used to crush clay), a *cortadera* (wire to cut blocks of clay), a *sanaguador* (polishing stone to smooth surfaces), a *ruca* (scraper), and a *pluma* (chicken feather to apply slip).

Traditional pottery is made by the pinch-pot process, in which the ceramist opens a cavity in the ball of clay, using the thumb for small pieces, or the fist if the piece is large. The piece is then shaped by pinching it into a cylindrical form or a more open, bowl-like form, depending on what is being made. The piece is then placed on the turning bowl (*plato de bailar*, shortened to *plático*), which is used as a turntable. The *plático* is a footed concave plate that is some twenty-five centimeters in diameter. The pot that is being made is set on the *plático* on the ground. As the potter shapes the wall of the pot, she turns it. The potter must be very dexterous to keep the *plático* in motion while she is simultaneously controlling and shaping the pot. As the pot turns, the wall is pinched and scraped into a uniform thickness. The process is continued upward until the border is formed and smoothed. If the piece is to be taller, it is set aside until the next day; when it is firmer, coils are added to the top to achieve the desired height. The coils are pinched together, and the entire piece is scraped with a *ruca* (commonly a piece of gourd) until the surface is smooth and uniform.

Once the basic form is made, it is set aside to firm up, which can take as little as thirty minutes for smaller pieces. It is then returned to the *plático,* and the sides are smoothed and scraped until they have the final shape. As soon as the piece is sufficiently firm, handles (*orejas*) and modeled designs are added, and it is scraped one last time to insure the uniformity of the finish. The inside surface is polished with a smooth river stone to seal it, but the outside surface is not sealed. During the dry season, pieces are left outside to dry, but if there is the possibility of rain they will be placed under a roofed storage area or inside the house, and the children help to move pieces from one drying place to another. In the dry season, the pieces will dry in two or three days, but in the rainy months it may be a week or more before they are ready to fire.

The contrast between the sealed inner surface and the porous outer surface of these pots creates an insulation that functions to keep liquids cool. The heavily tempered, porous claybody permits the pot to sweat slightly, and that humidity accumulates in the porous outer surface and insulates the cool water inside from the warmer air outside. This maintains the water at a lower temperature than the outside air. The porous wall is also resistant to the thermal shock of rapid heating and cooling that occurs in direct-flame cooking. Thus these pots, made in remote rural areas by techniques that are centuries old, have complex physical properties that make them ideally suited to the purposes for which they have been historically used.

Doña Mercedes Makes a Cooking Pot

*Doña Mercedes Bautista works outside on the ground in the space between her kiln, the storage room, and the mixing tank. To start a large cooking pot she cuts approximately fifteen kilos of clay (*mojón*) from the pile in the storage room and, working on her hands and knees, wedges (or kneads) it on a board on the ground some twenty to twenty-five times. When she has finished, the clay is in the shape of a log approximately forty centimeters long and twenty centimeters in diameter. She places the wedged clay log upright on a turning plate or* plático, *which sits on a board on the ground. The* plático *is a slightly concave ceramic plate of twenty-five centimeters in diameter, made with a solid foot.*

Next she begins turning the clay quickly with her left hand, and with her fist she makes a hole down the center. Without stopping she continues turning the clay and making the opening larger and larger, stretching out the clay until it is thirty centimeters in diameter and sixty centimeters high. At that point the walls are approximately five centimeters thick and the outside surface still shows the rough texture of recently wedged clay.

Once the basic form is established, she works on the rim of the mouth, evening it with her right hand as she turns the piece with her left. The upper eight centimeters of clay are turned inward, and she uses a palm-sized river stone to smooth the outside surface around the mouth. Then, holding it between her fingers, she smooths the edge of the rim as the piece turns on the plate. With the first stage completed, she takes the pot off the turning plate and sets it in the storage room to firm up until the next day, when it will be ready for the finishing steps.

When she resumes work, she smooths the inside wall of the pot with the river stone and pushes out the wall while applying counterpressure on the outside and turning the pot with her left hand. As she turns the pot on the turning plate, she stretches out the walls until the diameter at the shoulder is approximately sixty centimeters, and she maintains the height at forty centimeters. The outside surface has expansion cracks, reflecting the effects of the stretching of the clay, but the basic shape of the pot has been achieved.

Around the bottom of the pot a rough foot of unworked clay remains in place, a lumpy chunk that is the untransformed bottom of the original clay log. She leaves it in place for now while she attends to the sides of the pot, scraping them with a piece of gourd to even out the walls and fill in the expansion cracks. Then she props three large shards around the pot to support it because the wide upper third has made it unsteady. She brings a small chunk of clay from the clay pile and rolls out a thick coil, approximately twenty centimeters long and five centimeters in diameter. She

Making a cooking pot with a pinch-pot technique: After wedging a clay log (*mojón*), Doña Mercedes places it upright on the *plato de bailar*, the turning bowl, and she puts her fist down through the middle of the clay to make an opening. She turns the clay clockwise while putting pressure between her two hands and opens the clay up into a pot shape. She moistens her hands for working the clay, using water in the small pot beside her.

Completing the shape of the cooking pot: Continuing the process, Doña Mercedes stretches the pot to more than double its previous size. Pressing the clay between her hands, she pushes the wall out to its full extension, making the pot top-heavy so that it requires supports to hold it up. The rim is finished, and the walls are scraped to make them even.

Doña Mercedes and her daughter, María Lucila, carry a large water bottle, a *múcura*. The handles are placed at two different angles to facilitate carrying the bottle between two people. Doña Mercedes' granddaughter, Diana, can be seen in the background, as can the adobe and stone kiln. The *múcura* is sixty-five centimeters high and forty-five centimeters in diameter.

affixes one end to the upper side of the shoulder and stretches it between her fingers, thinning and shaping it into a flat strap handle. She turns it, gives it a twist, and attaches the other end to the pot, completing the handle. She adds a pinch of clay around both joints to strengthen the connection. Then she puts an identical handle on the other side and sets the pot in the sun to firm up more.

When the pot is ready, she removes the heavy base of original clay with the gourd scraper. Seated on the ground, she holds the pot in her lap and scrapes off thick layers with her right hand as she turns the pot with her left. Feeling with her left hand along the inside surface, she can tell when she is down to a wall of one centimeter thick, which is normal for Ráquira pottery. She continues to cut off uneven places and scrape the surface until the base is round and smooth. At that point she gives the entire surface a final scraping and sets the pot down on its rim, which is firm from sitting in the sun. The soft bottom is left in the sun to dry for the remainder of the afternoon. Her last touch will be to paint around the mouth of the cooking pot with a thin dark slip, forming spontaneous brush strokes to complete the concept of the pot.

Nearing the End of a Style?

Today the production of domestic pottery by women is largely in the hands of the older generation, and the continued existence of this millennia-old style is in jeopardy because most women of the younger generation do not make ceramics. Although some social values are changing (there is less physical abuse by husbands of wives now), others remain intact (the kiln should still be fired by a man), and the same holds true for ceramics. Some craft design practices are also changing, such as more extensive use of molds, while some traditional ones are preserved, such as the hand-modeling of country-style cooking pots. In rural workshops located near the town itself, the tradition of women's domestic pottery is rapidly giving way to the influence of the men's workshops, where mass-produced ware is made. Commercial success is a powerful incentive to change traditional cultural assumptions about work.

Men's Production Techniques

Men's workshops are characterized by molds, mechanization, and mass production. For them, pottery making is a full-time job, and they engage in it for its commercial value. They are interested in productivity, and they hire workers to increase it. They have adopted the industrial approach to mass production, and in the process pottery has become more of a proletarian than a craft activity. In the factories jobs are completely specialized, so that one person mixes and mills the clay, another drives the horses,

Town workshop production. The pieces in the foreground are representative of mold-produced pieces in a town workshop, and farther back are traditional cooking pots. All are receiving a last sun drying before being loaded into the kiln. The coal pile for the firing can also be seen next to the truck.

mules, or oxen that run the mill, others make pieces in molds, and still others may do the trimming.

The workshops run by men are divided into two types: the male-only, mass-production type using hired workers, which is usually devoted to planter production, and the husband-wife type in which the man takes the lead in a nuclear-family workshop. Mass-production techniques, primarily molds and electric potters' wheels, are used in men's workshops, and even press-mold machines have been tried. These techniques have improved productivity and the economic status of many potters, but they have also led to a loss of the hand-crafted quality of the traditional pottery. The change from handicraft to mass production has shifted the local potters from a craft orientation of being responsible for each step of the production process (that is, digging clay, making, firing, and selling the pieces) to a proletarian orientation of being responsible only for a specialized step in the production (for example, throwing pots on the wheel).

Spanish Origins of Men's Working Techniques

The male potters in the town of Ráquira use a technology and work organization that are primarily Andalusian in origin. It is a model similar to those used in Morocco (Lister and Lister 1987:259, 270, 279; Jereb

1995:117), Pakistan (Rye and Evans 1976:168), and other Muslim countries. The Mediterranean kiln used in Ráquira was called the *horno árabe*
(Arab kiln) in Spain. The walls are made of broken bricks, stones, and
pottery fragments that are mortared together with clay (Lister and Lister
1987:51). There is no archaeological or historical documentation indicating that Spanish-style wheel-thrown pottery was made in Ráquira during
the colonial period, which suggests that Ráquira men were not making
pottery. When men began to adopt the techniques of mass production in
the 1940s and 1950s, they copied the Andalusian model used in other
areas of Boyacá. That model includes:

1. The Mediterranean kiln. This updraft kiln design with the firebox directly under the ware chamber has a long history in Spain,
having been used by Romans, Visigoths, and Muslims (Lister and
Lister 1987:52). Since men have traditionally fired women's pottery,
they had adopted this kiln long before they began making pottery
themselves.

2. The potter's wheel. The Andalusian sidesaddle potter's wheel is
used in other areas of Boyacá, and a few men potters in Ráquira also
use it. (See photograph on page 36.) The potter sits to the right of
the wheel and throws to his left. The wheel that is most commonly
used in Ráquira today is the single-speed electric production model
introduced by Artesanías de Colombia.

3. The horse-powered clay mill. Like the potter's wheel, this was
added to Ráquira pottery making in recent decades as men became
more involved in production. It is essentially an open barrel that has
a wooden shaft with spokes. The shaft is turned by a horse walking
in a circle around the barrel. The design is also used in Morocco. See
figure on page 167.

4. Donkey sidesaddles. The donkey sidesaddle design for carrying
clay, wood for the firing, and pots is also from southern Spain, used
in Andalusia and Extremadura (Llorens and Corredor 1979:76). It
consists of two L-shaped wooden holders, one hanging on each side
of the animal and tied together across the donkey's back.

5. Working at tables. In Spanish pottery making, people work at
tables (Lister and Lister 1987:258), in contrast to the prehispanic indigenous tradition of working while seated on the ground.

6. Lead glazes. Following the Spanish tradition, men formerly used
lead glazes to seal and decorate pieces rather than adhering to the
indigenous tradition of using slips. These have now been replaced by
safer glazes.

In this century Ráquira men have added two-part plaster molds to this Andalusian pottery system, which guarantees them high volumes of production; but the reliance on the potter's wheel and molds also brings limitations. First, the wheel-made pieces are limited to small, simple, rounded shapes such as bells, cups, pitchers, and candleholders. For this reason the pottery becomes homogeneous and standardized in shape. Second, molds are expensive, which means that potters are slow to change forms because of the capital they have invested in the existing ones. Molds also occupy substantial amounts of space, requiring larger workshops for their use.

Mold-made Pieces

Molds are used primarily in workshops managed by men, who make the large pieces, such as planters, themselves. Smaller pieces, such as piggy banks or horses, are made by women, and both men and women may trim pieces after they come out of the mold. Mold-made pieces are valued for the industrial quality of their finishing, and they have come to dominate the mass production destined for the urban market. People are pleased with the uniform shapes and the smooth, partially sealed surfaces of mold-made pieces, which are quite different from the pitted textures of the earthenware cooking pots made by country potters. Since the ceramics made for the urban market will not be used for cooking, less temper is added to the claybody, resulting in a smoother texture. As the mold draws the water out of the clay in the drying process, it floats a layer of clay to the surface of the piece, producing a smooth finish that is highly valued locally. Most mold production is done with press molds, but some workshops have used slip molds for special pieces like tea sets and nativity scenes. The lack of knowledge of sodium carbonate or sodium silicate to deflocculate (that is, make clay particles float in the water) slip and make it set up faster frustrated early attempts to use poured slip molds. This and other technical problems in producing slip led potters to use press molds, so that they could work with claybodies with which they were familiar.

Mold Production of Planters in a Town Workshop

In most town workshops the workers making molded planters are contract employees, and they are paid on a per-piece basis. They do not have to come to work every day, and, in fact, they may take off one day and work extra hours on other days to earn the level of income they need. In a day of concentrated work, which may mean twelve to fourteen hours, a good mold worker can make seventy-five or more planters of fifty centimeters in height. That represents an average of one planter every

Inside a town workshop. To the left is a mound of mixed clay waiting to be worked into a column of clay one meter by eighty centimeters. After that it will be cut into slabs for the molds. Finished planters are stacked in the background.

nine to ten minutes, or six to seven planters per hour. However, on a normal day the output is closer to fifty planters.

Workers may arrive as early as 6:00 A.M. and work until 4:00 P.M., but on days of intense work they may stay later. During rush periods additional workers may be contracted, but production is limited by the number of molds the workshop has. The mold workers are men, and most come from the neighboring rural areas.

The moldero *(press molder) works from a waist-high block of clay, which he keeps covered under a plastic sheet. The two halves of a plaster mold are laid open next to each other, and clay slabs of approximately one centimeter in thickness are cut from the block by a hand-pulled wire cutter. Then the clay is cut according to the dimensions needed for each half of the mold, and it is carried to the open mold and laid in place. A* poma *or* pounder, *made of heavy cloth filled with sand, is used to press the clay against the mold wall and to compact the clay. The two halves of the mold are put together, and the* moldero *works through the open mouth of the planter to fuse the seam line at the union of the two halves of the piece. Rope-like strands of clay are rolled out and added to the line of union to reinforce it, and one is also added around the lip of the piece to strengthen it.*

The planter is left in the mold for three to four hours, but when it is removed it is still soft. It is left out to air dry overnight, and then it is placed under a plastic sheet for two or three days to dry slowly until it is leatherhard. After the third day, it is trimmed by the husband or wife of the family or another employee. Then the piece is placed for several days near the kiln or along the outside edges of the workshop shed, where it receives the wind and finishes drying. It will then be placed in the next kiln firing. The cycle of making, drying, and firing a piece to be ready for delivery usually takes a minimum of two weeks, and three weeks are more common for many smaller workshops because they do not have the volume of production to fill kilns as quickly.

People express frustration about the expense of changing molds, either to replace old ones or to add new designs. They are expensive by local standards, with a two-part mold costing between fifteen and twenty thousand pesos ($18.75 to $25.00 U.S.), which in 1995 represented most of a week's salary. As a result, family workshops are limited to a few molds and a few designs, making it difficult for them to compete with the well-financed large planter factories.

Most commonly used in Ráquira are two-part press molds made of plaster of paris. The claybody used in the molds is mixed with more temper than the claybody used in hand building, which results in less shrinkage as the clay firms up inside the mold. As the clay is brought into the work-

Worker making a planter in a mold. The worker lays a slab of clay in each half of the open two-piece plaster mold and presses the slab until it fits the mold perfectly. When the two halves of the mold are fitted together, the unions and the rim are reinforced. A *poma* or pounder, a cloth bag filled with sand, is used to compact the walls.

José Vicente Vargas and his wife Gloria de Vargas trim the mold marks off planters that were made the day before by the man who works for them. This is a town-style planter workshop run by the husband-wife team with one employee. The production fills their workshop.

shop from the mixing mill, it is worked into a massive block approximately one meter by eighty centimeters and one and one-half meters high. The top and sides are shaped to be perfectly flat and smooth. Larger workshops calculate the size of this clay block so that each slab that is cut off will be large enough for the two sides of a fifty-centimeter planter.

The mold must be relatively dry to work well, and the idea is that the dry plaster will draw the water out of the clay, drying it and firming it up. But the people of Ráquira work on a narrow economic margin and they usually overwork their molds, trying to obtain maximum production. Molds are air dried overnight in a sheltered outdoor work area, but since the cool night air does not dry as well as the warm daytime air, molds are usually worked without being totally dry. During the rainy season this problem is compounded by the increased humidity in the air.

Several hundred pieces can be made from each mold over its lifetime, but as a mold gets older, decorative detail becomes more blurred, and the mold actually loses some of its bulk, which means that the pieces made in it become a little larger (Frith 1985:51). People in Ráquira complain about the molds becoming "tired" (*fatigados*), which leads to a decline in production, and potters may reach the point of making only one piece per day in a mold instead of the two or three pieces that are possible in better circumstances. The only solution is to make new molds, but because of the cost, people put off that decision as long as possible. Making molds is one of the most important skills, and few know how to do it well. Usually the potter goes to a specialized mold maker, taking an example of the pot for which a mold is needed. Molds are expensive by Ráquira standards because each one is made individually.

Molds are not only made to replace existing forms, but sometimes new forms are added to the production of a workshop. Mora mentions three sources of the new forms that are added to the repertoire of an individual potter or workshop (1974:33):

1. When people are making a form that is commonly made in many workshops and there is no individual ownership of the form (such as the papaya, armadillo, turtle, or rabbit), a new mold is made when the old one is worn out without any special consideration of others who may use the same shape.

2. A ceramist who has a new idea for a shape (which may be original or copied from some other pottery community) takes it to a mold maker to produce, and that version of the shape belongs to that potter.

3. A ceramist may copy a shape made by someone else in the community with a small variation on the original idea and have a new mold made to produce it. For example, the potter may change the angle of the profile or make a thicker lip. Any variation on the original model is sufficient to claim creative distinctiveness, and these minute differences are sufficient for the rest of the community to distinguish one maker from the other.

Molds can speed up the production process and facilitate making odd-shaped pieces, which permits some variety from the traditional globular shapes. Today even some of the traditional figures, such as the horse, are made in molds, which leads some traditionalists in Colombia to complain that Ráquira is losing its authenticity. Potters, however, see the use of molds as a means of increasing their productivity and income.

Wheel-made Pottery

Although men are primarily the ones who throw on the potter's wheel in Ráquira, a few women do also. The potter's wheel was not used in Ráquira until the 1950s, when men began making mass-produced pottery, and

Néstor Reyes is throwing small bells
"off the hump," which means that a
single cone of clay is centered on the
wheel and several pieces are formed,
one after the other, off the top of the
cone of clay until it is used up. He is
working on a constant-speed, stand-
up, production-type potter's wheel.

most of the wheels in use today are electric constant-speed production
wheels. Records from Artesanías de Colombia show that in 1990 there
were fifty-three electric wheels in use in Ráquira, another five that were
manually operated, and three traditional kickwheels (Gómez Contreras
1990:46), for a total of sixty-one wheels in 201 workshops. Most of the
workshops using the potter's wheel own just one, which means that only
30 percent of all workshops in the township have a wheel. However, most
of the wheels are concentrated in town, where well over half of the workshops have one; probably no more than 10 percent of the women's workshops in the rural areas have them. Although throwing on the wheel is
considered to be men's work by most people in the town, a number of
rural women are now using the wheel to speed up their production.

Professional throwers make small and medium-sized planters, working
on a constant-speed, stand-up electric production wheel. The *tornero*
(thrower) usually works with an assistant, who wedges the cones of clay
that he throws. The assistant brings the cones of clay to the wheel and
carries the completed planters away to a drying area, so that the throwing
is never interrupted. In less than two minutes, the *tornero* centers the clay,
opens the center cavity to a diameter of twenty centimeters, and pulls the
straight walls up to twenty-five centimeters in height. At that rate he can
make 250 to 300 planters per day. Slight irregularities are left uncorrected
because the emphasis is on speed, not exactness of shape. Throwers regu-

larly work two-hour shifts before taking a break, and they normally work four two-hour blocks in a day. There is no collected information on re-petitive-motion injuries among these workers. However, the fact that most professional throwers do not continue that occupation (even though it is the most lucrative) past the age of thirty-five indicates the physical limita-tions of the job.

Pottery is considered legitimate work for men when pots are made by mold or by machine (using the potter's wheel or press-mold machine, which is discussed below). During this research, no man was ever observed using the women's techniques of pinch pots and coiling. Doña Mercedes Bautista of Pueblo Viejo said that men did not know how to make ceram-ics in the past because they could not learn the women's way of working, but she pointed out that since they learned to throw pots on the wheel, many men began making pottery.

Machine-made Pottery

Few machines are used to make ceramics in Ráquira, but when they are, men run them. One of the first mechanized workshops was set up in the early 1970s by Miguel Suárez, brother of the elder Reyes Suárez, and he used a German press-mold machine to make flower pots. Clay is laid into

Part of Néstor Reyes' morning pro-duction of bells. They are drying to the leatherhard stage for trimming, which he and his wife will share.

Table 7.3. Number of products per workshop

	Urban*		Rural**	
No. of products	No. of workshops	%	No. of workshops	%
1	13	17.11	13	30.95
2	16	21.06	10	23.80
3	18	23.68	15	35.71
4	12	15.78	2	4.77
5 or more	17	22.37	2	4.77
Totals	76	100.00	42	100.00

*Complete survey of urban workshops
**Sample of three *veredas*
Source: Bonilla et al. 1992:49, 76

a mold, and the machine presses it to the shape of the pot to be made. This rapid industrial process can produce more planters in one day than the women's pinch pot and coiling process can in weeks. However, there are problems. The small sizes of the planters that are made by the press-mold machine are not as marketable as the larger sizes that the buying public prefers, and the simple, slant-sided, V-shaped pieces made by machine have neither the complexity of form permitted by the mold nor the rich texture achieved by hand building pots. Although potters have experimented with press-mold machines to increase their productivity, the buying public retains esthetic values with respect to form and texture that are related to the hand-and mold-forming techniques. The forms produced by the press-mold machine do not have the hand-crafted quality valued by the public, and as a result the use of machines has not been successful.

Gender, Location, and Production

A comparison of volume and kinds of production between the men's town workshops and the women's rural workshops indicates the different cultural attitudes toward the craft of the two genders. Most (90 percent) of the rural workshops produce a narrow range of pots, usually a cooking pot (*olla*), water bottle (*múcura*), or country pitcher (*chorote*). Since most rural workshops have only one potter, production is limited to the repertoire of that person. The town workshops produce a greater diversity of forms, and over one-third make four or more different products, such as planters, mobiles, lamps, and banks. The larger number of workers in the

Straight-walled planter or *matera,* which is the principal form produced in the large town workshops in the 1980s and 1990s. This middle-sized planter is forty-five centimeters high by forty centimeters in diameter. There are both larger and smaller sizes. Collection of the author.

men's workshops permits the wider range of production, which gives them greater diversity for marketing.

Volume of production is also indicated by the amount of clay consumed in the workshops. Over half of the women's rural workshops were in the lowest-use category of under two thousand kilos per month, and, in fact, most of that group was under a thousand kilos. The town workshops were more evenly distributed between two and ten thousand kilos per month, but the largest single group were the users of over ten thousand kilos per month with some in the twenty thousand kilo range (Bonilla et al. 1992:33, 69).

The volume of monthly production of pieces per workshop demonstrates the greater productivity of the town. More than half the rural workshops are in the lowest production category, making fewer than five hundred pieces per month, while only a few town workshops are in that category. In contrast, twenty-one of the large producers making over three thousand pieces per month are in town, but only three of the sample of rural workshops are in that group (Bonilla et al. 1992:49, 77). By 1983 Gumercindo Rojas Escobar found that 92 percent of town workshops already used either molds or some kind of mechanical equipment, such as a potter's wheel. In comparison, 70 percent of the rural workshops made no

A son is adding handles to small bowls thrown and trimmed by his mother. The Londoños have a family-style workshop, which does mold production of piggy banks, planters, bowls, and other forms. Their house-workshop is located on the edge of town going to Pueblo Viejo.

use of molds or mechanical equipment, preferring entirely manual processes (1983:18f).

In the latter half of the twentieth century, the process of ceramics production in Ráquira gradually changed from craft work to machine and mold work marked by technological diversity. Dean Arnold suggests that ceramics communities with the greatest range of technological choice and diversity have a greater chance of economic viability (1989:54), and the Ráquira data support this observation. Ráquira's economic growth as a ceramics center has coincided with the expansion of its technological base.

Growth in Production

In the twenty-six years from 1966 to 1992, the number of town workshops grew from 16 to 76, a 475 percent increase representing an average of 2.3 new workshops each year. In 1966 there were 16 workshops in town (Mora 1974:23), in 1983 there were 49 (Rojas Escobar 1983:39f), and in 1992 there were 76 (Bonilla et al. 1992:9). In 1983 there were 90 workshops in the rural area (Rojas Escobar 1983:17–18), and twelve years later there were an estimated 120, representing an increase of 33 percent.

The increase was not only in the number of workshops but more dramatically in the volume of sales and production.

Artesanías de Colombia has documented sales to estimate production per month (Rojas Escobar 1983:33), and the pieces that constitute the greatest volume of sales in town workshops are planters, candlesticks, planter plates, toys, bell chimes, banks, flower vases, salt bowls, ashtrays, nativity sets, horses, and butter dishes. In the early 1980s it was estimated that 101,931 pieces were produced per month in the town workshops (ibid.), and the 55 percent increase in the number of workshops between 1983 and 1992 suggests a comparable increase in production

The fact that production is dominated by large industrialized and semi-industrialized workshops managed by men has a number of consequences for the wider community. One is that their production is so large that the prices for which they sell their pieces controls prices for everyone else. They also hire away the younger workers, leaving the smaller family workshops in the hands of the older generations. And since the 1970s, when this process started, people have been learning factory techniques and transforming the independent craft potters of earlier generations into proletarian factory laborers.

The output of rural workshops operated by individual women potters and husband-wife teams is consistently lower than that of the industrialized town workshops (Bonilla et al. 1992:35–36). Half of the women's country workshops fall into the category of the smallest producers, and they account for only one-tenth of the total rural production. The largest single rural workshop produces more than twice as much in one month as do the twenty-two smallest ones combined. The smaller workshops are primarily run by women who do domestic chores and agricultural tasks in addition to making pottery, and many of them do not make more than sixty or seventy pots per month. The three largest country workshops produce from four to twelve thousand pieces per month each, an estimated half of all rural production (ibid.). This reflects the same situation as the town, in which a few large workshops dominate the market and the craft, setting production standards, defining styles, and establishing prices.

The Potters' Problems

The growth in production over the last two decades has changed the world of Ráquira pottery from a traditional rural craft to a twentieth-century production-oriented business with the accompanying problems of urban markets, intermediaries, and large-volume competitors. When asked to identify the problems they face in the 1990s, many potters mentioned typical technical problems of pottery making, but others mentioned the new circumstances of pottery as a business (Bonilla et al. 1992:84).

Problems of marketing were mentioned by over one-third of the potters, including sale of production (27 percent), unfair competition (6 percent), and low profits (5 percent) (Bonilla et al. 1992:84). Just over one-third of the potters gave technical problems as the most important: clay problems (17 percent), chipping or cracking (11 percent), kiln problems (3 percent), low production (3 percent), and the cost of fuel (2 percent). A smaller group of potters had communal concerns, including environmental pollution (reported by 14 percent), a reflection of the problem of coal firing in town (ibid.), and the lack of a trade organization (3 percent). The others did not identify problems. Thus economic and technical problems are the most frequent problems plaguing Ráquira potters, and they seem to apply almost equally to men and women.

Cultural Factors That Shape Production in Ráquira

The working patterns of Ráquira ceramics have been forged in a crucible of historical, environmental, and social factors as each new generation learns the existing ceramic culture and modifies it to fit their circumstances. As an expression of material culture, pottery making is a cultural behavior, and the organization of production is a cultural construction.

In the women's and men's workshops, there are different rules about how to organize the pottery makers' work. In both gender traditions, pottery styles have changed in recent generations. Kinspeople are the primary collaborators for potters in both kinds of workshops, with the difference that among women work is cooperative, reciprocal, unpaid, and domestic, while in the men's workshops labor is bought and sold. The differences in work patterns between Andalusian and prehispanic ceramics constitute a cultural chasm that continues to be expressed in the contrasts between men and women and between town and rural people. Because men have adopted the Spanish commercial approach more than women, and because of their gender advantages in the patrifocal society, they have occupied higher positions than the women in the social hierarchy. These differences in social status have shaped the cultural history of the two genders, setting up the contrasting styles of behavior that characterize them in ceramics today.

8

The Technology of Clays and Kilns

The technology of Ráquira ceramics making is largely the work of men. Although the basic elements of clays, kilns, and firing procedures are common to both women's and men's pottery, men normally mix the clay and fire the kilns whether a woman or a man is the potter. Male control of clay preparation and firing is common to every style of Ráquira ceramics, overriding differences of gender and generational styles. Over the last five hundred years there have been two primary periods of technological change in Ráquira, and men were probably responsible for both of them. The first occurred shortly after the Conquest, when Mediterranean kilns were adopted (Therrien 1991:71), and the second occurred in this century with the adoption of electric potters' wheels, molds, and downdraft kilns as part of the men's complex of pottery making.

Clays, Claybodies, and Stains

Similar raw materials are used in making Ráquira ceramics in the rural women's workshops and in the semi-industrialized town workshops of the men. Until recently, people mined their own clay, built their own kilns, and cut their own firewood, but today materials are usually bought by the truckload from specialized suppliers. The newer kilns are now made by specialized builders according to high-tech designs developed by engineers, all of which are measures of the social changes occurring in Ráquira.

Obtaining Clay

There are clay deposits in the ten lower *veredas* of Ráquira, and ceramics are made in all of them. In contrast, nine out of the ten higher *veredas* did not have clay deposits, and ceramics are not made in those areas. This 95 percent correlation between making ceramics and the presence of clay deposits nearby shows the dependency of the potter on accessible clay deposits. The most direct arrangement for obtaining clay occurs in the coun-

Ráquira and its surrounding *veredas*. The ten darker, outlying *veredas* are located in the highest altitudes, where there are no clay deposits and no ceramics production. The ten lighter *veredas* clustered in the lower areas do have clay deposits, and potters are active in each of them.

tryside, where potters can mine clay on their own farm and transport sand from the river for temper. One quarter (26 percent) of the rural potters do, in fact, mine their own clay (Bonilla et al. 1992:68). However, the ceramists who live in town have to buy clay, and traditionally they paid a fee to the owner of a clay deposit for the right to mine the clay they needed. In the family workshops, it has been primarily the responsibility of the husband or older son to go to the mine and dig out the clay with a pick and shovel, although in some circumstances the woman would do it. Usually they could find a clay deposit within one kilometer or so of the workshop (see appendix).

Mining clay in Resguardo Occidente. The eight-man crew works for Don Aristóbolo Rodríguez, owner of Todo Ráquira. Clay is mined for his planter factory and for families who sell their production to him. A field of wheat is growing behind the clay pit.

As the larger workshops evolved into small industrial operations in the 1980s, they required larger supplies of clay, which gave rise to the specialized support businesses of digging and delivering clay. By the mid-1990s many rural and town potters were buying clay directly from specialized haulers, who delivered dump-truck loads to their workshop. Aristóbolo Rodríguez, the owner of the large pottery warehouse named Todo Ráquira (or All Ráquira), supplies the clay for many family workshops, and in return they promise to sell their production to him. He has a specialized team of ten or so workers who dig the clay by pick and shovel out of open clay quarries and hand load the dump truck for his own personal factory and for distribution to workshops that are his clients. During the rainy seasons, water accumulates and floods these clay pits, so clay is only mined during the two dry seasons, which are approximately June to August and December to February.

The price of a load of clay includes the cost of the delivery to the workshop, which may come to more than the clay itself. The cost (1994 prices) of one truckload (eight tons for yellow, red, or black clay; six tons for white clay) at the mine is 20,000 pesos ($25.00 U.S.). Loading and trucking the clay to town is 30,000 pesos ($37.50 U.S.), for a total cost of 50,000 pesos ($62.50 U.S.). Since a quarter of the rural potters mine clay on their own property, there is no direct cost for them, and many other rural potters are located close to commercial mines and have minimal delivery costs. However, most rural potters (52 percent) buy clay by the truckload, as the town potters do (Bonilla et al. 1992:68), and some rural potters are located at great distances from the mine and have expensive delivery costs. The cost of trucking the clay to rural workshops varies from 30,000 pesos ($37.50 U.S.) to 70,000 pesos ($87.50 U.S.) according to the location.

The Claybody

Locally there are deposits of white clay (called *caolín*, or kaolin) in the *veredas* of Mirque and Roa. Red, yellow, and black clays are mined in the other eight low-lying *veredas*. (The colors indicate the presence of iron oxide and other minerals.) The four clays are mixed together in specific proportions to make the claybodies used in the various styles of ceramics. The general rule in the formulation of the claybody is that it should contain a minimum of two different clays. This not only means mixing clays of different colors but also clays from different deposits.

The town workshops and factories working with molds add feldspar, silica, and zinc to their claybodies to alter the firing temperatures, shrinkage rates, plasticity, and color. Many also buy a white clay from commercial mills in Bogotá that has already been prepared with the particle sizes they prefer. This commercially prepared clay can be bought at the same price as the local *caolín*, but the commercial version is ready to mix and requires no additional treatment. Red, yellow, and black earthenware clays are still bought exclusively from local mines.

Claybodies are composed of varying mixtures of clay and temper (sand) according to the kind of pottery being made. The traditional cooking and storage pottery is made with heavily tempered red or yellow earthenware clay. Finer pieces, which are to be modeled or carved, are made without tempering material, but they do include various colors of earthenware clays and *caolín*. Earthenware clays from alluvial deposits are noted for their plasticity, which is important for those who throw on the wheel and build with coils. Of the four types of clay used, white clay is the most popular among town potters; 78 percent of the workshops use it in the claybody (Bonilla et al. 1992:30). White and yellow clays are the two most common ingredients of claybodies. Three-quarters of the town workshops used these two ingredients exclusively, and almost all used one or the other in their claybodies (ibid.:31).

In the rural areas, when small pieces are to be made from a claybody, it is lightly "salted" with sand, which means 20 to 25 percent temper is added. Cooking pots and large storage pots may contain as much as 45 percent temper, based on a proportion of seven measures of clay to six measures of sand. This heavily tempered claybody has a high resistance to thermal shock, which makes it appropriate for direct-flame cooking, and it also insures against breakage in the kiln since the porosity diminishes the stress associated with firing large, heavy pieces. Ráquira potters believe that organic material will cause pieces to crack in the kiln, so they carefully clean the clay of any straw or wood that might contaminate it. Broken pottery is ground up to mix a special claybody for making saggars, which includes equal parts of clay, sand, and pulverized pottery.

Mixing the Clay

The preparation of the mined clay begins with the drying process, and then it is beaten with a heavy club or hoe to break up large chunks. In the nuclear family workshops, small children may join in the process of pulverizing the clay, but it is a game for them and an adult's strength is necessary to reduce the dried clay lumps to the smaller sizes that will dissolve in the soaking tank before being milled. The factory workshops have hammer mills to pulverize the clay. Once the clays are dry and pulverized, they are mixed according to the kind of pottery being made and according to the specific formula of the workshop. The number of *arrobas* (11.25 kilos) of clay are balanced with a specified number of *arrobas* of sand for temper.

Traditionally, each workshop had a pit dug into the ground where the clay was moistened, but today the pits have largely been replaced by brick holding tanks built above ground in the form of a half circle. These tanks hold a ton or more of clay, which is shoveled into the tank in dry powder form. Water is added, and the clay is mixed with a shovel or board-like paddle. Fresh water is preferred to mix the clay, which presents no problem for people who live near the river or who have running water. However, in much of the countryside fresh water has to be carried from considerable distances. Many avoid using stagnant water from a pond or stored water to mix clay because they believe it will cause them to develop rheumatism or other diseases as they work with the clay.

The clay is soaked for a day or so until it is well moistened, and additional powdered clay and sand (temper) are added to thicken it to the right consistency for putting through the horse-powered barrel mill, which is located next to the tank. The mill consists of a spoked axle that turns inside of a barrel and mixes the clay. One end of a three-to four-meter-long pole is affixed to the top of the mill axle and the other is attached to a horse, which walks in circles, turning the axle. One person stands in the soaking tank and scoops handfuls of soft clay into the barrel mill as the animal turns the axle with its mixing spokes. The soaked clay is dumped in the open top of the barrel and mixed by the spokes; then it feeds out a hole on one side of the barrel at the bottom. This process binds the newly moistened particles into a unified claybody and produces as much plasticity as is possible from an unmatured, tempered claybody.

The mixed and milled clay is extruded from the bottom of the barrel in a few minutes, where another worker gathers it up and adds it to the clay ready to work inside the workshop. This clay is covered with a sheet of heavy plastic to seal in the moisture. Since clays are not aged in Ráquira, it is ready for hand wedging after it comes out of the mill. If smaller amounts of clay are used, which is especially the case in women's workshops, it may be soaked in old cooking pots reserved for that purpose. With this system the woman does not have to depend on the assistance of a man and can mix small amounts as needed for a day's work. The clay may be mixed in the morning, then wedged and used later in the day. After the clay has soaked, it is mixed with sifted dry clay to obtain the consistency necessary to work by hand.

Wedging the Clay

The traditional process was to remove the clay from the pit and lay it out on a cleaned floor that had previously been covered with powder from

In a town workshop clay is mixed in an ox-powered mill. The man on the right keeps the oxen moving; the boy in the middle shoulders a chunk of mixed clay to carry inside; and the man in the pit feeds moist clay into the mill for mixing.

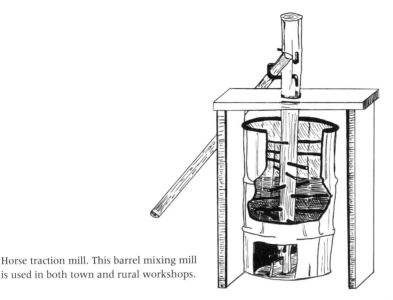

Horse traction mill. This barrel mixing mill is used in both town and rural workshops.

the same claybody. A square of clay was laid out that measured up to two meters square and fifteen to twenty centimeters thick. The clay was dusted with a layer of dry clay, and one of the women wedged it by walking back and forth on it; additional powdered clay was mixed in until a workable consistency had been reached. As the woman's feet wedged the clay, her movements took on the rhythm of a soft dance. This is a Spanish process that was still used in Spain until recently (Llorens and Corredor 1979:23). Foot wedging traditionally completed the mixing process, but it is no longer needed because the barrel mill is so effective.

After the mixing there is a final stage of hand wedging in which the clay is first rolled into a log shape, sixty centimeters long and fifteen centimeters in diameter, called a *mojón.* If a woman is wedging, she will sit on the ground and rock forward with the weight of her body to give force to the wedging. The log-shaped clay roll is folded in on itself as it is wedged, gradually eliminating the air pockets that could cause the piece to break during the firing. Children from eight to twelve years old may help the adults with the wedging, but an adult will always complete any hand wedging done by children to guarantee that no lumps or air pockets remain.

If the clay is to be used for traditional coil-built forms, it is hand wedged only ten or fifteen times. Since the coils will be pinched together, that process will remove any air that remains. However, clay to be used in finer urban market ceramics will be wedged twice as much to guarantee that all air pockets are eliminated. If the clay is to be used for figurative forms, which may be modeled with little pressure, it also receives additional wedging.

Oxide Stains and Glazes

Watery oxide stains have traditionally been used to draw designs on the surfaces of pots, and in recent years potters have begun to make their own stains with commercial oxides. By the 1990s thirty-four (45 percent) of the town workshops used commercial red iron oxide to make stain (Bonilla et al. 1992:36), but in the country workshops people still make stain from ocher-colored pebbles (limonite, $Fe_2O_3H_2O$); the stain is an opaque manganese-like dark charcoal brown. The pebbles are easily available and can be gathered along the road; then they are placed in the wood or coal fire of the cooking stove for a couple of days, which transforms them to a red color (ferric oxide, Fe_2O_3). They are then pulverized and mixed with water to make the stain. A "white" stain was traditionally made with white clay, but it is rarely used today.

Glaze is used to seal and decorate the surface of tableware. People value the finished appearance of glazed pieces, and glazing has always been reserved for special work. In the 1980s people began experimenting with commercial glazes from Bogotá, and the Museo de Artes y Tradiciones Populares offered a course on glazes and colorants. In 1995 two workshops in town were using commercial glazes, and they were used on tea sets and dinnerware fired in electric kilns. Commercial glazes are made with frits, which are lead fused with silica or other materials to make the glazes safe for handling by the potter. The exchange potter from Japan also introduced information on glazes in the early 1990s.

Formerly, glazes were made from a simple mixture of lead and clay, and the lead was produced locally using the plates of old car batteries, but more recently it has been purchased in fritted form (or occasionally as lead oxide) from chemical companies. Because most people are aware of the toxicity of lead, they have changed to fritted lead glazes. The traditional fired color of this lead glaze ranges from green to yellow, and the two colors can be mottled. Because lead-based glazes must be protected from the direct flame, lead-glazed pieces are placed in locally made saggars if they are fired in a traditional kiln, but today most glazed ceramics are fired in electric kilns.

Commercial Paint

Commercial paints and varnish have been used by some people to decorate the surfaces of nonutilitarian pieces, which allows them to avoid the difficulty of controlling glazes. This was often done in the 1960s and 1970s with the mold-made forms, such as the armadillo or the turtle. Sometimes the pieces to be varnished are first stained with dark shoe polish to alter the natural clay color. In the early 1990s twenty-seven town workshops

Loading the kiln. This is an older Mediterranean-style updraft kiln made of adobe blocks. The man is in the ware chamber positioning the Indian-motif planters that his wife is passing to him. The fire chamber can be seen below. The flue opens on two sides of the stubby chimney, and a Christian cross is placed on top.

(36 percent) were using commercial paint on ceramics (Bonilla et al. 1992:36)

The 1994 house-painting campaign instigated by the mayor of Ráquira had a spin-off in the painting of ceramics. At least one workshop began painting vases with monochrome iridescent, metallic colors (dark purples, blues, and reds) that seemed to be drawn from the color schemes for the houses. Local potters had mixed opinions about these brightly painted vases, which represented a break from the earth tones of the slips and claybodies that are normally used.

Firings and Kilns

Since the man's primary role in the production has been the firing, kiln design and management are men's issues. Women have never been very involved with this aspect of ceramics, and the introduction of large coal-fired downdraft kilns in recent decades reflects men's interests in technological innovations to expand production and control costs.

Firing

The loading of the kiln is an activity in which all of the family members participate. A layer of pot shards is placed along the floor of the ware chamber to protect pots from the flames that come up through the brick grillwork from the fire chamber. Pots are then stacked one on top of another, making each kiln loading a unique process. The pieces are positioned in such a way that each receives even pressure during the firing from the pieces around it. The largest pots are placed on the bottom level, and smaller pots and objects are placed on top of them to form a second level. Finally, flat pieces, such as toasters (*areperos*), and other small pieces are placed in the very top of the kiln. If glaze is used, the foot, rim, and any other parts that might come in contact with other pieces are wiped clean to prevent fusing by the glaze, and the pieces are placed in saggars. The smallest and most fragile pieces are placed inside unglazed larger ones or set at the very top of the stack of pots.

The man is normally the stacker, and he sits inside the ware chamber as his wife and older children bring the pots to him one by one. He stacks the backside of the chamber first, and as it fills up, he backs toward the door of the kiln. Once the chamber is filled, the door is sealed with adobe blocks or bricks, similar to those in the kiln wall, and the cracks between them are filled with clay. Saint Anthony or Saint Dimas may be implored to watch over the firing and to prevent rain until it is finished. Santa Rufina or Saint Ignatius may be asked to keep the pieces from breaking in the kiln, and someone in the family may light a candle in front of a picture of one of the saints. Many families have a cross permanently installed on the top of the kiln as a request for God's protection against the unpredictability of the firing process.

If the kiln is loaded during the morning hours, a small warming fire is started in the mouth of the firebox as soon as it is full. The warming fire will continue for five or six hours to remove any moisture remaining in the pots. When the kiln is warm and all the pots are completely dry, the main fire begins. If the kiln is loaded during the afternoon, the warming fire will be lighted overnight, and the main firing will start in the cool predawn hours of the next day. The greenest wood is used during the initial stages of the firing, so that it will start slowly, and the older and drier wood is introduced later when the kiln is hot inside.

Temperatures vary greatly from one firing to another, and Ráquira potters do not precisely measure the heat in the kiln. The new downdraft kilns can be fired more or less consistently to a thousand degrees centigrade; however, the traditional kilns usually fire between six and seven hundred degrees centigrade, with fairly wide differences between hot and cold areas within the kiln. Mora measured the temperature of thirteen kilns in 1966 and found that twelve of them fired only to six hundred degrees centigrade, and just one reached a thousand degrees centigrade (1974:39). The traditional adobe kilns are quite porous and inevitably have cracks in the kiln walls and around the door, which can complicate temperature control.

The man who is firing the kiln decides when the right temperature has been reached (or when "el horno está al punto") according to the time elapsed, amount of fuel used, color and sound of the fire, and color of the pots being fired. Dean Arnold mentions that similar factors are also used by potters in Quinua, Peru, to determine the completion of the firing (1993:106). During the height of the firing of a Ráquira kiln, flames and smoke leak out from a number of places, giving a good idea of the color of the fire inside and the amount of heat. Some potters also put small pieces of clay or small pots in the firebox and examine them during the firing. When they reach a brownish-red color, they are considered ready. Potters also refer to the *bramido* of the kiln, which can be translated as a bellowing or roaring; the same word is used for the bellowing of a bull. So when the sound of the kiln reaches the deep-throated bellow of the bull, it is another indicator that the firing is complete.

The length of a firing depends on the size of the kiln and the density of the load. Smaller Mediterranean-style kilns can be fired in eight hours, but the larger ones require much more time. When the potter estimates that the required temperature has been reached, he holds the fire at that level for a couple of hours, "soaking" (*caldeando*). Many then fire the kiln down by gradually reducing the fuel before totally ending the firing and closing the mouth of the firebox. One complete day is required for the small kilns to cool down, and on the morning of the second day after the firing, the kiln can be unloaded. The large, new, coal-fired downdraft kilns require thirty to forty hours for firing and three to four days for cooling down, but the timing may vary depending on the size of the kiln and other factors.

In the sixteen downdraft kilns in town, the firing is "salted" by throwing salt into the firebox when the kiln is at the peak of temperature, near a thousand degrees centigrade. Not enough salt is added to glaze the pieces, but it is enough to produce flashes of reddish coloring on the sides of pots, which are highly valued. Two kilos are thrown into each of the four fireboxes, and the salt vaporizes instantly. Sodium acts as a flux, or melting agent, and imbeds itself in the side walls of pots, producing the flashing. Highly toxic chlorine gas goes out the chimney, contributing to the respiratory illnesses that have been prevalent in Ráquira in recent years. The esthetic and monetary value of the flashing is achieved at the price of weakened lungs and respiratory infections.

The unloading may be a happy event or a sad one, according to how the firing has gone. When the kiln is opened and the husband, wife, and older children unload it, their spirits rise if it was a good firing. But it can be a sad occasion if many pieces are broken. The pots are commented on as they come out of the kiln: the fire produced nice flashing on one, the form of another is particularly well done, and this figure looks like old Señora Suárez down the street. There may be smiles and even a few jokes. The pieces placed closest to the firebox receive the direct flame and are darker and have more flashing or coloration from the flame, and these pots are the most highly valued and sell for higher prices. Racial attitudes appear in the particular care that is taken to locate the figures of the baby Jesus and the Virgin Mary in a place protected from the flame, because it is said that they should never be dark.

When the firing has been bad, the ceramist sees weeks of work lost in the cracked and broken pots that come from the kiln. The pieces that can be saved may only be enough to pay for the next cycle of work, and even food may have to be purchased on credit. It can be a precarious way to earn a living, but no more so than agriculture, the other alternative that the people of Ráquira have to earn income.

Some people do not have a kiln and must sell their unfired production, or they may rent a kiln to do the firing themselves. Women who live alone frequently sell their unfired production rather than hire a man to fire it, and some older men do the same to avoid the rigors of firing. A young couple that does not yet have a kiln will usually rent a kiln or borrow one from other family members to do their own firing. The ideal is for each nuclear-family working unit to have its own kiln, and most do. Many workshops have two kilns, usually a large one for regular firings and a smaller one for urgent or overload firings.

Firing the Ráquira-built Mediterranean kiln is an unpredictable process for most potters because the kiln tends to fire too hot in some places, leaving other areas underfired and the pots unusable. But the most serious problem is breakage. Ten to 15 percent breakage rates are common, but a bad firing or a windy day may cause losses up to 50 percent. Breakage rates run slightly higher in country workshops, and that may be due to the cracks normally found in the walls of the traditional adobe kilns, which permit excessive drafts in the ware chamber that can crack pottery. Some believe that a densely packed kiln leads to more breakage, and they pack the kiln loosely to avoid it.

Fuel

Historically, most Mediterranean kilns have been fired with wood, but the sixteen new brick downdraft kilns are fired with coal. Of the eighty Mediterranean kilns in the town itself, most are fired with a mixture of wood and coal, but some are still fired solely with wood. Since the coal-fired kilns are large and the wood-fired kilns are small, much more coal is consumed in the town. In 1990 Emiro Gómez Contreras recorded the amounts of fuel consumed by the town workshops and found that 207 tons of coal were used per month compared with only 24 tons of wood (1990:44). He also estimated that a hundred Mediterranean kilns in the rural areas were being fired with an average of 600 kilos of wood per firing for a total of 60 tons of wood consumed per month (ibid.). The 84 tons of wood used each month in Ráquira for firings represent almost that number of trees being cut each month.

The firing of an average-sized Mediterranean kiln requires at least one well-formed tree (estimated at 500 to 600 kilos), but the large kilns may require twice as much. Hanna Bibliowicz (1978:15f) reports that twenty *cargas* (horseloads), which is approximately a hundred *arrobas* (or 1,125 kilos), are required to fire larger kilns. Andean oak (*roble*) is the preferred wood for firing because "it burns longer" and the firing can be completed with less wood, but it is the most expensive. Eucalyptus is the softest wood, generating fewer BTUs than other woods, and it is the least expensive. The other woods fall in between, and each is preferred by some potters for its cost or proximity.

The Spanish Mediterranean-type kiln requires two or three times as much fuel to fire the same amount of pottery as does the precolumbian open-air firing. Thick, mature tree trunks and branches are required for the slower fire needed to heat this heavy kiln, and the larger trees that are cut down for this style firing take longer to replace. The result has been the denuding of the tree cover around town, and after centuries of firing kilns with wood, the landscape of the region is barren and eroded. Wood is now scarce and expensive. Since Colombia has extensive deposits of coal, which is much cheaper than wood, the economic incentive is to switch to coal. By 1980 Ráquira men potters needed greater amounts of fuel because of the rapid expansion in production, but at the same time the limited wood resources were becoming more scarce. As a result, they began

Three kilns of the Reyes family workshop. Many families have two kilns (one large and one small), but the Néstor Reyes family, located just outside of town, has three. This permits the family to fire the kiln that is the best size for the amount of work they have. The kilns are built of adobe and covered with pottery shards to protect them from the rain. The tops are closed in a domed shape that terminates in the chimney funnel, which makes them similar to the Spanish beehive (*colmena*) shaped kilns.

switching to coal. Although the rapid success of the new fuel led many people to adopt it, wood is still used by many to preheat the firebox and kiln, which allows the coal to burn more efficiently. Ráquira kilns are always fired in oxidation (a rich flow of oxygen into the combustion chamber), and as a result very few have dampers or any system to control draft.

By 1988 air pollution and health problems had become critical in the town as a result of the increased prevalence of coal firing, and the town council prohibited the construction of any more coal-fired kilns within the city limits (Acuerdo 023 of 1988, Consejo Municipal). Potters who want to build the larger coal-fired kilns now have to do so in one of the rural districts outside of town. In 1995 Artesanías de Colombia was experimenting with a version of the downdraft coal kiln designed to reduce air pollution, but the cleaning mechanisms interfered with the draft, causing it to malfunction. A new design has been developed in consultation with Ecocarbón, a Colombian agency established to encourage the use of coal, and the projections indicated that it could dramatically reduce air pollution.

Kilns

Four types of kilns are normally used in the township of Ráquira: the Mediterranean updraft kiln, beehive kiln, domed downdraft kiln, and electric kiln. In addition to these, open-air firings still occur in some scattered areas in the region surrounding Ráquira. The Mediterranean kiln is the traditional one used in rural areas and smaller town workshops, while the domed downdraft model is the kiln of choice for the factory workshops. The seventy-six workshops in the town itself have a total of 111 kilns, a average of 1.46 kilns per workshop. In fact, thirty-five of the seventy-six workshops have a second, usually smaller, kiln for specialized firings. In some cases it is an old kiln that has been kept in case it is needed after the family has built a new one.

Almost three-quarters of the kilns in town are Mediterranean-type updraft kilns (eighty, or 72 percent), and all of the rural kilns are of this type. The Mediterranean kilns and beehive kilns are usually built of adobe, but the new domed downdraft kilns are always made of brick. Sixteen (14 percent) of the town kilns are of the new downdraft design. Fourteen (13 percent) of town families have electric kilns, primarily for the "fine" glazed ceramics. Although most town kilns are of a traditional Mediterranean design, over one-quarter of them represent some innovation in design and fuel.

The type of kiln used has a direct relationship to the gender of the potter, his or her place of residence, and the socioeconomic level of the workshop. The kilns that represent technological innovations (the domed downdraft kiln and the electric kilns) are regarded locally as having the highest status, and both are used to fire men's work. The Mediterranean kiln, beehive kiln, and the open-air firing are used primarily to fire women's work, and they have the lowest status.

Each type of kiln also represents different historical periods in the community. The domed downdraft kilns and electric kilns are innovations of the last two decades. They were introduced by Artesanías de Colombia and represent the industrialization of Ráquira ceramics. The former is used almost exclusively for firing industrial loads of planters, and the latter is used for firing glazed tableware and other small speciality items. These two kilns are state-of-the-art technology for Ráquira in the 1990s. They signify substantial capital investment, and they are found in family and industrial workshops run by men.

Colonial Spanish technology is represented by the Mediterranean kiln and the beehive kiln, which were introduced shortly after the Conquest (Therrien 1991:71). Until recently the Mediterranean kiln was the standard for kiln technology in the region, but today it is used in family workshops that have low capital investments, low productivity, and middle to lower levels of income. The oldest firing technology in the community is open-air firing, which represents prehispanic influences preserved by women potters in remote rural areas, and it is associated with a minimal level of capital investment and the lowest levels of productivity and income.

Mediterranean Kiln

The kiln used by most family workshops has been the Spanish-styled, Mediterranean updraft kiln. It is divided into two chambers, the lower one being the firebox, which is separated from the upper ware chamber by a brick grillwork floor. The fire is pulled directly up through the ware chamber and vented through a short rooftop chimney. This style of kiln can be traced back to Roman models (Lister and Lister, 1987:14), and it is the same as the basic Middle Eastern model used in Egypt and Iran (ibid.:51). This kiln has also been used in Spain since the Moorish period (ibid.:52), and in the areas of strongest Spanish influence in Latin America (P. Arnold 1991:54; Litto 1976:136, 139). Louana Lackey describes an open-topped cylindrical kiln used in precolumbian Mexico, which she calls a "Mediterranean" kiln (1989:119), but that type of open-top kiln is not used in Ráquira. The term "Mediterranean" is used here to refer to the Spanish-Muslim design of an enclosed kiln.

There are many variations on the size and shape of the traditional kiln. Although most are cylindrical, they may also be square or domed, and these are the same three shapes used in Spanish versions of this kiln (Lister and Lister 1987:51). The design of Mediterranean kilns has never been very exact, and people have continual problems with such things as the weakness of the brick grillwork floors, uneven temperatures within the kiln, insufficient draft, and the lack of a system to control the draft. Philip J. Arnold III reported similar problems with Mediterranean kilns among potters in Las Tuxtlas, Mexico (1991:54).

A survey of forty-two rural workshops by Artesanías de Colombia identified sixty-one Mediterranean kilns; most were fired with wood, although some used a mixture of wood and coal. Fifty-nine were cylinder-shaped Mediterranean-type kilns, and two were domed versions called beehive (*colmena*) kilns (Bonilla et al. 1992:52ff), which are used in the more remote rural areas. Almost all (97 percent) of the rural kilns are of the Mediterranean type, and most are built with adobe and fired with wood. Cultural change in the choice of fuel is indicated by the 40 percent of potters who have begun to use coal (ibid.:53, 57). Economic reasons largely account for this change, but potters sometimes also mention the ecological advantages of protecting the remaining trees.

The building technique of combining adobe, brick, and rock to make the kiln wall is similar to the traditional Spanish practice in Andalusia (Lister and Lister 1987:51). Since adobe blocks are usually homemade and represent little or no cost, a low-income potter may prefer using them to buying bricks. The dry adobe building blocks are mortared together with a wet adobe and clay mixture, which later dries to form a continuous seal. The outside wall may be plastered with the same mixture. Adobe has also been the traditional building material for houses, but, as with kilns, brick is now the preferred material for those who can afford it. The cost of bricks and cement for a small traditional kiln is about $250.00 U.S.; the labor to construct the kiln represents an additional expense. Ordinary red bricks and common portland-type cement are used, and the latter is mixed with molasses to enable it to withstand heat and to minimize cracking. The Mediterranean kiln is normally built out of doors, and it is covered with a brick tile roof to protect it from the rain. Keeping it dry is important because wet kiln walls slow down the firing and require more fuel.

Many people know how to build kilns, but there are specialists, normally older man, whom potters consult or contract to build them. Both levels of the kiln consist of arches, following the general design of the original Roman versions. The lower level is the firebox and has a vaulted arch roof that is composed of five or six parallel arches, which are separated by thirty to forty centimeters each. A brick gridwork is laid on top of these arches to make the floor of the ware chamber, which is on top. Both the arches and the floor that covers them are anchored in the outside walls of the kiln for stability. The upper-level ware chamber is built the same way, as a series of arches.

The measurements of the interior diameter and height and the chimney height of the Mediterranean kiln indicate the sizes commonly built. Eighty-four percent are under two meters in diameter and height (Bonilla et al. 1992:12–13). In the smaller kilns the height is often greater than the diameter, creating a high dome profile in the ware chamber. The chimneys of the Mediterranean kilns are short, all under one meter (ibid.), with the shortest no more than a minimal exhaust flue (.20 cm). Forty-eight (96 percent) have no system to control the draft in the kiln (ibid.:15).

Open-Air Firings

Some rural women potters near Sáchica, Sutamarchán, Tuaté, and other places have continued doing open-air firings until recently. This common prehispanic indigenous firing technique has been preserved by the women, much in the same way they have preserved traditional pot-making techniques. In the open-air firing, pots are laid out on the ground, with the larger ones placed on the bottom to form a circle and smaller pots placed in layers on top of these to form a dome-shaped pile. Smaller pieces may be placed inside larger ones or between pots. Wood is inserted between the pots on the ground and over the entire pile. Large pot shards or pieces of sheet metal are placed on top of everything to enclose the fire and retain the heat during the firing. This firing is fast, only an hour or two depending on the size of the pottery pile and the amount of wood. By the third hour a pot may be cool enough to be taken out of the pile. This fast firing process and exposure to drafts requires a heavily tempered clay body.

Electric Kilns

Electric kilns are used primarily for glazed dinnerware produced by men in town workshops. This type of kiln was introduced by the Artesanías de Colombia center in the early 1970s, and two potters bought them at that time through a special financing program sponsored by the center (Mora 1974:76), and today fourteen workshops have them. The Museo de Artes y Tradiciones Populares also had a technical-assistance program in Ráquira for a number of years that fired small glazed items like candlesticks in electric kilns.

Pieces to be glazed are first fired in a low-temperature bisque firing, which hardens the piece and facilitates the later application and absorption of the liquid glaze. The bisque firing lasts about six hours and reaches approximately eight hundred degrees centigrade. A second firing of the glazed pieces reaches a thousand degrees centigrade, and commercial kiln shelves are used to separate the pieces for this firing. Although electric kilns solve many of the problems of underfiring and hot and cold spots that Ráquira potters have always experienced with the Mediterranean kiln, their adoption has been slow because they are expensive to buy and operate. Urban buyers see Ráquira ceramics as an inexpensive country craft, and few are willing to pay the higher prices required for glazed ware fired with electricity.

Dome-shaped Downdraft Kiln

The industrial-sized, dome-shaped downdraft kiln came into common use in the 1980s and is used in the sixteen largest town workshops, all of which are run by men. It is fired with coal contained in four fireboxes, which are evenly distributed around the outside floor of the kiln. The design of this

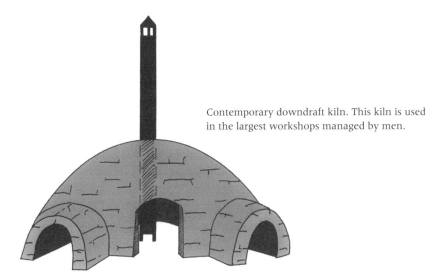

Contemporary downdraft kiln. This kiln is used in the largest workshops managed by men.

kiln permits a much larger ware chamber, greater control over temperature and higher kiln temperatures, and more even firings than the traditional Mediterranean kiln.

The dome is built with common red bricks, and a one-half-inch steel cable is bound around the dome about one meter above the ground to stabilize it. The height of the chimney depends on the size of the kiln, but it can range from seven to ten meters high. Tall chimneys are necessary at this altitude to create the proper draft to fire the kiln. The grating in the fire boxes is made of one-meter-long sections of train rails, placed closely together (five centimeters apart). There is little or no control over the amount of air entering the fireboxes, and potters evaluate the progress of the firing by the fire in the box and the smoke from the chimney.

Most domed downdraft kilns are approximately four meters in diameter, although a few are five meters, and the interior height at the peak of the dome ranges from 1.9 meters to 2.2 meters. Since the diameter of these kilns is considerably greater than the height, they appear to be the top quarter section of a larger sphere. It is a broad dome with a long, slow slope, in contrast to the higher-pitched domes associated with the older, beehive-shaped Mediterranean design. The broad, domed shape of these kilns makes it impractical to built a roof onto the kiln itself, as is done with the Mediterranean kilns, so they are built under roofed areas to keep them dry. These kilns symbolize the change in Ráquira from village craft pottery to the incipient industrialization of pottery.

Men, Technology, and Change in Ráquira

Technology is the responsibility of men in Ráquira, according to the cultural construction of gender, and they have used their position in recent decades to transform the technology of pottery production in this town. While they have retained some elements of the centuries-old tradition to which they are heir, they have abandoned many others. From the colonial period to the present, technological change has been the hallmark of men's involvement in Ráquira ceramics. The changes of recent decades form part of the capital-intensive effort of men to industrialize pottery making in order to increase productivity, volume of sales, and profits. These technological changes have opened a new era in Ráquira ceramics, making it much more profitable than it had been in the past.

9

Economics and Marketing

Both women and men potters in Ráquira are concerned about the economics of making and marketing their craft. For women, ceramics is a part-time, noninvasive occupation practiced as a supplement to their other domestic activities. They invest little in the craft, and their profits are minimal. On the other hand, men use ceramics as a profit-making occupation, and they dedicate full time to the craft and invest as much capital as is possible for the family. Young men with no capital are usually hired workers, but older men who do have capital invest in their own workshops and are capitalists.

Domestic versus Corporate Economics

The pottery-making families of Ráquira are peasant farmers, rural proletarian workers, and small-town entrepreneurs, and they can be divided into two groups, based on their orientation toward the market economy. Women potters engage in the production of ceramics to supplement family needs, and they do so in conjunction with other domestic responsibilities. In contrast, the men of Ráquira adopt ceramics as an occupation when they see that it is economically viable, and their market orientation to the craft is to maximize income and profits. Nola Reinhardt recognized these two orientations—namely, "subsistence household production" and "market-oriented production" (1988:19)—in her study of small farmers in Colombia, which indicates that the patterns apparent in Ráquira are found among other rural populations in the country.

Peasant Society and Economy Theory

In the last half of the twentieth century, anthropologists have made a number of attempts to explain the special characteristics of the subsistence household production associated with peasant farmers and craftspeople in Latin America, spawning an extensive literature on these groups (Mintz

1979; Roseberry 1995; Wolf 1955, 1979). From the 1950s through the 1970s, the prominent theories explaining the economic behavior of small farmers and rural craftspeople were based on the concepts of culture or cognition (that is, mindset).

George Foster made the first in-depth ethnographic study of a village potter community in Latin America in Tzintzuntzan, Mexico (1967), and he explained economic behavior with the "image of the limited good." According to his interpretation, peasant farmers and potters see all of the desirable things in life (land, wealth, health) as existing in finite quantities that are insufficient to meet the minimal needs of the community. Furthermore, there is no way that the supply of good can be increased, which means that the individual or family can increase their wealth only at the expense of others in the community (ibid.:123–24). In this system, economic success is a result of fate or luck, and it has little or nothing to do with hard work, energy, and thrift. In fact, Foster confirms that, in a subsistence economy, hard work does not create greater wealth, nor is there any surplus with which a person can be thrifty (ibid.:150). According to the concept of the limited good, the community's economy is like a pie with a finite number of pieces, so that if one person becomes wealthier, he or she is in essence taking the piece of someone else, which leads to envy and hostility (Duncan 1975a:86).

In her study of small farmers and potters in the township of Amatenango de Valle, Mexico, June Nash goes beyond Foster to say that the motor that drives economic change in the community is consumer behavior (1985:68). Thus, people make adaptations in traditional production as a way to increase their incomes and pay for attractive new consumer goods. This change in behavior is a conscious choice to improve personal standards of living. Although the shift toward acquiring consumer goods from external markets changes the material good available to people, it does not change the pattern of community life (ibid.:96). This suggests that the essential patterns of community continue intact although the kinds of pottery made and the marketing strategies change, so Nash perceives a process of economic change that Foster did not see.

According to Nash, traditional pottery production did not lead to the accumulation of wealth nor to the formation of social classes. Potters understood that their work would permit them to survive at their existing level of poverty, but it was not expected to be a means of accumulating wealth. Any surplus that was produced was absorbed into the ritual and ceremonial obligations of the community, which served to maintain its economic and social balance. Increased income to acquire the new consumer goods had to come through wage labor rather than traditional production practices (1985:71). The changes in pottery making observed in Ráquira are, in fact, tied to the desire to increase income and improve the economic well-being of the family, as suggested by Nash.

However, men and women in Ráquira have a different approach to increasing income. While men's economic choices have a more unidimensional orientation toward maximizing profits, women's choices are more complex. They are required to balance monetary considerations with the social reproduction of the family, most notably their responsibilities for nurturing and caring for children, spouses, and older parents. This balancing act is explained by the theory of household economics, as developed by Gudeman (1986), Gudeman and Rivera (1990), Annis (1987), and Chayanov (1966).

Family and Household Economic Theory

Based on research in Colombia, Stephen Gudeman and Alberto Rivera suggest that the rural family economy is a household economy in which people understand that the earth is the source of strength and that it is given by the supernatural. The house is the center of material culture, and it is the metaphor for the household economy. Good management of the family economy means that after the required expenditures are made, there will be a surplus for other uses. The house is not expected to make money but rather to make savings, in contrast to the corporation, which is intended to make a profit (1990:2).

In the household economy, people save and hoard excess capital, while in the corporate economy people invest more than they hoard (Gudeman and Rivera 1990:161). Shelton Annis (1987:61) describes a similar pattern of economic thinking among Mayan small farmers and artisans, in which economic decisions are based on considerations of household need rather than the maximum possible yield. These studies suggest that one pattern of economic decision making among Latin American small farmers and artisans emphasizes the maintenance of the family group more than the attainment of maximum economic benefits.

Earlier research by A. V. Chayanov in Russia also pointed out that much of the economic behavior of rural families was not market oriented. His work among peasant farmers suggested that the motive of their economic decisions is to produce a livelihood for the family rather than to earn a profit. His model of peasant economic behavior suggests a self-replicating family farm, limited to subsistence consumption and production goals. The purpose of production is qualitative (to meet the family's needs) rather than quantitative (to achieve the highest production possible) (1966:4f). Chayanov also suggests that people in the peasant economy overexploit themselves to achieve subsistence incomes, accepting lower than minimum-wage returns on their work. In situations of economic shortage, families increase their workloads to maintain subsistence income levels, even though this means accepting reduced remuneration for their work (ibid.:113). He concludes that the peasant family economy would not necessarily be replaced by the corporate-oriented economy, but that the latter could economically dominate the peasant family (ibid.:257ff).

Chayanov sees the role of crafts as being a "residual activity" within the peasant farm economy that is undertaken when there is a shortage of land or some other impediment to farming (1966:5). He also suggests that craft production increases when there are more consumers than producers in the family. He assumes that men are the producers and women and children the consumers, and that the men will have to produce more to support the women and children. In contrast to Chayanov's expectation, June Nash (1993:137) points out that when women are the producers, craft production decreases when there are more consumers (that is, women and children) because her domestic responsibilities increase and leave her less time for producing pottery.

The family-livelihood economic models developed in the work of Gudeman and Rivera, Annis, and Chayanov describe the economic behavior of Ráquira women and their understanding of saving and subsisting, in contrast to the men's approach of investing and expanding. Both approaches to economics play important roles in Ráquira. On one hand, men have pushed the craft toward the technological changes that have made it more economically productive, but on the other, women have preserved a balance between economics and the social reproduction of the family.

Ceramics as Domestic Economy among Women Potters

The distinction between "house" and corporate models of economic decision making can be seen between the women potters of rural Ráquira and the men potters of the town. Women potters make minimal investments in their production and save their profits for household (that is, family) needs, similar to the "house economy" models suggested by Gudeman and Chayanov. Although their profits are limited, they do not make investments in infrastructure or equipment that would be seen as taking money away from the family. For them, making pottery is not a business, and it should not interfere with the family's space in the house, nor should it absorb the earnings that are intended for the family.

In the domestic-economy orientation of Ráquira women potters, the purpose of making pottery is not to maximize profits but rather to provide for the family. For the woman it is another nurturing activity akin to preparing meals and washing clothes. As an economic process, it is more about domestic family issues than market issues. Although the rural-style women potters do not strive to maximize their profits and accumulate capital, they are concerned to earn money to meet the economic needs of their families. In contrast, the men potters in the town of Ráquira have a "capitalist" orientation to investing the family's money in the means of production as a way to increase their income. The capital that remains after expenses have been covered is invested in primary materials or infrastructure for the purpose of expanding the family workshop or business.

Gender and Socioeconomic Hierarchy

Socioeconomic status in Ráquira ceramics correlates with the gender and economic orientation of the potter. In male-dominated societies generally, women's work does not have as much prestige as men's (Deere 1990:286; Ehlers 1990:20; Moore 1988:14), and that holds true in Ráquira. The "corporate" orientation of the men is granted high social status because it is more successful economically, while in contrast the women's orientation to the domestic economy has low status. The low valuation of women's hand-built pottery combined with their low productivity results in low incomes.

In general, a woman's income declines if she is of the older generation or if she produces styles, such as cooking pots, that have traditional indigenous associations. Men who work in ceramics have higher incomes, are generally younger, and produce a style of work oriented toward urban markets. Women potters from rural Ráquira earn incomes that are below the minimum wage, while the men potters in town may earn three times that amount or more. Although crafts are the most consistent source of income for rural women in much of Latin America, that income is usually the lowest that is earned in the local economy.

As goods are produced in society, value is added to them from various sources, especially labor, technology and capital investment, and social prestige. However, for most village potters the only value that is added to their production is that of their labor. Since women potters have minimal capital investment in their production techniques, that adds little to the value of their pots, and their low social status does not add value.

In addition to gender, the social and economic status of women's work in Ráquira is measured by residence, ethnicity, and generation. Women potters live in rural areas, and people who are rural and poor in Colombia are considered uneducated and unsophisticated by the larger society. Women potters also use indigenous handicraft techniques, which are negatively valued because they are associated with the non-European cultures of Colombia. Generation is a negative factor because many women potters are older and they make traditional rural-style pottery, which does not have the prestige of the newer styles made by the younger generation. These factors combine to reduce the social and economic status of women and to devalue their work, which in turn limits their income so that women actually earn less than the minimum wage.

The negative social status of pottery production is accepted by many potters themselves, who consider their craft a dirty, unpleasant occupation. This negative self-perception has also been reported by George Foster in Tzintzuntzan, Mexico, as well as for other groups cross-culturally (Foster 1967:46–47). Even though potters are hard workers, have low overhead, and are highly productive (all ingredients of success in the corporate world), the economy of village ceramics yields low returns, and this is partially due to the low market valuation of their craft. However, despite these negative attitudes, the modest economic rewards are sufficient to make their occupation worthwhile for many. Gonzalo Cárdenas of the *vereda* Resguardo Occidental remarked, "Pottery is a dirty occupation, but it does give enough money to buy soap to clean up."

To offset the low rates of remuneration they receive for their work, women frequently draw upon the unpaid labor of their children and other family members in order to increase the value of their production. The economic logic of rural women potters is to minimize expenditures (by making no capital investments in pottery production), expand labor (work as many hours as possible and enlist the assistance of family members), and accept subsistence-level incomes (in the absence of alternatives)— strategies that are similar to the models described by Chayanov (1966:4f) and Gudeman and Rivera (1990:2).

In contrast, the economic logic of the men emphasizes increasing investment and technical capacity with the expectation that it will lead to expanded production and income, as well as high socioeconomic status. A social hierarchy is recognized within the community according to the market valuation of one's product, one's level of investments, the extent to which one employs technical versus manual methods of production, and one's income. Since the women's rural workshops have low investments and low to moderate returns, their work has lower status locally. Although women potters recognize the higher social and economic status of the men's mass-production workshops, they are consistent in maintaining a traditional approach to making and selling pottery.

Marketing

Ráquira has a large, pluralistic pottery tradition with many marketing venues, each of which specializes in certain design styles. For example, the traditional cooking pots are sold in regional markets, while sculptural or mold-made market figures are sold to intermediaries for urban markets. Banks and other small ceramics are intended for tourists who visit the region, and factory-made planters go to city buyers. This plethora of styles and marketing venues also produces a hierarchy of incomes that correlates with the socioeconomic classes of potters.

Marketing Women's Domestic Pottery

Country pottery is typically distributed through two different marketing outlets: intermediaries and the local markets. When country pottery is sold to an intermediary, the man usually sells his wife's production; he may keep part or all of the profits himself. However, some rural women potters sell directly to intermediaries, which reduces the husband's role as seller and controller of the money. The man or woman may also sell part of the production in the local markets in the region, such as the one in Villa de Leyva. The woman does the direct market selling more frequently than the man, a situation commonly found among craftswomen in Latin America (Ehlers 1990:162). Some women prefer to sell their pottery in the weekly town markets since they do not have to pay a percentage to an intermediary nor give the money to the husband. However, the volume of sales in these open-air markets is limited and never comparable to the much larger orders that are made by intermediaries.

Preparing to go to market is also complicated for a rural potter, beginning with the problem of distances. She may live an hour's walk from the nearest road, and the first obstacle is to transport the pottery from the house to the road to catch a ride to the market. If the family has a horse or donkey, it will carry the load of pots; otherwise, the man of the house may have to carry the ceramics on his back in seemingly unwieldy loads weighing up to a hundred pounds. The pottery is wrapped in rope-mesh nets for transportation, and ferns and other leaves are placed between the pots to minimize breakage. None of these families own cars, so they stack their ceramics at the side of the narrow dirt road and wait for a ride into town. The few vehicles that travel these country roads are mostly trucks hauling goods to or from town for hire. On a market day a truck will pass through the *vereda* on a prearranged schedule to pick up the people going to the market. Once a truck arrives, the pots are loaded into the back, and the potter climbs on to ride alongside the ceramics. The truck gradually fills with agricultural produce, pottery, and people going to the market. At the end of the market day the truck returns with the people and their purchases and unsold goods.

The country markets start at 6:00 A.M., and the women who sell their pottery in the market have to leave their houses as early as 2:00 or 3:00 A.M. to arrive on time. Some of the women have relatives or godparents who live in the town, and they may arrive the day before and spend the night with them in order to be at the market early enough to get a good position. Sometimes the potter will store her production at the house of the relative or godparent and let them sell it for her.

Pots wrapped for shipment to market. The traditional potter wraps her pots for market in straw or ferns and bundles them together in a rope net. These bundles have been brought in from the countryside and left in front of the house of a friend or relative to await transportation to market.

Pottery market in Villa de Leyva. Traditional pottery from the Ráquira area is sold in the Villa de Leyva market along with baskets and other products from the region. Women from this region typically dress in black shawls, as seen here. Both men and women wear fedora-type hats to protect them from the intensity of the sun at this altitude and latitude.

Villa de Leyva Market

Villa de Leyva, a neighboring town, has one of the most important regional markets. Saturday is market day, and the trucks that bring the foodstuffs, pottery, and other goods sold here begin arriving between 4:00 and 5:00 A.M. The marketplace is a large, open field up the hill from the main plaza of this colonial town, which has changed little over the last four hundred years. All of the buildings around the plaza and in the town retain the Spanish colonial-style architecture, with thick whitewashed walls and red tile roofs. The large town plaza is the size of four city blocks, and the plaza and the streets are paved with cobblestones. Along the upper side of the plaza is the simple, squat country church with its stubby bell tower. Although the population of the town is primarily made up of rural and small-town people, some people from Bogotá also have vacation houses there.

As the trucks reach the marketplace and begin unloading, the sellers select a place to spread out their goods. The sellers of dry goods, such as pottery, tools, and clothes, occupy the outer perimeter of the market ground, along the sides and lower end. Meat, vegetables, and fruits are sold in the center of the market. Canopies are set up with tables and benches along the upper side of the market for outdoor lunch stands, and potatoes, meat, and corn on the cob are cooked for the standard Boyacá lunch. From 6:00 A.M. to early afternoon, the townspeople come with baskets and bags to buy their week's supply of food, and weekend tourists from Bogotá and other cities visit to see an example of the classic small-town market day. The pottery that is sold here is primarily functional, and the buyers are mostly farmers from nearby communities. They buy cooking pots in various sizes and storage pots for holding water, guarapo *(the sugar-cane drink), or* chicha *(the corn drink), and they also buy jugs that will be used for serving the same drinks.*

➤ ◆

Even when the woman potter sells her own pieces in the market to avoid paying a percentage to the intermediary, the prices are only slightly above the subsistence level. In the market she can sell a large cooking pot for five dollars, which is double what she would have received from the intermediary but still half of what the piece will go for in the city. Most of these pots are bought by low-income farmers who cannot pay higher prices, but if a city person from Bogotá expresses interest in a pot, a slightly higher price will be asked. If the woman's pottery has not sold by the end of the day, she will have to pack up what remains to take home; some women will lower their prices at that point in hopes of selling the last pieces.

The Villa de Leyva market, like the other markets in the region, permits the traditional woman potter from Ráquira to sell her production for the best price that the local economy can support. At the same time that it gives her some degree of independence from the intermediaries, it also provides a rich social environment in which she can visit with friends and relatives from other towns. The market's cornucopia of pottery, hand-woven, poncho-like *ruanas,* and homemade aprons, sandals, and baskets represent the home-based economy of the craftswomen from this region.

Men and Intermediaries

Today most ceramics are sold by the man of the family to an intermediary who is also a man, which means that the negotiations are almost always done man to man. Male control of wholesale businesses is common in other Latin American craft traditions as well (Ehlers 1990:162). The intermediary usually picks the work up at the workshop and resells it in Bogotá or another city. The potter typically receives only one-fourth of the final sales price of a pot. The primary complaints of the potters about this system is that they cannot negotiate prices, and that the potter is forced to accept the price set by the intermediaries.

A woman is contemplating buying a toasting pan (*arepero*), and beside her is a basket of onions that she has already bought. She is wearing a traditional women's shawl, and the man in front of her wears a *ruana* (a Colombian-style, open-front wool poncho).

It is a common practice for the intermediary to pay the potter only after the pottery has been resold. That means that the potter may have to wait weeks or even months after a sale is made before receiving final payment, which creates serious cash-flow problems. During that time the money may lose 5 to 7 percent of its original value in the inflationary economy of Colombia, and the ceramist has no capital with which to work. As a result, most family workshops are usually cash starved.

Women potters can wait through these delays because the basic subsistence of the family comes from the food produced on the farm, and their income is considered supplemental. However, for the husband-wife workshops, in which the man works along with the woman in the production, these delays can create serious financial problems. They are the ones who most complain about the intermediary system being prejudicial to them and forcing the family to live in precarious circumstances.

Most Ráquira potters sell their work through traditional godfather-type relationships in which the parties are loyal and support each other, which can lead to a debt-patronage system. A potter contributes his or her labor and production, and the intermediary consistently buys from that potter,

Loading area for traditional pots and planters that will be shipped to urban markets. A truckload of ferns is being unloaded; the ferns will be used to repack the truck with pottery.

guaranteeing his or her income, and may even supply raw materials on credit. So the potter may be in debt to the intermediary for raw materials, and the intermediary may delay paying for the last load of pottery, creating a cycle that guarantees the dependency of the potter. In this way, intermediaries can maintain potters hooked in dependent economic relationships for long periods of time. More than one-third of the town workshops still choose to sell to one primary intermediary, even though they have marketing leverage because of their location in town and could negotiate between intermediaries. They prefer the *patrón* system because it guarantees commitment and sales, even though the profit margins are less.

Don Aristóbolo Rodríguez and the Factory Owners

The dominant intermediary is Don Aristóbolo Rodríguez, who controls close to half of the local market and has developed a godfather-like relationship with many women potters and some husband-wife workshops. He arranges with them to deliver dump-truck loads of clay and coal, and in turn they sell to him most or all of their production. He dominates the market in such a way that he can solve almost any business problem that a pottery family has, but that power also means that potters have little

Table 9.1. Sale of Ceramics

Channel	Urban		Rural	
	No. of workshops	%	No. of workshops	%
One intermediary	30	39.47	29	69.05
Multiple intermediaries	37	48.68	13	30.95
Direct sales	9	11.84	0	00
Totals	76	99.99	42	100.00

Source: Bonilla et al. 1992:81

leverage to negotiate with him. When he began as an intermediary, he had one small truck that he used to visit every rural district around Ráquira buying ceramics from family workshops. Now he has thirteen trucks with which to deliver raw materials, buy pottery, and ship it to town markets. Largest of his fleet is a tractor-trailer truck, which he uses to ship to Bogotá and other cities.

He also owns one of the planter factories, and the marketing networks through which he sells planters can also be used for reselling the pottery he buys as an intermediary. The owners of the other large town work-shops and factories can negotiate special arrangements with intermediaries because of the larger volume of their orders. They work on a contract system in which they produce orders of thousands of pieces according to a preset price schedule and delivery date. They can demand half of the contract price at the time the order is placed, with the balance due on delivery. In contrast, the rural family workshops produce the pieces and then must find buyers after they are made. So the small family workshops are at a financial disadvantage in relation to the larger businesses because they cannot always predict the final selling price of their pieces.

The large volume of their work permits the planter factories to lower their production costs and accept lower profit margins per piece. This forces the smaller family-workshop potters to lower their prices as well, which in turn requires them to work harder to maintain their incomes, essentially making them poorer. They survive by accepting the subsistence-level lifestyle permitted by their marginal profits. Many small workshops focus on the niche markets for specialty pieces, such as nativity scenes, banks, or bells to avoid competing with the factories in the broader market for planters.

Town Marketing Venues

Ráquira has become a tourist center for crafts, and entering one of the crafts stores along the main street going into Ráquira today, the tourist can find international crafts from various Latin American countries. Four-teen crafts stores are located in the space of two blocks, all but one in houses converted to commercial use. They can be divided into four kinds of businesses.

1. Crafts warehouse (one). Todo Ráquira (All Ráquira) is a ware-housing operation, the Sam's Club of Ráquira ceramics, but other regional crafts, including basketry and weaving, are also sold there. Don Aristóbolo Rodríguez is the owner. The front of Todo Ráquira is a house with some twelve meters of street front, which is large by Ráquira standards. In the front display room smaller ceramic pieces are shown, including strings of hanging bells, small pots, and fig-ures. Behind the house and extending through the block to the next street is an open-sided warehouse containing hundreds of planters, traditional pots, and the newer decorative ware made with tradi-tional techniques, such as the large *múcuras,* all stacked to heights of two meters.

Todo Ráquira controls much of the national market for Ráquira ceramics, and it has also created an international market, exporting container loads of fifteen hundred or more pieces to the United States, Israel, Aruba, and elsewhere. The exports typically consist of larger pieces of traditional pottery, mostly closed-vessel shapes such as cook-ing pots, pitchers, and bottles. The municipal government has im-posed a tax of 25,000 pesos ($31.25 U.S.) on each container that is shipped from Ráquira and another tax on each load of clay taken from the mines. Both taxes directly affect the multiple businesses of Don Aristóbolo. Teresa Suárez, manager of the Todo Ráquira store, complained that the taxes were excessive and that they were hurt-ing sales. But the dominant position of Aristóbolo Rodríguez in the Ráquira economy makes his businesses obvious targets for taxation.

2. Ceramic speciality shops (two). Across the street from Artesanías de Colombia are two businesses specializing in ceramics, including glazed and decorated wares. They also carry ceramics brought from other centers of production in the country. These shops specialize in table and household ceramics.

3. General crafts shops (eleven). Eleven general crafts shops carry less expensive items designed to appeal to the tourists visiting Ráquira.

Planters and traditional pottery are stacked in the warehouse of Todo Ráquira, waiting for shipment. Ferns used for packing material are piled to the right.

Craft shops are located along the two blocks of the street entering Ráquira from Tinjacá and Sutamarchán. Some potters with workshops on this street have their own showrooms. There are three craft shops in a row in this photograph, each selling basketry, weavings, and ceramics.

Patio of Artesanías de Colombia in Ráquira, with traditional pots in the foreground and planters in the background stacked and ready for purchase.

In 1995 the entrances to these shops were dominated by sets of hanging bells, which the customer had to push aside to enter. Inside hundreds of items of diverse crafts were displayed, including pottery, basketry, textiles, and wooden wares. These stores also sell imported merchandise, including textiles from Guatemala and Ecuador, ceramics from various parts of Colombia, as well as Ráquira basketry and ceramics. Curiously enough, Ráquira ceramics have a secondary role in these shops.

    4. The Artesanías de Colombia center (one). This center is the largest building along the main street entering town, and it includes a shop that sells ceramics, basketry, and weaving from the region. The shop carries Colombian "fine" craft ceramics, glazed tableware, including the better-glazed Ráquira pieces and dinnerware from Carmen de Viboral. The Artesanías de Colombia complex is an attractive contemporary building of colonial design. Its two stories are organized around a colonnaded central patio, and the largest and most dramatic pots for sale from the local potters are displayed around this patio. The center also includes a large production area equipped with electric wheels and both electric and diesel-fired kilns, and it offers workshops on glazes, claybodies, kilns, and marketing. The center promotes the marketing of traditional handcrafted pottery as well. The Museo de Artes y Tradiciones Populares is located in the center, and it includes examples of Ráquira ceramics from various periods throughout the twentieth century.

Cooperative Marketing

Although many Ráquira potters mention the inequities of the intermediary system, they have not been able to create effective communal or cooperative organizations to replace it. Nor have the marketing efforts of Artesanías de Colombia and the Museo de Artes y Tradiciones Populares been sufficiently successful to provide an alternative to the intermediaries. In 1994 another attempt was made at organizing a cooperative association among Ráquira potters, called the Asociación de Artesanos de Ráquira (Association of Ráquira Craftspeople), or ASOMUISCA. (The abbreviated name honors the Muiscas, the precolumbian people who lived in this area and who were the first to make pottery here.) Ángel Custodio Hernández of Artesanías de Colombia has been active in organizing the association, but its work has been hampered by a lack of economic resources. The association requested economic assistance from the mayor of Ráquira, in order to promote alternative marketing plans and direct selling arrangements with businesses in Bogotá and other cities. Although prior attempts at cooperative organizations have failed in the community, some think this attempt may be more successful.

Economics and Income

Ráquira potters complain that their incomes are lower than they should be, considering the long hours, harsh working conditions, and hard work their craft requires. Incomes vary widely, with traditional women potters earning the least and men production potters the most. Although rural women potters do not keep an exact accounting of their monthly expenses, they can be estimated from the cost of raw materials, which are clay, firewood, and coal. In 1995 prices, a dump-truck load of wood delivered to a rural workshop in the central *veredas,* where most of the ceramists live, cost 100,000 pesos ($125.00 U.S.). A load of coal cost 75,000 pesos ($94.00 U.S.). Both could be expected to last six months or longer. Each eight-ton load of clay cost 50,000 pesos ($62.50 U.S.) and would last approximately six months, depending on the potter's work schedule.

The costs for a woman's monthly work cycle (including fuel, clay, and hiring a man to do the firing) are estimated to be 40,000 pesos ($50.00 U.S.), and the value of the pots fired is estimated to be 100,000 pesos ($125.00 U.S.), which gives her a monthly profit from ceramics of approximately 60,000 pesos ($75.00 U.S.). If the rural potter has a husband or other male relative to fire the kiln for her, she can save the cost of hiring a man to do it.

The profits from figure making are greater than for traditional pottery. Javier Sierra Rodríguez has said that in a month's time he can complete a figure sixty centimeters high, which he sells for 80,000 pesos ($100.00 U.S.). He sells them as fast as they are made, giving him an income approximately equal to the minimum wage in Colombia, which is considered a good income. However, if he were a trained urban artist of a "European" or "good" social class, he could sell his figures for ten times more than he does.

The mold-made nativity sets and other figures made by Fabio Sierra sell for less, but he produces a large quantity of them, so he makes money on the volume of production. The nativity sets are Fabio's main source of income, and he sells them for 12,500 pesos ($15.63 U.S.) for a painted set, 8,000 pesos ($10.00 U.S.) for a slip-painted set, and 6,000 pesos ($7.50 U.S.) for a plain earthenware set. He also makes large, bare-breasted reclining mermaids about ninety centimeters long, a true fantasy figure for a young male craftsman in the isolated and conservative world of rural Boyacá. Like his nativity sets, these are intended for urban buyers; each one sells for 30,000 pesos ($37.50 U.S.).

Most of Fabio's income occurs in the October–December quarter of the year as people buy nativity scenes in preparation for Christmas. His income varies from year to year, but he makes and sells approximately 175 sets a year, mostly of the plain earthenware type (estimated at 100), half as many slip-painted sets (50), and half again as many painted sets (25). At that level of production, his annual income is 1,312,500 pesos ($1,640.63 U.S.) or 109,375 pesos ($136.72 U.S.) per month, giving him a gross income slightly higher than Javier's. He also has some occasional sales of mermaids and other figures during the year. However, he has far higher expenses than Javier in the purchase of plaster for molds, higher clay costs, and the salary of the person who paints the polychrome nativity sets, which means that his net income is probably much closer to that of his brother.

The industrialized mass-production techniques used in town increase the productivity and the earnings of potters. Within the community, people say that for every twenty-five pieces made by hand, a potter can make a hundred mold-made pieces or three hundred pieces on the wheel. A full-time salaried worker in one of the planter factories earns approximately $100 U.S. per month, plus full benefits (health insurance, sick leave, pension, vacations, annual bonus, and job security), which can increase the value of the salary by one-half. A contract worker with no benefits may earn from $100 to $175 U.S., according to the job. The high-wage star of

Table 9.2. Day-Wage Pay Scale in 1995

Job	Colombian Pesos	U.S. Dollars*
Trim and finish	4,000	5.00
Decorate	4,500	5.63
Mix clay	5,000	6.25
Press molder	6,500	8.13
Fire the kiln	9,000	11.25
Throw on wheel	12,000	15.00

*$1.00 U.S. equals 800 Col. pesos.

this system is the thrower making pots on the wheel, who can earn over $300 U.S. per month. The full-time family workshops can earn $500 U.S. per month or more. Figures were impossible to obtain from the large industrial operations, but local estimates indicate sales can range up to $10,000 U.S. per month.

From Country Markets to Tourist Boutiques

Selling the production is always the single biggest problem for a potter, and it is the most frequently identified problem by Ráquira ceramists. Traditionally, pottery was sold during the weekly market days in towns in the region (Fiori 1990:19). Potters would load the ceramics on a horse, mule, or ox for the trip to the market or, if necessary, they would carry them on their own backs. After the advent of the buses and trucks, people began traveling farther to sell their products, even to Bogotá.

By the late 1960s and early 1970s families with town workshops were selling their production from the front rooms of their houses. The Reyes Suárez family had the most important workshop and store on the main street, along with another workshop owned by the Rodrigo Lorenzo family. Both were located across the street from the Artesanías de Colombia complex, and they sold to the few day tourists who visited Ráquira.

Ráquira ceramics have always been sold in the Villa de Leyva market, but in the last few decades tourists have been coming to Ráquira itself in greater numbers to buy crafts. The growth in the tourist market compared to the traditional local markets has changed the commodity production, and new items have been introduced to appeal to a new set of buyers. As a result, in Ráquira the traditional production for local market days and the patron saint festivals has declined, and production has been reoriented to satisfy the tastes of urban buyers and their intermediaries. In this quiet revolution, intermediaries have assumed the primary role for marketing the production of family workshops.

These changes in the marketing infrastructure, combined with the increases in productive capacity of the workshops, have had a major influence in transforming Ráquira ceramics in the last half of the twentieth century. In the past, Ráquira pots were primarily sold in the local region, but today they are known and sold in most regions of Colombia and are exported internationally, even being available in fashionable boutiques in New York and other world cities.

Gender and Economics

As in the past, men continue to control the economics of Ráquira ceramics while women have marginal roles of subsistence craft producers. Men are the owners and managers of the most productive workshops and factories, and they are the intermediaries who buy from the small family workshop to resell in the city. Men set the prices to be paid in Ráquira, and they decide which work to buy from women potters and when they will be paid. Men profit from managing their own enterprises and from reselling the work of the family-based potters. Women are the underpaid, marginal producers who continue working in the craft because it is their only alternative source of income. In a context of marginal family agriculture, where there are no other economic options, women potters continue their traditional craft as a means of contributing to the well-being of their families.

10

Gender and Culture in
Ráquira Ceramics

In Ráquira gender defines the cultural construction of work and economic decision making for potters. The economic expansion of recent decades and the incorporation of small craft producers, such as the Ráquira potters, into global capitalism has made gender inequities starkly apparent. The combination of a culturally constructed gender ideology and the socially disinterested nature of incipient capitalism has led to a behavioral system that has marginalized women economically and socially. Gender has become the primary determinant of an individual's working style and position within the social hierarchy of Ráquira.

Men have been structurally favored by the expansion of capitalism in Ráquira because their full-time work patterns can be more easily adapted to maximizing profits than can women's part-time work patterns. Within the patrifocal society of the town, women are isolated into male-dominated nuclear families, and in the absence of any supportive matrifocal group to share their social-reproduction responsibilities, they are prohibited from dedicating the hours to pottery making that men do. The extended family support groups that do exist are patrifocal and support the men's working pattern.

Since Ráquira men are engaged in profit-oriented mass production, they generate more income than women do, but their support of the family is primarily monetary and unidimensional. In contrast, women who are potters dedicate so much of their time to the social reproduction of the family (caregiving, food, and cleanliness) that their economic production in ceramics is less than that of the men. Women balance family maintenance with profit. However, the success of capitalism in producing economic wealth for the men's workshops has overshadowed the importance of the balance maintained by women between economics and family.

Gender and Pottery Making Cross-Culturally

The division of labor by gender in Ráquira falls within cross-cultural norms as revealed in a study done by George P. Murdock and Caterina Provost. They compared 185 societies from every major world region, and they found that pottery is exclusively or predominantly a women's activity in 80 (43 percent) of these societies, exclusively or predominantly a men's activity in 19 (10 percent), and equally shared by males and females in 6 (3 percent). No pottery was made in 80 (43 percent) of the societies (1973:207).

Of the 105 societies in which pottery is made, women are the potters in three-quarters (76 percent) of them. In South America the percentage is even higher. There women are the potters in 89 percent of the cases, and pottery ranks with other tasks that constitute the core of women's work: spinning (90 percent), laundering (91 percent), water fetching (95 percent), cooking (92 percent), and preparation of vegetal food (96 percent) (Murdock and Provost 1973:209). In spite of the predominance of women in craft making cross-culturally, their role has been neglected in research until recently (Feldman 1991:77), and few ethnographies have discussed the issue of gender in pottery making (Foster 1967:41ff and Nash 1985:48ff).

The fifty tasks studied by Murdock and Provost were compared to establish the major correlations between gender and characteristics of the tasks, and they identified the following rules:

1. Raw materials. Men work with hard or tough materials, including metal, wood, stone, bone, horn, or shell. Women work with soft or pliable materials, which are used in the crafts of leather-working, basket making, mat making, loom weaving, pottery making, and spinning (1973:211–12).

2. Use. The gender that uses the finished craft product tends to be the one to make it (ibid.:212). In Ráquira, women prepare, cook, and store the food and water, so they are the ones who normally use traditional domestic pottery, which is made by women potters.

3. New technology. When a new, more complex technology replaces an older and simpler one, the new task is more consistently assigned to men (ibid.:212, 216). This can be observed in Ráquira with the introduction of molds and the pottery wheel.

4. Occupational specialization. When the division of labor becomes more complex, the more specialized tasks are assigned to men (ibid.:213). This can be observed in the specialized production tasks

of the town workshops in Ráquira, where 67 percent of the workers are men (Rojas 1983:9).

Based on the research in Ráquira and a review of economic change in other Latin America craft towns (Annis 1987; Ehlers 1990; Nash 1993), a fifth rule can be added to the four identified by Murdock and Provost.

5. Capitalist expansion. When the craft markets expand significantly beyond the local area, men introduce new technologies to expand production and assume top-down authority over ceramics making, marginalizing the role of women.

Murdock and Provost summarize the patterning of gender preferences in the following way. Across the 185 societies there is a masculine preference for tasks that call for great physical strength, or brief bursts of concentrated physical energy, or for travel distant from home (1973:211). There is a feminine advantage for work that is close to home, compatible with child care, and not dangerous. Women's tasks tend to be repetitive, and they can be performed in spite of interruptions and can be easily resumed. They are often tasks that require continuous, daily attention (ibid.). Pottery making as a domestic traditional craft fits this cross-cultural profile of women's work, but mass-produced ceramics based on complex technology and specialized labor fits the profile of men's work. The development of contrasting gender styles in ceramics in Ráquira coincides with the cross-cultural pattern described by Murdock and Provost.

Gender, Ethnicity, and Rural-Town Contrasts in Ráquira

Rural women have retained the domestic culture associated with the indigenous heritage, while men have adopted the Spanish elements of public culture. Following the Spanish model of gender ideology, men in town have become the primary economic support for the family. As the mestizo cultural system was being constructed as a synthesis of indigenous and Spanish influences, the present division of work and pottery styles based on gender came to exist in Boyacá and eventually in Ráquira. The cultural construction of gender has shaped craft, family organization, work, and economics.

Along with gender and ethnicity, place of residence in Ráquira is an important marker of cultural difference. Rural families are characterized by shared tasks and gender complementarity in agricultural and pottery work, in contrast to the hierarchical organization of families and workshops in town. The rural areas historically were the havens of the indigenous population, and in the mestizo culture of today, rural people retain more indigenous behaviors, in contrast to the greater influence of Spanish patterns in town behavior.

The contrast of gender cultures in ceramics has been described in other parts of Latin America, including Mexico (Hendry 1992:112) and Guatemala (Reina and Hill 1978:200). In each case, women use labor-intensive hand-building techniques with traditional technologies that represent minimal capital investment, and their production is part-time and interwoven with other domestic responsibilities. In contrast, men work full-time in the craft and use pottery wheels and other mass-production technology that represents a capital investment. There are exceptions to this general pattern, and recently some women have begun to work with the potter's wheel.

In each of these Latin American societies, there is a pattern of male dominance in the larger society that defines the gender division of labor, confining women to domestic pursuits and assigning economic primacy to the man along with authority in the public sphere. In the mestizo society that developed in Ráquira following the Conquest, this gender division came to characterize local behavior. As economic primacy and authority were confirmed for men in the emerging mestizo world, women consolidated their control of domestic matters and indigenous identity. There are, however, some communities where women and men have developed symmetrical roles.

Gender Culture and Ceramics

The women potters of Ráquira have to solve the same problems of the cultural definition of work, expected gender behaviors, and socioeconomic status as other women potters have to do in Colombia. The comparison of gender culture and ceramics with other communities shows that some have developed more symmetrical roles for women and men. The other traditional pottery community that has a comparable reputation of importance is La Chamba in the state of Tolima. The women and men of La Chamba have developed cultural arrangements for work, gender, and status that are very different from those of the potters in Ráquira. In La Chamba, women are the potters, and the role of men in pottery making is marginal. Women work in the domestic-economy workshop style; they procure (buy or gather) their own raw materials; and they sell their own production directly to intermediaries. Women prefer that men fire the kiln, but the firing of the ceramics does not give the man a claim to it, nor can he sell it. The basic style in La Chamba is traditional cooking pots, as it is in rural Ráquira. However, as the market has declined for those pots, La Chamba potters have developed new styles that are oriented toward the urban markets of Bogotá. They continue to use the same indigenous techniques of making ceramics by hand building that are traditional to their community. Women in La Chamba are frequently the head of the nuclear household, and some organize themselves into matrifocal residential clusters that are, in fact, women-oriented support groups. The women of La Chamba are more empowered than those of Ráquira, and they can have symmetrical relationships with their husbands.

The capitalist expansion of pottery making in recent decades has also been felt in La Chamba, but the local men have continued their agricultural work rather than becoming potters, nor have they challenged the domestic economic style of their wives' work. However, the women of La Chamba do have problems with the low remuneration that is offered to them as home-based producers who are at the bottom of national and global contracting and subcontracting chains, and they struggle with poverty because of the low return they receive for their work. Nevertheless, their struggle is with the larger economic system of global capitalism; their problems are more from poverty than from the cultural construction of gender and family, as it is in Ráquira.

The women of La Chamba have more control over their work and have relatively strong roles within their families, much as the rural women potters in Ráquira do. What explains the empowered roles of women in La Chamba and rural Ráquira, in contrast to the disempowered roles of town women in Ráquira? Ideological and cultural differences traceable to ethnic history, coupled with contrasting physical environments that lead to differing economic structures, help account for the different roles of these women.

First are the ideological and cultural differences, with the women of La Chamba and rural Ráquira following indigenous-derived behavioral patterns and the women of the town of Ráquira following Spanish-derived mestizo behaviors. The indigenous tradition of both towns has gender symmetry, whereas the Spanish tradition is patriarchal. The resulting differences in the cultural construction of gender ideology produce contrasting behaviors.

Second, there are marked differences between La Chamba and Ráquira in terms of physical setting and the resulting local economic structure. La Chamba is located in the rich agricultural valley of the Magdalena River. Although most of the good agricultural land is owned by large landowners, there is a constant demand for agriculture labor, and the men of La Chamba can earn cash income for most of the year. The economic situation has never forced them to cross the gender line in the division of labor to work in ceramics. In contrast, the agricultural lands around Ráquira are located on arid mountainsides that have low productivity. For many small farmers, their crops provide little more than subsistence-level living. This precarious agricultural base has prompted the men of Ráquira to cross the gender line and create a men's style of ceramics production.

The combination of ideology, environment, and economics creates a structure of behavior that has produced markedly different systems, one that permits women to have fuller, more active roles that confer social and self respect, and another that marginalizes women and limits their social participation. The cultural context of life for Ráquira women presents them with the tensions between indigenous Colombia and Spanish Colombia, and the unfavorable physical environment of their township offers them few economic opportunities. Within these limitations men and women strive to create a life for themselves and their children, using the possibilities at hand and the internal logic of their cultural assumptions.

Culture and Style in Crafts

The definition of gender ideology is cultural, and the internal logic of that ideology in turn shapes people's decisions about culturally appropriate work patterns. In craft behavior, such decisions mean the cultural construction of style, work organization, and marketing as well as other aspects of the craft. When a man stands in front of the potter's wheel or a woman puts a log of clay onto her turning bowl and begins to shape a piece, each draws upon collectively held community models in deciding how to proceed. But it is the individual potter who reconfirms each step in that model, either consciously or unconsciously.

In the specific case of Ráquira, ceramics reflect the gender ideology of the local community. Culture and ideology are not fixed and unified wholes, however. They exist in a state of flux as men and women potters choose and change their behaviors in relation to their society, physical habitat, and inherited traditions. Essentially, each potter in Ráquira behaves in terms of his or her own perspective on the shared social, environmental, and cultural contexts (a perspective especially influenced by gender and place of residence). Each one works with a learned heritage of ceramics appropriate to his or her gender, and each will use his or her cultural assumptions about shape, texture, color, line, and other technical concerns to make decisions about the crafting of ceramics. These considerations lead to the creation of the distinctive styles of ceramics.

The theorist David Bidney sees culture as the product of human choices (1967:xxvi), and he suggests that people do not create it ex nihilo but out of their sensory experience of nature, setting up a cyclical feedback between their experience and cognition. A cognitive map is built from our sensory experience of the world around us, and it is the primary cultural achievement of a group (ibid.:xxii). If we apply Bidney's terms, the culture of craft making is a matter of choices about the style to be used, the specific forms to be made, and the visual qualities each piece will have. In each case, the potter draws from a cognitive map of possibilities based on his or her cultural formation and experience with the visual world. Culture influences craft production because the basic pattern of decision making used in culture is the same one used to make craft decisions.

The forms of the ceramic style are learned and stored in the cognitive map of the craftsperson and become a part of the structure and mode of thinking of that person. A style suffers from fatigue when innovation stops and the traditional forms no longer correspond to needs within the community. Such forms will eventually be dropped from the repertoire, or people may cease to make that style altogether. If the craft as a whole becomes irrelevant for the people, there will be no reason for them to continue using it. However, it may take on new symbolic meaning, as happened with the traditional cooking pots and water bottles in Ráquira after the introduction of metal cooking pots and plastic water bottles.

The craftsperson works on two levels, one of which is the Chomskian deep structure, or feeling experience, of line, color, texture, light, or other visual elements that are conveyed to the surface structure, which is the visual experience of the object itself (Chomsky 1965:6). For example, the potter can translate his or her feeling about color or texture (deep structure) into a pot by using the medium (clay) and the cultural rules of the style in which the person is working, such as women's domestic pottery in Ráquira (surface structure). When the craftsperson translates his or her deep structure (feeling about visual characteristics such as color or texture) into the visual style (surface structure) that is known culturally, she or he can make a pot that is appreciated by other members of the society. According to Bidney, behavior reflected in the "artifacts of a culture," such as crafts, is the culture of a group (1967:401). In making pottery or weaving, the craftsperson is acting out her or his culture.

Innovation and Style

If culture is the result of the human capacity for choice (Bidney 1963:34), in the crafts that usually means choices about style or technology. The craftsperson can change elements in his or her set of assumptions about craft making, and that in turn can lead to a change of style or medium. As social needs, the economy, or technology change, potters develop new models of working to respond to the new conditions. Changes in residence or marital status may also lead the Ráquira potter to change the style with which he or she works. For a woman in Ráquira, these changes are usually family related. She may enter her post-child-rearing years, when less money is needed, or her husband may join the business and begin to make commercial ware. When production potters adopt the new designs or techniques developed by innovative ceramists, new community styles are born. Although innovation and change do occur in village craft ceramics, only a few isolated individuals are known as innovators.

Explaining why some potters are innovative and others are not, Dean Arnold suggests that high-status people innovate to establish leadership and maintain their uniqueness, while low-status people innovate to improve their socioeconomic position within the system (1985:220). Furthermore, he suggests that women rarely innovate in ceramics because they see it as a supplemental income-producing activity for the family (ibid.) and not a primary activity that would justify the investment of time and energy necessary for innovations.

The low social status assigned to pottery makers in Latin America (Arnold 1985:127) also works against innovation. Village ceramics communicate ruralness with the associated ideas of poverty, indigenous roots, and foreignness to the Eurocentric national cultures. In Colombia village crafts do not have prestige as an occupation, either for the craftspeople themselves or the larger public. For example, Ráquira men prefer to manage other workers or work in agriculture rather than make ceramics themselves, but young men who do not have the experience or capital to open their own workshops are obligated by economics to work in pottery production.

Gender and Innovation

Since Ráquira men have not had a tradition of working in ceramics and they are not limited by the domestic constraints that have affected women, they have been able to develop new ways of making and selling ceramics and new attitudes toward the medium of clay. When the availability of new ideas was combined with expanded market outlets, many men adopted the new alternatives, initiating social change that led to a conservative-liberal tension between women's and men's ceramics.

The women potters have been more conservative, playing a key cultural role in maintaining contact and coherence with existing traditions in technique, form, and attitude toward the craft. This conservative position provides a stable platform, a point of reference, to which the men relate as they introduce innovations. Coherent change occurs when there is a clear definition of what has existed before. This is a viable and vital process in which cultural continuity is maintained, and yet change introduces the economic vitality that is necessary for the community to survive. The fact that women continue making traditional pottery may be due to the cultural conservativeness expected of women, which seems to be accentuated in communities with indigenous backgrounds like Ráquira.

Arnold identified four barriers that impede the acceptance of innovation in pottery communities, all of which can be observed in Ráquira. One is that the motor behaviors required in the innovation may conflict with motor behaviors that already exist in the community (1985:221). This may be one of the reasons for the resistance of women to adopting the potter's wheel in Ráquira. Second, the work patterns of pottery making in the community may conflict with the requirements of the innovation (ibid.:222). The leaders in introducing the innovations of recent decades have been men who had not previously made pottery and had no established work patterns in ceramics. On the other hand, women, who have been the traditional potters with established work patterns, have been slow to adopt the changes. Third, the lack of capital to finance innovations can also be a factor blocking innovation (ibid.), and the most conservative potters in Ráquira are rural women, who have the least access to capital. Whatever capital their family has is usually controlled by the male head of household, who invests it in his own occupation. And fourth, community solidarity organized around attitudes and beliefs can also block innovations (ibid.:223). This was apparent in Ráquira when the pottery school was blocked and when the first attempts were made by outsiders (that is, the Cárdenas family) to set up a pottery factory. Reina described a similar case in which community solidarity blocked innovation (1963:28). When innovation does occur, it goes through the individual potter's own personal repertoire of color, line, texture, and form.

Style and the Craftsperson's Culturing System

Styles are the cultural alternatives in craft that are available to the potters, and their choice to work in one style or another indicates who they are and the influences that have shaped them. The cultural context in Ráquira provides each craftsperson with opportunities to choose between styles, but once that choice is made, it limits the individual to a constricted range of behaviors. For example, a rural woman potter lives in a context of obligations to her family and expectations from the community that she will make traditional domestic pottery. Once she has learned the style of traditional pottery, it structures her visual ideas (shape, texture, and color), her knowledge of pottery forms (cooking pots, water bottles, toasting pans), and her motor skills in working (coiling and pinching, for example). After she has established that style as her guide for working, she will probably continue with it until some fundamental change occurs in her life, or she may never change.

Cultural forms are a central part of the identity of the potter, just as gender is. Although culture is collective, the acting out of culture occurs at the individual level, which reinforces this personal identification with culture. Edward Lucie-Smith points out that people do this with their craft by identifying themselves according to the medium used (for example, "I am a potter"), and in so doing they identify their persona or self according to their skills and work (1981:11) as well as their gender.

The personal culturing system is the means by which the craftsperson creates and acts out the actions, ideas, and artifacts that make up the crafts. The styles of a craft are cultural and include forms of design, shape, color, and texture, which may be learned from others or invented by the craftsperson. Stephen Gudeman (1986:28) says that models of livelihood (such as crafts) are cultural constructions, and he goes further to say that humans are "self-constituting" beings who culturally construct their behaviors based on critical reflection of the past and future (ibid.). In the crafts, people make choices about the style, shapes, and techniques that they will use in their work, and the decisions to change their choices lead to variations in style.

The cultural construction of craft behavior permits the flexibility required to adapt to changes in time and place. By nature of its arbitrariness, craft knowledge and skill will vary as it is taught from one person to another, and individual craftspeople can also vary their interpretations of the principles of design from time to time, leading to new styles. The craftsperson draws from the repertoire of visual elements that are culturally available to produce individual and group styles. The individuality of the potter and the social and economic contexts in which he or she lives and works are key reference points around which craft is shaped, and the dynamics between them affect whether the potter is an innovator, a commodity producer, or a domestic-oriented producer.

Ráquira at the End of the Twentieth Century

The men and women of Ráquira have created parallel cultural styles within their local society that reflect their history and gender ideology. They have constructed contrasting systems of work within their defined cultural parameters, which demonstrate the powerful role of gender in behavior. As hundreds of men and women have taken up work in ceramics, they have consistently recognized and chosen gender-appropriate versions of the craft in formulating their own behaviors. Although the burst of cultural change in Ráquira over the last few decades has been dynamic, tradition has also been impressive for its persistence.

Since culture is constantly changing and never static, the gender and ceramics behaviors portrayed here from the late 1980s to the mid-1990s provide only glimpses of the emerging trends in factory production and national tourism, which are being actively promoted by the town elite. These are new factors coming onto the amalgam of Ráquira culture, which will clearly continue the process of change for the foreseeable future. The potters of Ráquira have been Muisca potters, Spanish colonial potters, and Boyacá country potters, and some are now becoming potters in the global economy. It remains to be seen whether the traditional design principles and working techniques will survive this transition, and more importantly whether women will find an equitable role within the new capitalist version of Ráquira ceramics.

Appendix:
Sources of Clay in Ráquira

Owner of the mine	Type of clay
Vereda Resguardo Occidental	
1. Pascual Buitrago	Red and yellow
2. Gabriel Castillo	Yellow
3. José Cárdenas	Yellow and black
4. Félix Salinas	Red
5. Fideligno Torres	Yellow
6. Simón Ruiz	Red and black
7. Dionisio Martínez	Yellow
8. Margarita Ruiz	Yellow and red
9. Flaminio Forero	White
10. Álvaro Romero	Yellow
Vereda Pueblo Viejo	
1. Adán Valero	White
2. Agustín Valero	White
3. Samuel Rodríguez	Yellow
4. Juan Gómez	Yellow
Vereda Farfan (Alto de los Nevados)	
1. Juan Ávila	White
Vereda Mirque	
1. Antonio Albañil	Yellow and white
Vereda Torres	
1. Julio Ibaque	Yellow
Vereda Roa	
1. Evaristo Rodríguez	White

Glossary

Adobe: A mixture of clay, earth, and straw that is commonly compacted into blocks and used for building walls.

Arepero: A toasting pan with a slightly rounded bottom, which is used to toast thick corn pancakes (*arepas*).

Cazuela: In Ráquira it refers to a bowl-like cooking pan with a handle.

Chicha: A fermented corn drink.

Claybody: Two or three different natural clays are mixed together to form a working clay that has the characteristics needed by the potter.

Coiling: The process of building up the walls of pots with ropelike coils of clay.

Comadre: A close friend and ally who is the godmother of a person's child.

Compadre: A close friend and ally who is the godfather of a person's child.

Deflocculate: To make clay particles float in the water. This is important to successfully slip cast ceramics.

Don: An honorific title used for older, respected men in the community.

Doña: An honorific title used for older, respected women in the community.

Downdraft: The exhaust draft for a kiln exits into the chimney near the bottom of the kiln. The heat from the fire first rises in the kiln, but the exhaust pulls it down to exit. This design guarantees a flow of fire and heat in the kiln.

Earthenware: Pottery made of low-fire clay, which frequently includes red iron oxide, giving it a reddish-beige "terracotta" color.

Encomienda: The Spanish colonial practice of assigning a district of the country to a Spanish person to control and collect tribute in the name of the crown.

Flashing: The changes in coloration produced by the flames from a wood fire as they lick around a pot during the firing.

Form: This refers to a particular vessel shape, such as the cooking pot or water bottle.

Frit: An industrially produced fusion of lead oxide with silica or other oxide, which is made for glazes.

Greenware: A piece of ceramics that has been made and dried but not yet fired.

Guarapo: A fermented sugarcane drink.

Leatherhard: The stage of drying of a pot in which the clay has the consistency of firm leather.

Licorera: A bottle used to store and serve rum or aguardiente, a locally distilled anise-flavored drink.

Loza de arena: Pottery made from common earthenware clay tempered with sand.

Loza de suelo: Pottery made from common earthenware clay.

Múcura: The prehispanic-style bottle that is still made in Colombia.

Oxidation: A firing environment in which the fire consumes oxygen naturally from the air.

Olla: The traditional pot used for cooking and storing of food.

Open-air firing: Pots to be fired are stacked on the ground, surrounded by wood, and covered by metal sheeting. Formerly they were covered by broken potsherds.

Orton cones: Laboratory-prepared cones used by ceramists for precise measuring of temperatures. Orton cones are made of ceramic material, and they soften and bend when the heat in the kiln reaches the temperature for which they are made. They are more practical in some situations than a temperature gauge.

Paila: A shallow, wide bowl.

Saggars: Containers in which pottery is placed for the firing.

Slip: Liquid clay of a thick, milk-like consistency.

Sprig mold: A special mold for making small, delicate pieces, which are combined to make a complete piece or applied to the surfaces of larger pieces.

Style: A type of ceramics defined by the use of similar designs, techniques, and forms.

Temper: Sand or pulverized pottery that is mixed into clay to give it porosity and strength.

Thermal shock: The rapid increase or decrease of temperature that is characteristic of wood fires. Rapid changes in temperature can crack pottery if it is not made for such conditions.

Tinaja: A water-storage jar.

Updraft: The exhaust for the heat of a kiln is located in the uppermost part of the kiln.

Vereda: A rural district or community.

Wedging: Applying pressure to the clay in a repeated, systematic pattern to guarantee an even mixture and consistency and to eliminate air pockets.

Bibliography

Alonso, José A. 1983. "The Domestic Clothing Workers in the Mexican Metropolis and Their Relation to Dependent Capitalism." In *Women, Men and the International Division of Labor,* ed. June Nash and M. Patricia Fernandez-Kelly, 161–72. Albany: State University of New York Press.

Ancízar, Manuel. 1956. *Peregrinación de Alpha* (The alpha pilgrimage). Bogotá.

Annis, Sheldon. 1987. *God and Production in a Guatemalan Town.* Austin: University of Texas Press.

Archivo General de Indias, Seville, Spain. N.d. Audiencia de Santafé (Audience of Santa Fe). Legajo (File) 164.

———. N.d. Audiencia de Santafé. Legajo 187.

———. N.d. Audiencia de Santafé. Legajo 370.

———. N.d. Audiencia de Santafé. Legajo 769.

———. N.d. Protocolos. Legajo 1932.

———. N.d. Sección de Contaduría (Section of Accounting). Legajo 1775.

———. 1584. Patronato (Guardianship) 196. "Relación que don Diego de Torres, Cacique, hace a su Majestad sobre los agravios que a los naturales del Nuevo Reino se hacen por las personas en quienes su Majestad los tiene encomendados y de la manera que se consumen y acaban, las cosas que conviene remediar y el poco fruto que con ellos se ha hecho en su conversión." (Account that Don Diego de Torres, Chief, gives to his Majesty about the serious acts inflicted on the natives of the New Kingdom by the persons chartered by his Majesty and in such a way as to ravage and destroy them, things that should be corrected and the little progress that has been made toward their conversion.)

Archivo Histórico Nacional de Bogotá (AHNB). N.d. Fondo de caciques e indios (Collection of chiefs and Indians). Vol. 63, Folio (Leaf) 1035.

Arizpe, Lourdes, ed. 1996. *The Cultural Dimensions of Global Change: An Anthropological Approach.* Paris: UNESCO.

Arnold, Dean E. 1993. *Ecology and Ceramic Production in an Andean Community.* Cambridge: Cambridge University Press.

———. 1989. "Technological Diversity and Evolutionary Viability: A Comparison of Pottery-Making Technologies in Guatemala, Peru, and Mexico." In *Ceramic Ecology, 1988: Current Research on Ceramic Materials,* ed. Charles C. Kolb, 29–59. BAR International Series 513. Oxford: B.A.R.

———. 1985. *Ceramic Theory and Cultural Process.* Cambridge: Cambridge University Press.

Arnold, Philip J., III. 1991. *Domestic Ceramic Production and Spatial Organization: A Mexican Case Study in Ethnoarchaeology.* Cambridge: Cambridge University Press.

Babb, Florence E. 1989. *Between Field and Cooking Pot: The Political Economy of Marketwomen in Peru.* Austin: University of Texas Press.

Bibliowicz, Hanna. 1978. "Ráquira, pueblo de olleros" (Ráquira, town of potters). Artesanías de Colombia, Bogotá.

Bidney, David. 1967. *Theoretical Anthropology.* 2d ed. New York: Schocken Books.

———. 1963. "The Varieties of Human Freedom." In *The Concept of Freedom in Anthropology,* ed. David Bidney, 11–34. The Hague: Mouton and Company.

Bonilla, Fernando. 1989. "Cerámica de Ráquira, Boyacá" (Ceramics of Ráquira, Boyacá). Artesanías de Colombia, Bogotá.

Bonilla, Flor Ángela. 1980. "Estudio socioeconómico de Ráquira" (Socioeconomic study of Ráquira). Bogotá: Museo de Artes y Tradiciones Populares.

Bonilla, Manuel Antonio, María Cristina Baquero, and Carlos Augusto Manrique. 1992. "Sustitución de la leña por el carbón en la quema de cerámica: Diseño y fabricación de un horno con carbón" (Substitution of coal for wood in the firing of ceramics: Design and building of a coal-fired kiln). Artesanías de Colombia, Bogotá.

Bossen, Laura. 1984. *The Redivision of Labor: Women and Economic Choice in Four Guatemalan Communities.* Albany: State University of New York.

Boster, James S., and Susan C. Weller. 1990. "Cognitive and Contextual Variation in Hot-Cold Classification." *American Anthropologist* 85, no. 4: 826–47.

Bourdieu, Pierre. 1993. *The Field of Cultural Production.* New York: Columbia University Press.

Bradley, Harriet. 1989. *Men's Work, Women's Work: A Sociological History of the Sexual Division of Labor in Employment.* Minneapolis: University of Minnesota Press.

Buckley, Thomas, and Alma Gottlieb. 1998. *Blood Magic: The Anthropology of Menstruation.* Berkeley: University of California Press.

Bushnell, David. 1993. *The Making of Modern Colombia: A Nation in Spite of Itself.* Berkeley: University of California Press.

Cardale de Schrimpff, Marianne. 1989. "La naturaleza del cambio" (The nature of change). In *Historia y culturas populares: Los estudios regionales en Boyacá* (History and popular culture: Regional studies in Boyacá), ed. Pablo Mora Calderón and Amado Guerrero Rincón. Tunja: Instituto de Cultura y Bellas Artes de Boyacá.

Ceballos, Alberto. 1987. "Estudios de hornos de leña en Ráquira" (Studies of wood-fired kilns in Ráquira). Artesanías de Colombia, Bogotá.

Céspedes del Castillo, Guillermo. 1992. *América hispánica (1492–1898)* (Hispanic America [1492–1898]). Barcelona: Editorial Labor.

Chayanov, Alexander Vasilevich. 1966. "Peasant Farm Organization." In *A. V. Chayanov: The Theory of Peasant Economy,* ed. Daniel Thorner, Basile Kerblay, and R. E. F. Smith. Homewood, Ill.: Richard D. Irwin.

Chomsky, Noam. 1965. *Aspects of the Theory of Syntax.* Cambridge: M.I.T. Press.

Clarke, Michael, ed. 1996. *Velázquez in Seville.* Edinburgh: National Gallery of Scotland.

Colmenares, Germán. 1970. "La provincia de Tunja en el Nuevo Reino de Granada: Ensayo de historia social (1539–1800)" (The province of Tunja in the New Kingdom of Granada: Essay on social history [1539–1800]). Bogotá: Facultad de Artes y Ciencias, Departmento de Historia, Universidad de los Andes.

———.1969. *Haciendas de los jesuitas en el Nuevo Reino de Granada siglo XVIII* (Jesuit haciendas in the New Kingdom of Granada in the eighteenth century). Bogotá: Tercer Mundo.

Deagan, Kathleen. 1987. *Artifacts of the Spanish Colonies of Florida and the Caribbean, 1500–1800.* Vol. 1, *Ceramics, Glassware, and Beads.* Washington, D.C.: Smithsonian Institution Press.

Deere, Carmen Diana. 1990. *Household and Class Relations: Peasants and Landlords in Northern Peru.* Berkeley: University of California Press.

Duncan, Ronald J. 1996a. "De mariposas a madonas: Arte y diseño prehispánico" (From butterflies to madonnas: Prehispanic art and design). In *Gran enciclopedia temática,* 333–43. Bogotá: Grupo Editorial Norma.

———. 1996b. "Orfebrería prehispánica: De chamanes a caciques" (Prehispanic goldwork: From shamans to chiefs). In *Gran enciclopedia temática,* 344–54. Bogotá: Grupo Editorial Norma.

———. 1993. "Arte precolombino" (Precolumbian art). In *Gran enciclopedia de Colombia,* vol. 6, *Arte,* 15–26. Bogotá: Círculo de Lectores.

———. 1992. "Precolumbian Art and Design in Nariño Ceramics." In *Arte de la Tierra: Nariño,* ed. Alicia Eugenia Silva, 27–31. Bogotá: Fondo de Promoción Cultural.

———. 1986. "Crafts and Development in Latin America." Paper presented at the International Symposium on Handicrafts, International Development Research Centre, Singapore.

———. 1985a. "El niño rural como trabajador: Estudio de caso en La Chamba" (The rural child as worker: Case study in La Chamba). Research report for the International Development Research Centre, Ottawa, Ontario, Canada.

———. 1985b. "Cuatro siglos de cerámica en Colombia" (Four centuries of ceramics in Colombia). In *Gotas de antaño: Introducción a la cerámica en Colombia* (Traces from yesteryear: Introduction to ceramics in Colombia). Bogotá: Centro Colombo-Americano.

———. 1985c. "Diseño y técnica en la cerámica de La Chamba" (Design and technique in La Chamba ceramics). Research report for the Program of Art. Bogotá: Universidad de los Andes.

———. 1984. "Ceramics as Art in Colombia." *Craft International: Journal of the World Crafts Council* (New York) (July): 4.

———. 1983. "Traditional Craft Ceramics in Colombia." Paper presented at the Latin American Regional Meetings of the World Crafts Council. San Juan, Puerto Rico.

———. 1975a. "Comment" on "Image of the Limited Good, or Expectation of Reciprocity?" by James R. Gregory. *Current Anthropology* 16, no. 1: 86.

———. 1975b. "Informe Barrio Unión Vivienda Popular" (Report on the Barrio Unión Vivienda Popular project). Cali: Universidad del Valle.

———, ed. 1979. *The Anthropology of the People of Puerto Rico.* 2d ed. San Juan: Inter-American University of Puerto Rico.

Duncan, Ronald J., Jaime Bernal, and Ignacio Briceño. 1993. *El arte del chamanismo, la salud y la vida: Tumaco–La Tolita* (The art of shamanism, health, and life: Tumaco–La Tolita). Bogotá: Instituto Colombiano de Cultura Hispánica.

Durrenberger, E. Paul, ed. 1984. *Chayanov, Peasants, and Economic Anthropology.* New York: Academic Press.

Ehlers, Tracy Bachrach. 1990. *Silent Looms: Women and Production in a Guatemalan Town.* Boulder: Westview Press.

Ehrich, Robert. 1965. "Ceramics and Man: A Cultural Perspective." In *Ceramics and Man,* ed. Frederick E. Matson, Viking Fund Publication in Anthropology no. 41. New York: Aldine.

Fairbanks, Charles H. 1972. "Cultural Significance of Spanish Ceramics." In *Ceramics in America,* ed. Ian Quimbay. Winterthur Conference Report 1972. Charlottesville: University Press of Virginia.

Falchetti, Ana María. 1975. Arqueología de Sutamarchán (Archaeology of Sutamarchán). Bogotá: Biblioteca Banco Popular.

Feldman, Shelley. 1991. "Still Invisible: Women in the Informal Sector." In *The Women and International Development Annual,* vol. 2, ed. Rita S. Gallin and Anne Ferguson. Boulder: Westview.

Fiori, Lavinia. 1990. "Las vírgenes de Doña Otilia: De la artesanía tradicional al arte popular" (The virgins of Doña Otilia: From traditional craft to popular art). *Revista Cultural Popular* 2: 14–24 (Tunja: Instituto de Cultura y Bellas Artes de Boyacá).

Flórez, Carmen Elisa, and Elssy Bonilla. 1991. "The Demographic Transition in Colombia." In *Women, Households and Change,* ed. Eleonora Masini and Susan Stratigos, 55–88. Tokyo: United Nations University Press.

Foster, George. 1988. "The Validating Role of the Humoral Theory in Traditional Spanish-American Therapeutics." *American Ethnologist* 15, no. 1: 120–35.

———. 1967. *Tzintzuntzan.* Boston: Little, Brown.

Friede, Juan. 1976. *Fuentes documentales para la historia del Nuevo Reino de Granada* (Documentary sources for the history of the New Kingdom of Granada). Vol. 6. Bogotá: Biblioteca Banco Popular.

———. 1969. "De la encomienda indiana a la propiedad territorial y su influencia sobre el mestizaje" (From the Indian *encomienda* to the territorial property and its influence on the mixing of races). In *Anuario colombiano de historia social y de la cultura* no. 4. Bogotá: Universidad Nacional de Colombia.

Friedemann, Nina S. de. 1993. "Arte étnico" (Ethnic art). In *Gran enciclopedia de Colombia,* vol. 6, *Arte,* 145–54. Bogotá: Círculo de Lectores.

Frith, Donald E. 1985. *Mold Making for Ceramics.* Radnor, Penn.: Chilton Book Company.

García Canclini, Néstor. 1990. *Culturas híbridas: Estrategias para entrar y salir de la modernidad* (Hybrid cultures: Strategies for entering and leaving modernity). Mexico City: Editorial Grijalbo.

Gestoso y Pérez, José. 1903. *Historia de los barrios vidriados sevillanos desde sus orígenes hasta nuestros días* (History of the glaze barrio district of Seville from its origins to today). Seville: Tipografía la Andalucía Moderna.

Giral, María Dolors. 1993. "Talavera de la Reina y Puente del Arzobispo" (Talavera de la Raina and Puente del Arzobispo). In *Museo de Cerámica: Palacio de Pedralbes Barcelona*, ed. Trinidad Sanchez-Pacheco, M. Antonia Casanovas, and María Dolors Giral, 57–63. Belgium: Ludion.

Goggin, John M. 1970. *The Spanish Olive Jar.* New Haven: Yale University Press.

———. 1968. *Spanish Majolica in the New World: Types of the Sixteenth to Eighteenth Centuries.* New Haven: Yale University Press.

Gómez, Tomás. 1984. "Vida cotidiana y trabajo indígena en Tunja y Santa Fe (siglos XVI y XVII)" (Everyday life and indigenous work in Tunja and Santa Fe [sixteenth and seventeenth centuries]). In *La Ville en Amérique espagnole coloniale*, comp. Seminaire Interuniversitaire sur l'Amérique Espagnole Coloniale, 171–91. Paris: Service des Publications, Université de la Sorbonne Nouvelle.

Gómez Contreras, Emiro. 1990. "Estudio y evaluación de la artesanía cerámica en Colombia" (Study and evaluation of craft ceramics in Colombia). Artesanías de Colombia, Bogotá.

Gottlieb, Alma. 1988. "Menstrual Cosmology among the Beng of Ivory Coast." In *Blood Magic: The Anthropology of Menstruation*, ed. Thomas Buckley and Alma Gottlieb. Berkeley: University of California Press.

Gudeman, Stephen. 1986. *Economics as Culture: Models and Metaphors of Livelihood.* London: Routledge and Kegan Paul.

Gudeman, Stephen, and Alberto Rivera. 1990. *Conversations in Colombia: The Domestic Economy in Life and Text.* New York: Cambridge University Press.

Gutiérrez Escudero, Antonio. 1992. "La primitiva organización indiana" (The primitive Indian organization). In *Historia de Iberoamérica*, ed. Manuel Lucena Salmoral. Madrid: Ediciones Catedra.

Harris, Olivia, ed. 1983. *Latin American Women.* London: Minority Rights Group Ltd.

Hendry, Jean Clare. 1992. *Atzompa: A Pottery-Producing Village of Southern Mexico in the Mid-1950s.* Publications in Anthropology, no. 40. Nashville: Vanderbilt University.

Herlihy, David. 1990. *Opera Muliebria: Women and Work in Medieval Europe.* New York: McGraw-Hill.

Hernández de Alba, Gonzalo. 1988. "La Nueva Granada en 1809 y 1810" (New Granada in 1809 and 1810). In *Historia de Colombia*, vol. 7, 787–810. Bogotá: Salvat Editores Colombiana.

Herrera Rubio, Neve. 1976. "Historia y factores de la artesanía" (History and aspects of craftwork). Artesanías de Colombia, Bogotá.

Holguín, Cecilia Iregui de. 1983. *El hombre y su oficio* (Man and his work). Bogotá: Instituto de Investigación de la Expresión Colombiana.

Jaramillo Uribe, Jaime. 1964. "La población indígena de Colombia en el momento de la conquista y sus posteriores transformaciones" (The indigenous population of Colombia at the time of the Conquest and its subsequent transformation). *Anuario colombiano de historia social y de la cultura* 1, no. 2 (Bogotá).

Jereb, James F. 1995. *Arts and Crafts of Morocco.* London: Thames and Hudson.

Kolb, Charles C. 1989. "Ceramic Ecology in Retrospect: A Critical Review of Methodology and Results." In *Ceramic Ecology, 1988: Current Research on Ceramic Materials,* ed. Charles C. Kolb, 261–375. BAR International Series 513. Oxford: B.A.R.

Kolb, Charles C., and Louana M. Lackey, eds. 1988. *A Pot for All Reasons: Ceramic Ecology Revisited.* Special Publication of Cerámica de Cultura Maya. Philadelphia: Laboratory of Anthropology, Temple University.

Kramer, Carol. 1997. *Pottery in Rajasthan: Ethnoarchaeology in Two Indian Cities.* Washington, D.C.: Smithsonian Institution Press.

Lackey, Louana. 1989. "Following the Book: Lessons from Piccolpasso." In *Ceramic Ecology, 1988: Current Research on Ceramic Materials,* ed. Charles C. Kolb, 117–54. BAR International Series 513. Oxford: B.A.R.

———. 1982. *The Pottery of Acatlán.* Norman: University of Oklahoma Press.

Langebaek, Carl Henrik. 1987. *Mercados, poblamiento e integracíon étnica entre Muiscas* (Markets, settlements, and ethnic integration among the Muiscas). Bogotá: Banco de la República.

Las Casas, Bartolomé de. [1552] 1992. *A Short Account of the Destruction of the Indies.* Edited and translated by Nigel Griffin. New York: Penguin Books.

Lauer, Mirko. 1984. "La producción artesanal en América Latina" (Craft production in Latin America). Ottawa: International Development Research Centre.

Leghorn, Lisa, and Katherine Parker. 1981. *Woman's Worth: Sexual Economics and the World of Women.* London: Routledge and Kegan Paul.

León, Magdalena. 1987. "Colombian Agricultural Policies and the Debate on Policies toward Rural Women." In *Rural Women and State Policy,* ed. Carmen Diana Deere and Magdalena León, 84–104. Boulder: Westview Press.

León, Magdalena, and María Viveros. 1983. "Rural Women in Colombia: Invisible Labour and the Double Day." In *Latin American Women,* ed. Olivia Harris, 9–10. London: Minority Rights Group Ltd.

Lewenhak, Sheila. 1980. *Women and Work.* New York: St. Martin's Press.

Lister, Florence C., and Robert H. Lister. 1987. *Andalusian Ceramics in Spain and New Spain: A Cultural Register from the Third Century B.C. to 1700.* Tucson: University of Arizona Press.

Litto, Gertrude. 1976. *South American Folk Pottery.* New York: Watson-Guptill.

Llorens Artigas, Josep, and J. Corredor-Matheos. 1979. *Cerámica popular española* (Spanish folk ceramics). 3d ed. Barcelona: Editorial Blume.

Lucie-Smith, Edward. 1981. *The Story of Craft: The Craftsman's Role in Society.* Ithaca: Cornell University Press.

Martínez Carreño, Aida. 1985. *Mesa y cocina en el siglo XIX* (Table and cookery in the nineteenth century). Bogotá: Fondo Cultural Cafetero.

Mathews, Holly F. 1983. "Context-Specific Variation in Humoral Classification." *American Anthropologist* 85, no. 4: 826–47.

Matson, Frederick E., ed. 1965. *Ceramics and Man*. Viking Fund Publications in Anthropology no. 41. New York: Aldine.

McKee, Lauris. 1997. "Women's Work in Rural Ecuador: Multiple Resource Strategies and the Gendered Division of Labor." In *Women and Economic Change: Andean Perspectives*, ed. Ann Miles and Hans Buechler, 13–30. Arlington, Va.: American Anthropological Association.

Méndez Valencia, María Alexandra. 1993. "Las artesanías en Colombia." In *Gran enciclopedia de Colombia*, vol. 6, *Arte*. Bogotá: Círculo de Lectores.

Mies, Maria. 1982. *The Lace Makers of Narsapur*. London: Zed Press.

Miles, Ann, and Hans Buechler. 1997. "Introduction: Andean Perspectives on Women and Economic Change." In *Women and Economic Change: Andean Perspectives*, ed. Ann Miles and Hans Buechler, 1–12. Arlington, Va.: American Anthropological Association.

———, eds. 1997. *Women and Economic Change: Andean Perspectives*. Arlington, Va.: American Anthropological Association.

Mintz, Sidney. 1979. "The Role of Puerto Rico in Modern Social Science." In *The Anthropology of the People of Puerto Rico*, ed. Ronald J. Duncan, 5–16. San Juan: Inter-American University Press.

Mitchell, Timothy. 1990. *Passional Culture: Emotion, Religion, and Society in Southern Spain*. Philadelphia: University of Pennsylvania Press.

Montoya de la Cruz, Gerardo. 1990. "Comunidad artesanal de La Chamba: Aproximación a los componentes socioculturales" (The artisan community of La Chamba: Approximation to the sociocultural components). Artesanías de Colombia, Bogotá.

Moore, Henrietta L. 1988. *Feminism and Anthropology*. Minneapolis: University of Minnesota Press.

Mora Calderón, Pablo, and Amado Guerrero Rincón, eds. 1989. *Historia y culturas populares: Los estudios regionales en Boyacá* (History and popular culture: Regional studies in Boyacá). Tunja: Instituto de Cultura y Bellas Artes de Boyacá.

Mora de Jaramillo, Yolanda. 1974. *Cerámica y ceramistas de Ráquira*. Bogotá: Banco Popular.

Moreno y Escandón, Francisco. 1985. *Indios y mestizos de la Nueva Granada a finales del siglo XVIII* (Indians and mestizos of New Granada at the end of the eighteenth century). Vol. 124. Bogotá: Biblioteca Banco Popular.

Murdock, George P., and Caterina Provost. 1973. "Factors in the Division of Labour by Sex: A Cross-Cultural Analysis." *Ethnology* 12, no. 2: 203–35.

Nash, June. 1993. "Maya Household Production in the World Market: The Potters of Amatenango del Valle, Chiapas, Mexico." In *Crafts in the World Market: The Impact of Global Exchange on Middle American Artisans*, ed. June Nash, 127–53. Albany: State University of New York Press.

———. 1985. *In the Eyes of the Ancestors*. Prospect Heights, Ill.: Waveland Press.

———, ed. 1993. *Crafts in the World Market: The Impact of Global Exchange on Middle American Artisans*. Albany: State University of New York Press.

Nash, June, and M. Patricia Fernandez-Kelly. 1983. *Women, Men and the International Division of Labor.* Albany: State University of New York Press.

Olsen, Fredrick. 1983. *The Kiln Book: Materials, Specifications and Construction.* 2d ed. Radnor, Penn.: Chilton Book Company.

Orbell, John. 1995. *Los herederos del cacique Suaya: Historia colonial de Ráquira (1539–1810)* (The heirs of Chief Suaya: Colonial history of Ráquira [1539–1810]). Bogotá: Banco de la República.

Osborn, Ann. 1979. *La cerámica de los Tunebos.* Bogotá: Banco de la República.

Patiño, V. M. 1990. *Historia de la cultura material en la América equinoccial* (History of the material culture of equinoctial America). Vol. 5. Bogotá: Instituto Caro y Cuervo.

Perdomo Escobar, José Ignacio. 1965. "Gracia y permanencia de la cerámica en Colombia" (The grace and permanence of ceramics in Colombia). *El Tiempo* (Bogotá), August 1: 4–5.

Pescatello, Ann, ed. 1973. *Female and Male in Latin America.* Pittsburgh: University of Pittsburgh Press.

Pinto Escobar, Inés. 1988. "La inestabilidad social: Los comuneros" (Social instability: The communalists). In *Historia de Colombia,* vol. 6, 641–63. Bogotá: Salvat Editores Colombiana.

Rasmussen, Susan J. 1991. "Lack of Prayer: Ritual Restrictions, Social Experience, and the Anthropology of Menstruation among the Tuareg." *American Ethnologist* 18 (November): 751–69.

Reina, Ruben. 1966. *The Law of the Saints: A Pokomam Pueblo and Its Community Culture.* New York: Bobbs-Merrill.

———. 1963. "The Potter and the Farmer: The Fate of Two Innovators in a Maya Village." *Expedition* 5, no. 4: 18–31.

Reina, Ruben, and Robert Hill. 1978. *The Traditional Pottery of Guatemala.* Austin: University of Texas Press.

Reinhardt, Nola. 1988. *Our Daily Bread: The Peasant Question and Family Farming in the Colombian Andes.* Berkeley: University of California Press.

Rojas, M. 1978. *La plaza mayor: El urbanismo, instrumento de dominio colonial* (The central plaza: Urbanism as an instrument of colonial domination). Madrid: Muchnik Editores.

Rojas de Perdomo, Lucia. 1985. *Manual de arqueología colombiana* (Manual of Colombian archaeology). 2d ed. Bogotá: Carlos Valencia Editores.

Rojas Escobar, Gumercindo. 1983. "Diagnóstico de las artesanías en el municipio de Ráquira, Departamento de Boyacá" (A diagnostic study of the crafts of the township of Ráquira, state of Boyacá). Artesanías de Colombia, Bogotá.

Romero, María Eugenia. 1984. "Los misioneros de la orinoquía colombiana, siglos XVI a XVIII" (The missionaries of the Colombian Orinoco, sixteenth to eighteenth centuries). *Revista Javeriana,* no. 510 (Nov.–Dec.): 355–62.

Roseberry, William. 1995. "Latin American Peasant Studies in a 'Postcolonial' Era." *Journal of Latin American Anthropology* 1, no. 1: 150–77.

Rosselló Bordoy, Guillermo. 1992. "The Ceramics of al-Andalus." In *Al-Andalus: The Art of Islamic Spain,* ed. Jerrilynn D. Dobbs, 97–103. New York: Metropolitan Museum of Art.

Rubio y Moreno, Luis. 1917. *Pasajeros a Indias. Catálogo metodológico de las informaciones y licencias de los allí pasaron, existentes en el Archivo General de Indias. Siglo primero de la colonización de América, 1492–1592* (Passengers to the Indies. Methodological catalogue of the information and licences that exist in the General Archive of the Indies of those who passed there. First century of the colonization of America, 1492–1592). Colección de Documentos Inéditos para la Historia de Hispano-América, vol. 8. Madrid: Ibero-Americana de Publicaciones.

Ruiz Rivera, Julián. 1975. *Encomienda y mita en Nueva Granada* (*Encomienda* and *mita* in New Granada). Sevilla: Escuela de Estudios Hispano-Americanos.

Rye, Owen S., and Clifford Evans. 1976. *Traditional Pottery Techniques of Pakistan.* Smithsonian Contribution to Anthropology no. 21. Washington: Smithsonian Institution.

Safa, Helen. 1996. "Women and Industrialization in the Caribbean: A Comparative Analysis of the Global Feminization of Labour." In *The Cultural Dimensions of Global Change: An Anthropological Approach,* ed. Lourdes Arizpe, 135–54. Paris: UNESCO.

Seminaire Interuniversitaire sur l'Amérique Espagnole Coloniale (comp.). 1984. *La Ville en Amérique espagnole coloniale.* Paris: Service des Publications, Université de la Sorbonne Nouvelle.

Silverman, Helaine. 1993. "Style and State in Ancient Peru." In *Imagery and Creativity: Ethnoesthetics and Art Worlds in the Americas,* ed. Dorothea S. Whitten and Norman E. Whitten, Jr., 129–69. Tucson: University of Arizona Press.

Simón, Fray Pedro. [1627] 1981. *Noticias historiales de las conquistas de Tierra Firme en las indias occidentales* (Historical accounts of the conquests of Terra Firma in the West Indies). Vol. 3. Bogotá: Biblioteca Banco Popular.

Solano, Pablo. 1974. *Artesanía boyacense* (Craftwork of Boyacá). Bogotá: Artesanias de Colombia.

Sowell, David. 1992. *The Early Colombian Labor Movement: Artisans and Politics in Bogotá, 1832–1919.* Philadelphia: Temple University Press.

Stephen, Lynn. 1993. "Weaving in the Fast Lane: Class, Ethnicity, and Gender in Zapotec Craft Commercialization." In *Crafts in the World Market: The Impact of Global Exchange on Middle American Artisans,* ed. June Nash. Albany: State University of New York Press.

Stevens, Evelyn P. 1973a. "Machismo and Marianismo." *Society* 10, no. 6: 57–63.

———. 1973b. "Marianismo: The Other Face of Machismo in Latin America." In *Female and Male in Latin America,* ed. Ann Pescatello. Pittsburgh: University of Pittsburgh Press.

Stolmaker, Charlotte. 1996. *Cultural, Social and Economic Change in Santa María Atzompa in the Late 1960's.* Publications in Anthropology no. 49. Nashville: Vanderbilt University.

Therrien Johannesson, Monika. 1991. "Basura arqueológico y tecnología cerámica: Estudio de un basurero de taller cerámico en el resquardo colonial de Ráquira, Boyacá (Archaeological trash and ceramic technology: Study of a waster pile of a ceramic workshop in the colonial reservation of Ráquira, Boyacá). Degree thesis, Department of Anthropology, University of the Andes, Bogotá.

Tice, Karin E. 1995. *Kuna Crafts, Gender, and the Global Economy.* Austin: University of Texas Press.

Triana, Miguel. 1972. *La civilización Chibcha* (Chibcha civilization). Cali: Carvajal y Compañía.

Tsuji, Kaichi. 1972. *Kaiseki: Zen Tastes in Japanese Cooking.* Tokyo: Kodansha International.

Urrutia, Miguel, and Clara Elsa Villalba de Sandoval. 1971. *El sector artesanal en el desarrollo colombiano* (The craft sector in Colombian development). Bogotá: Universidad Nacional de Colombia, Centro de Investigaciones para el Desarrollo.

Vergara y Vergara, José Villalba María. 1866. *Almanaque de Bogotá i guía de forasteros para 1867* (Bogotá almanac and guide for foreigners for 1867). Bogotá: Imprenta Gaitán.

Villamarin, J. A. 1972. "*Encomenderos* and Indians in the Formation of Colonial Society in the Sabana de Bogotá, Colombia, 1537 to 1740." Ann Arbor: University Microfilms International.

Villamarin, J. A., and J. E. Villamarin. 1979. "Chibcha Settlement under Spanish Rule: 1537–1810." In *Social Fabric and Spatial Structure in Colonial Latin America,* ed. D. J. Robinson, 34–47. Ann Arbor: University Microfilms International.

Villegas, Liliana, and Benjamin Villegas. 1992. *Artefactos: Colombian Crafts from the Andes to the Amazon.* New York: Rizzoli International.

Whitten, Dorothea S., and Norman E. Whitten, Jr. 1988. *From Myth to Creation: Art from Amazonian Ecuador.* Urbana: University of Illinois Press.

———, eds. 1993. *Imagery and Creativity: Ethnoaesthetics and Art Worlds in the Americas.* Tucson: University of Arizona Press.

Wilkinson-Weber, Clare. 1997. "Skill, Dependency, and Differentiation: Artisans and Agents in the Lucknow Embroidery Industry." *Ethnology* 36, no. 1 (Winter): 49–65.

Wolf, Eric R. 1979. "Remarks on the People of Puerto Rico." In *The Anthropology of the People of Puerto Rico,* ed. Ronald J. Duncan, 17–25. San Juan: Inter-American University Press.

———. 1955. "Types of Latin American Peasantry." *American Anthropologist* 57, no. 3: 452–70.

Index

Ronald J. Duncan is professor of anthropology and studio ceramist at Oklahoma Baptist University. He is visiting curator of precolumbian art at the Mabee-Gerrer Museum of Art at St. Gregory's College and faculty coordinator of the Native American Heritage Association in Shawnee, Oklahoma. He is the author of *El arte del chamanismo, la salud y la vida: Tumaco—La Tolita* (1993).